A GORGEOUS GALLERY OF
GALLANT INVENTIONS

LONDON : HUMPHREY MILFORD
OXFORD UNIVERSITY PRESS

A Gorgeous Gallery
of Gallant Inventions
(1578)

EDITED BY

HYDER E. ROLLINS

North Central College Library
Naperville, Illinois

CAMBRIDGE

HARVARD UNIVERSITY PRESS

1926

COPYRIGHT, 1926
BY HARVARD UNIVERSITY PRESS

PRINTED AT THE HARVARD UNIVERSITY PRESS
CAMBRIDGE, MASS., U.S.A.

To

ADDIE FRANCES ROWE

*The good genius of an entire generation of Harvard men
In gratitude and friendship.*

CONTENTS

INTRODUCTION xiii
"A GORGEOUS GALLERY OF GALLANT INVENTIONS"
  FACSIMILE TITLE-PAGE 1
    A. M. UNTO ALL YOUNG GENTLEMEN IN COMMENDATION OF THIS GALLERY 3
    OWEN ROYDON TO THE CURIOUS COMPANY OF SYCOPHANTS . . . 3
    TO A GENTLEWOMAN THAT SAID ALL MEN BE FALSE 5
    THE LAMENTABLE LOVER ABIDING IN THE BITTER BALE OF DIREFUL DOUBTS TOWARDS HIS LADY'S LOYALTY WRITETH UNTO HER 7
    A LOVING EPISTLE WRITTEN BY RUPHILUS TO HIS BEST BELOVED LADY ELRIZA 9
    NARSETUS A WOEFUL YOUTH IN HIS EXILE WRITETH TO ROSANA HIS BELOVED MISTRESS 13
    THE LOVER FORSAKEN WRITETH TO HIS LADY A DESPERATE FAREWELL 16
    THE LOVER IN DISTRESS EXCLAIMETH AGAINST FORTUNE . . . 21
    ANOTHER COMPLAINT ON FORTUNE 21
    THE LOVER BEING NEWLY CAUGHT IN CUPID'S SNARES COMPLAINETH ON THE GODS OF LOVE 22
    THE LOVER EXTOLLETH AS WELL THE RARE VIRTUES OF HIS LADY BELOVED AS ALSO HER INCOMPARABLE BEAUTY . . . 24
    THE LOVER'S FAREWELL AT HIS DEPARTURE PERSUADETH HIS BELOVED TO CONSTANCY 25
    A PROPER DITTY. To the tune of Lusty gallant 26
    THE LOVER PERSUADETH HIS BELOVED TO BEWARE THE DECEITS AND ALLUREMENTS OF STRANGE SUITORS 27
    THE LADY BELOVED EXCLAIMETH OF THE GREAT UNTRUTH OF HER LOVER 28

CONTENTS

The Lover Declareth his Painful Plight for his Beloved's Sake	29
The Lover Having his Beloved in Suspicion Declareth his Doubtful Mind	30
An Excellent Sonnet Wherein the Lover Exclaimeth against Detraction. To the tune When Cupid scaled first the fort	31
The Lover in Bondage Looketh for Releasement and Longeth for the Relief of his Wedding-day	33
A Fine and Friendly Letter of the Lover to his Beloved	34
The Lover's Fatal Farewell at his Death	35
The Lover Complaineth of his Lady's Unconstancy. To the tune of I loathe that I did love	35
The Lover Having Sustained Overmuch Wrong at his Lady's Hand Wisheth Speedy Death	37
The Lover Exhorteth his Lady to be Constant. To the tune of Attend thee go play thee	38
The Lover Wounded with his Lady's Beauty Craveth Mercy. To the tune of Where is the life that late I led	39
A Caveat to Young Men to Shun the Snares of Cupid's Crafty Sleights	42
The Aged Lover's Note at Length to Learn to Die	44
The Desperate Lover Exclaimeth his Lady's Cruelty and Threateneth to Kill Himself	45
The Lover Being Blinded with the Faithless Love of his Lady is Contented to Remit her Fault	45
A Worthy Comparison of Virtue against All Worldly Pomp	46
Of a Happy Wished Time	47
The Lover Persuadeth Himself to Patience against Envy and Slanderous Tongues	48
The Lover Grievously Complaineth against the Unjust Dealing of his Lady Beloved	49

CONTENTS

The Lover in Great Distress Comforteth Himself with Hope	50
In the Commendation of Faithful Love	51
The Lover Wisheth Himself an Hart in the Forest (as Actaeon Was) for his Lady's Sake	52
An Epitaph upon the Death of Arthur Fletcher of Bangor	52
A Lady Writeth unto her Lover Wherein she Most Earnestly Chargeth him with Ingratitude	53
The Lover unto his Lady Beloved of her Disdainfulness toward him	55
The Lover in the Praise of his Beloved and Comparison of her Beauty	56
In the Praise of a Beautiful and Virtuous Virgin Whose Name Begins with M	56
The Lover Deceived by his Lady's Unconstancy Writeth unto her	57
A True Description of Love	58
The Lover to his Beloved by the Name of Fair and False	59
The Lover Describeth his Painful Plight and Requireth Speedy Redress or Present Death	59
The Lady Beloved Assureth her Lover to be his Own and not to Change	61
In the Praise of the Rare Beauty and Manifold Virtues of Mistress D.	63
Pretty Parables and Proverbs of Love	65
Of Patience	66
Of Lawless Lust	66
Of Will and Reason	66
Of Three Things to be Shunned	66
Of Beauty and Chastity	66
Of Wisdom	66
Of a Pure Conscience	67

CONTENTS

Of Friendship Found by Chance	67
Of Good Will Got by Due Desert	67
Of Flatterers and Faithful Friends	67
Of a Virtuous Life Age and Death	67
A Proper Posie for a Handkerchief	67
The Lover Being Overmuch Wearied with Servile Life Compareth it to a Labyrinth	68
How to Choose a Faithful Friend	69
The Lover Being Accused of Suspicion of Flattery Pleadeth Not Guilty	69
The Lover Describeth the Dangerous State of Ambition	70
The Painful Plight of a Lover Remaining in Doubtful Hope of his Lady's Favor	72
The Lover Recounteth his Faithful Diligence toward his Beloved	73
A Letter Written by a Young Gentlewoman and Sent to her Husband Unawares into Italy	74
A Letter Sent from beyond the Seas to his Lover Persuading her to Continue her Love towards him	77
Another Loving Letter	78
Pretty Pamphlets by T. Proctor	79
Proctor's Precepts	79
Invidus Alterius Rebus Macrescit Opimis	80
The Reward of Whoredom by the Fall of Helen	81
A Lover's Life	82
A Lover Approving his Lady Unkind is Forced Unwilling to Utter his Mind	83
A Gloze of Fawning Friendship	86
A Maze of Maidens	87
A Short Epistle Written in the Behalf of N. B. to M. H.	88
A View of Vainglory	89

CONTENTS

The Fall of Folly Exampled by Needy Age	91
A Proper Sonnet How Time Consumeth All Earthly Things	93
A Mirror of Mortality	94
A Brief Dialogue between Sickness and Worldly Desire	95
Aeger Dives Habet Nummos sed non Habet Ipsum	96
Win Fame and Keep it	98
Respice Finem	99
A Brief Caveat to Shun Fawning Friends	100
Beauty is a Pleasant Path to Destruction	101
T. P. his Farewell unto his Faithful and Approved Friend F. S.	102
The History of Pyramus and Thisbe Truly Translated	103
The Lamentation of Pyramus for the Loss of his Love Thisbe	113
The Lamentation of a Gentlewoman upon the Death of her Friend William Gruffith	116
MISPRINTS AND VARIANT READINGS	121
NOTES	143
INDEX OF FIRST LINES, TITLES, AND TUNES	209
GLOSSARIAL INDEX	214

INTRODUCTION

THE fashion for Elizabethan poetry was set in 1557, when Richard Tottel issued a small volume of *Songes and Sonettes, written by the ryght honorable Lorde Henry Haward late Earle of Surrey, and other*. This volume, familiarly known as Tottel's *Miscellany*,[1] was published on June 5, and a second edition, in which numerous changes and additions were made, was printed on July 31; other editions [2] appeared in 1559, 1565, 1567, 1574, 1585, and 1587. The influence of Tottel's *Miscellany* was more or less constant throughout the pre-Shakespearean period. Rival publishers, naturally enough, imitated Tottel, and in several cases with marked success.

The second genuine poetical miscellany — if we ignore such anomalous works as the extremely popular *Mirror for Magistrates*—was the lost predecessor of *A Handful of Pleasant Delights*, which Richard Jones prepared for printing and almost certainly printed in 1566. Only a single copy, and that fragmentary, of the 1584 edition of the *Handful* remains.[3] It was very popular indeed, and seems to have been a favorite with Shakespeare.

More popular, however, than any other miscellany was *The Paradise of Dainty Devices*, — containing poems by Richard Edwards, Lord Vaux the elder, the Earl of Oxford, William Hunnis, and many other court poets, — which came from the press of Henry Disle in 1576. The *Paradise* is said to have reached a second edition in 1577; it certainly appeared, with many additions, omissions, and corrections, in 1578, and by 1606 had reached at least a tenth edition.[4]

[1] Edited by Edward Arber, *English Reprints*, 1870.
[2] According to Arber's edition, p. v.
[3] Edited by Hyder E. Rollins, Harvard University Press, 1924.
[4] A variorum edition by the present writer is now in press.

INTRODUCTION

Beyond question it was the success of the *Paradise* that led to the publication, by Richard Jones, of *A Gorgeous Gallery of Gallant Inventions* in 1578. The manuscript may have been partly or completely ready as early as June 5, 1577, for on that day Jones secured from the Stationers' Company a license to begin the printing. The entry in the Register[1] is peculiar:

Richard Jones.
MEMORANDUM that this booke is intytuled by the name of ~~Delicate Dainties to sweeten lovers lips withall~~ a gorgious gallery of gallant invencons./

Receaued of him for his licence to imprinte *a handefull of hidden Secretes conteigninge therein certaine Sonetes and other pleasante Devises pickt out of the Closet of sundrie worthie writers and collected together by* R williams .... iiij ᵈ

Who R. Williams was is a mystery.[2] Possibly his name in the entry was due to a mistake on the part of the clerk; or he may have been asked by Jones to compile the work, being later displaced by Roydon and Proctor. In any case, the first title, *A Handful of Hidden Secrets*, points directly to that of *A Handful of Pleasant Delights*, the one miscellany to which the *Gorgeous Gallery* is most indebted. The entry indicates that Richard Jones first discarded this title in favor of *Delicate Dainties to Sweeten Lovers' Lips Withal*, before deciding on that of *A Gorgeous Gallery of Gallant Inventions*. The last title is the most appropriate and, from the point of view of the Elizabethans, the most pleasing. But even it was chosen with the complete title of the *Paradise of Dainty Devices* in mind.

The *Gorgeous Gallery* never won genuine popularity. In its own day

---

[1] Arber's *Transcript*, II, 313.
[2] He can hardly have been the ballad-writer, Richard Williams, whose *Poore Mans Pittance* (made up of three poems) is reprinted in *Ballads from Manuscripts*, ed. F. J. Furnivall, vol. II (1868).

INTRODUCTION

it was not, so far as is known, reprinted, and in modern times it has seldom been read and has not before been critically edited. For many years only one copy was known to be preserved. That passed from the possession of Dr. Richard Farmer to Edmond Malone, the Shakespearean scholar, with the remainder of whose books it found a final resting-place in the Bodleian Library. From this copy (Malone 464a) George Ellis in 1803 reprinted three stanzas of one of the poems in his *Specimens of the Early English Poets*.[1] Almost nobody else noticed it.

There has been no recent edition of the *Gorgeous Gallery*, and only one of any date — Thomas Park's edition in the first volume of *Heliconia. Comprising A Selection of English Poetry of the Elizabethan Age* (1815).[2] Two reprints, in severely limited numbers, have been published. The first of these appeared in *Three Collections of English Poetry, of the Latter Part of the Sixteenth Century*, — a work that contains also *A poore Knight his Pallace of priuate pleasures* (1579) and *A Speciall Remedie against the furious force of lawlesse Loue* (1579), — which was issued for members of the Roxburghe Club in 1845. To the *Three Collections* Sir Henry Ellis contributed an anonymous introduction, which, however, has little or no bearing on the *Gorgeous Gallery* itself. J.P. Collier's reprint of fifty copies appeared in 1867. Because of the early date of Park's edition and the small number of the reprints, so far as the general public is concerned the *Gorgeous Gallery* has never been reprinted at all. Copies of the Collier and Roxburghe Club reprints almost never come on the market, Park's *Heliconia* is itself difficult to find, and the prices of all three are prohibitive. For these reasons the present critical edition of the *Gorgeous Gallery* will, it is believed, supply a genuine need.

Park's text, based on Malone's copy of the *Gorgeous Gallery*, is very inaccurate, no doubt because Park relied solely on a MS. transcript

---

[1] Ellis (II, 393 f.) printed all but the first stanza of "The Louer deceyued by his Ladyes vnconstancy" (p. 57, below).

[2] On the separate title-page of the *Gorgeous Gallery* the date is given as 1814.

INTRODUCTION

and made no attempt to collate his proof-sheets with the original. In some cases, moreover, he has modernized the spelling and punctuation, while in others he has retained the spelling and punctuation of the text itself,—a curious and confusing editorial method. Worse still, he has omitted one leaf, or two pages. In his "Advertisement" he remarks, "One hiatus, occasioned by the loss of a leaf, occurs at p. 102, which it will be hopeless to supply;" but on turning to page 102 (page 62, between lines 17 and 18, of the present edition) one finds the more correct pronouncement, "A line appears to be here wanting in the printed copy." Sir Henry Ellis in 1845, accordingly, was misled into saying, "Park in his Introduction to the reprint of the Gorgious Gallery in the Heliconia speaks of a hiatus at p. 102 in the loss of a *Leaf*, but he meant a LINE." Strangely enough, Ellis did not notice that two entire pages[1] of the text are omitted after page 157 of Park's edition. At the bottom of that page Park printed a row of asterisks, but nowhere did he call attention to their significance. Undoubtedly, however, in the sentence quoted above he intended to say "p. 157" instead of "p. 102."

Park's remarks have misled all subsequent editors and bibliographers into believing that Malone's copy of the *Gorgeous Gallery* is imperfect. As imperfect, for example, it is described in Hazlitt's *Hand-Book* (1867).[2] In his *Extracts from the Registers of the Stationers' Company* (1849)[3] Collier remarks that the *Gorgeous Gallery* "is very carelessly reprinted in 'Heliconia,' vol. i, and from a copy which had the lamentable deficiency of a leaf." He then proceeds to reprint leaf Niii from another copy, which had four years earlier furnished the basis for the Roxburghe Club text. Collier further tells us that he gives the verses from leaf Niii "punctuation and all, precisely as they stand in the original." It is altogether characteristic, however, that in the bare forty-four lines of his reprint there should be sixteen or more variations

[1] Pages 101–102 of the present edition.   [2] Page 483.   [3] II, 39.

INTRODUCTION

from the original, so far as I can judge from the text at my disposal. For some reason or other, Collier knew almost nothing about the books in the Bodleian, and evidently had never seen Malone's text of the *Gorgeous Gallery*, which is perfect. In his *Bibliographical and Critical Account of the Rarest Books in the English Language* (1865)[1] he repeats the assertion that Malone's copy is imperfect, and again prints the two poems from leaf N iii that Park omitted. Here he outdoes himself by varying from his original fifty-five times within the forty-four verses. Apparently he did not think of collating his two reprints.

Returning to Park, it is but fair to say that, with all its faults, his edition has served a very useful purpose. Thanks to it, the contents of the *Gorgeous Gallery* have for more than a century been fairly accessible and fairly well known. In his "Advertisement" Park suggested that some day another copy of the miscellany might be found "lurking in the corner of a musty chest, a family-library, or neglected lumber-closet." Shortly afterwards, a second copy did come to light in the library of the Duke of Northumberland, and this formed the basis for the reprint made by the Roxburghe Club and, presumably, for that made by Collier.

The Roxburghe Club reprint follows the original text page by page and usually line by line; it is printed in black-letter type and, except for a few variations mentioned on page 123 below, purposes to be an exact reproduction. It is a handsome volume with a fairly accurate text, but it cannot be said ever to have been in circulation. Like most of the other publications of the Roxburghe Club, it is seldom found in the average public or private library, and in booksellers' catalogues it almost never appears.

Collier's reprint, in his series of *Seven English Poetical Miscellanies*, contributed nothing by way of preface, introduction, or notes; and his text—though it was intended to be an exact reproduction except

[1] II, 199.

INTRODUCTION

for pagination and typography — cannot be trusted. Collier does not say which text he followed, but no doubt it was the Northumberland copy. On the whole his reprint agrees with that of the Roxburghe Club, but there are enough variations between the two to show that both cannot follow the same original with accuracy.

I have been unable to see the Northumberland copy. Evidently it belonged to the same issue as Malone's. That there are differences of importance between the two copies seems altogether improbable. Perhaps some of the commas and periods that are blurred or doubtful in Malone's copy would turn out to be clear in the Northumberland copy, and *vice versa*. In the list of variant readings given on pages 123 ff. below, every variation between Malone's copy and the two modern reprints of the Duke of Northumberland's is set down; but a study of these variants indicates that they are due to Collier and Ellis rather than to the original texts, and that the Malone and Northumberland copies of the *Gorgeous Gallery* are identical.

The present text, based upon Malone's copy, aims to be an exact reprint, page for page, line for line, except in the following particulars: All obvious typographical errors (like inverted letters, *yrt* for *yet*, and so on), except those of punctuation, are corrected in the text but are listed among the "Misprints and Variant Readings." The long ʃ is everywhere printed *s*. In the text proper — and hence of course in the key-words relating to it — the black-letter of the original is represented by roman type, with roman words replaced by italic and italic by black-letter; but everywhere else — in the title-page, headlines, titles of poems (with the key-words relating to them), "finises," and signature-marks — the typography of the original is followed as closely as modern types permit. False rhymes, incorrect key-words, and bad readings in general are retained in the text, though emendations are suggested in the Notes. The numbering of pages and lines is, of course, an editorial addition.

Thomas Proctor, whose initials appear on the title-page of the

INTRODUCTION

Gorgeous Gallery, is thought to have been the son of John Proctor (†1584), first Master of the Grammar School at Tunbridge and a divine and historian of some note. He was probably the Thomas Proctor who, after an apprenticeship to the well-known printer John Allde, was made free of the Stationers' Company of London on August 17, 1584.[1] The probability of this identification gains from the fact that an obvious friendship existed between Proctor and Anthony Munday; for Munday had been apprenticed to Allde before 1582, and hence was very likely a fellow-apprentice of Proctor's when the *Gorgeous Gallery* was compiled. To that work he contributed complimentary verses, and Proctor returned the compliment in the following year (1579) by writing a poetical commendation for Munday's *Mirrour of Mutabilitie*.[2] In 1579, furthermore, both Proctor and Munday prefixed commendatory verses to *Newes from the North. Otherwise called the Conference between Simon Certain and Pierce Plowman*, by "T. F., Student," initials that are sometimes said to be reversed for "F. T.", that is, Francis Thynne.

Elizabethan printers frequently wrote and published their own poems and ballads. Proctor was, then, merely following the fashion. At least two other works of his are known,—*Of the knowledge and conducte of warres, two bookes* (1578), and *The Triumph of Truth* (no date). The first of these was printed by Richard Tottel; there are copies in the British Museum and the library of Mr. Henry E. Huntington. The second was "published by T. P." — no doubt Proctor himself — shortly after Proctor was actively admitted to the Stationers' Company in 1584; it was reprinted by Collier in 1866. Proctor has also been credited[3] with the authorship of *The Treatise of Heavenly Philosophy*,

---

[1] Arber's *Transcript*, II, 692; Collier's *Bibliographical and Critical Account*, II, 197; *D. N. B.*, *s. v.* "Proctor, Thomas."   [2] See below, p. 145.

[3] By Joseph Ritson, *Bibliographia Poetica*, p. 301, and by Collier, *Bibliographical and Critical Account*, II, 198. The error was noted as early as 1814 by John Fry (*Pieces of Ancient Poetry*, pp. 84–85).

[xix]

INTRODUCTION

which appeared under the initials "T. P." in 1578, but which was really written by Thomas Palfreyman. Nor can our T. P. have been the Thomas Proctor whose name was signed to *A Profitable Worke to this whole Kingdome* (1610) or to *The Righteous Man's Way* (1621).[1]

Evidently Proctor was at the height of his powers and reputation when the *Gorgeous Gallery* was printed. Several of the poems in that miscellany are signed with his name or initials, and he may have written others that are not signed. On the whole, his acknowledged poems are as good as the majority of those in the *Paradise of Dainty Devices*. He seems to have been of a sententious, contemplative bent, and he wrote with perhaps more gravity than inspiration on the commonplaces of Elizabethan poetry. But as a metrist he is not often inferior to his contemporaries, Spenser always excepted.

There are indications that Proctor fell heir to a work which Owen Roydon was "building up"; for the address to the critics (or "sycophants"), as well as the first poem, in the *Gorgeous Gallery* is signed with Roydon's initials. He may have written some of the other poems. In this connection it should be noted that Proctor's name first appears on leaf K iv (page 79), in the heading, "Pretie pamphlets, by T. Proctor." Since this heading displaces the usual phrase, "of gallant Inuentions," it seems to refer to the entire group of poems that follows. The first poem (on page 79) is called "Proctors Precepts," and of the next eighteen pieces ten are signed with the initials "T. P." The last two poems in the book are presumably not his work. From these facts it seems probable that Roydon collected and arranged the contents of the *Gorgeous Gallery* down to page 79, where Proctor took up the "building." Or perhaps the unknown R. Williams mentioned in the stationers' entry may have laid the first stones or added the finishing touches.

Because of his unusual surname, Owen Roydon is generally sup-

[1] They are attributed to him by Hazlitt, *Hand-Book*, p. 484, and *Bibliographical Collections*, III, 205; cf. also G. J. Gray's *General Index* to Hazlitt, *s. v.* "Procter."

INTRODUCTION

posed to have been related in one way or another to the well-known poet, Matthew Roydon, M.A. The relationship may have been that of father and son, but it cannot be proved. There is a sketch of Matthew Roydon in the *Dictionary of National Biography*. He was a friend of Sidney, Lodge, Chapman, and other Elizabethan poets, and is spoken of in complimentary terms in the epistle that Thomas Nashe prefixed to Robert Greene's *Menaphon* (1589), as well as in Francis Meres's *Palladis Tamia* (1598). His contributions to *The Phoenix Nest* (1593) make his name familiar even at the present day.

In addition to Roydon and Proctor, other (perhaps involuntary) contributors to the *Gorgeous Gallery* can be identified. Among them are Lord Vaux the elder, Thomas Churchyard, Thomas Howell, Clement Robinson, Jasper Heywood, "E. S.," and Master Bewe (whoever he may have been). In a real sense, then, the *Gorgeous Gallery* is as genuine a miscellany as is Tottel's or the *Paradise of Dainty Devices*. It should be noted that the title-page frankly admits that the poems were "first framed and fashioned in sundry forms by divers worthy workmen of late days," and that they were "joined together and builded up" by Proctor. In such an action there was, from the point of view of an Elizabethan, nothing especially dishonest or unethical. Proctor had read widely in the poetry of his time, and he (or his assistant or his publisher) simply collected from various sources poems that appealed to him, perhaps changing or supplying words and lines at his fancy, and to the whole adding original compositions of his own. If any objection had been made to his building, it would have come, not from the authors, but from the printers who held the rights to the poems.

The most striking source from which Proctor drew was Clement Robinson's *Handful of Pleasant Delights*. Since Richard Jones printed both the *Handful* and the *Gorgeous Gallery*, no doubt he authorized the wholesale borrowing from the *Handful* that characterizes Proctor's anthology. Four of the poems are frankly taken from six ballads in the

INTRODUCTION

Handful,[1] but the other cases of borrowing are not so simple. It is doubtful whether permission was secured for the inclusion of poems the rights to which Jones did not own. Very likely Proctor, or Jones, helped himself to pieces he wished to include without asking any one's permission. Thus, three poems are borrowed from Tottel's *Miscellany*[2] and three from the *Paradise*;[3] two are preserved also in a manuscript dating about 1500;[4] two others are the work of Thomas Howell and Thomas Churchyard;[5] several are mere street-ballads.[6] Probably the compiler secured a considerable number of his texts in broadside-ballad form.

Richard Jones became notorious for printing in a single volume poems by various hands and assigning them to one author. For example, he printed *Brittons Bowre of Delights* (1591) and *The Arbor of Amorous Devices* (1597)[7] as the work of Nicholas Breton, though most of the poems in them were not from Breton's pen. In one of his prefatory epistles to *The Pilgrimage to Paradise* (1592) Breton complained that the *Bower of Delights* "was donne altogether without my consent or knowledge, and many thinges of other mens mingled with a few of mine, for except *Amoris Lachrimæ*: an epitaphe vpon Sir Phillip Sydney, and one or two other toies, which I know not how he [Richard Jones] vnhappily came by, I haue no part of any of them."

Perhaps by following this policy of thievery Jones hoped to make the *Gorgeous Gallery* rival in popularity the *Handful* and the *Paradise*; but, if so, he was doomed to disappointment. The *Gallery* did not, apparently, reach a second edition; it had no traceable effect on Elizabethan writers, nor is it referred to more than once or twice by them.

---

[1] See pp. 28, 35 (lines 20 ff.), 38, 39, and the Notes.
[2] See pp. 31 (cf. 35), 45, 47, and the Notes.
[3] See pp. 52, 69, 72 (cf. 100), and the Notes.
[4] See p. 66 and the Notes. Cf. also 92.25 n.
[5] See pp. 7, 57, and the Notes.
[6] *E. g.*, pp. 26, 116, and all those cited in foot-note 1 above.
[7] This appears to have been licensed in 1594 as *The Arbour of Amorus delightes*.

INTRODUCTION

Possibly Nicholas Breton had it in mind when, in his *Floorish upon Fancie* (1582),[1] he says in a list of books, "Some Pretie Pamphlets are." Thomas Nashe[2] unmistakably refers to it in *The Unfortunate Traveller* (1594): "To tell you of the rare pleasures of their [the Romans'] gardens, theyr bathes, theyr vineyardes, theyr galleries, were to write a seconde part of the gorgeous Gallerie of gallant deuices." Thomas Dekker makes one of the characters in his *Satiro-mastix* (1602, ed. Hans Scherer, 1907, p. 21) say, "Why you bastards of nine whoores, the Muses, why doe you walk heere in this gorgeous gailery of gallant inuentions?" Neither in the sixteenth century nor in later days has the *Gorgeous Gallery* been praised. For this cold reception perhaps both its style and its subjects are to blame.

In spite of the various authors represented, the style of the book is more or less uniform. The diction is more archaic than that of either the *Handful* or the *Paradise*, as lexicographers have observed. Unusual words and phrases abound, and there are about a dozen words among them that furnish the only, or the earliest, examples given in the *New English Dictionary*. Greater reliance, too, is placed on alliteration than in either the *Handful* or the *Paradise*, and so artfully is the right letter hunted for that sometimes the lines are devoid of meaning. Love of alliteration accounts for the repetition of such phrases as "goring gripes," "pining pain," "doleful dumps," "grisly grief," the taste for which was apparently beginning to lose something of its savor even in 1578. Too much sententiousness and literary affectation, too much moralizing, too little lightness and sparkle, — these are some of the characteristics that may explain why the book did not succeed.

Since the subjects are, in the main, conventional, originality of treatment is not to be expected. There are, of course, as in most other Elizabethan miscellanies, bountiful examples of epistles sent to and from the love-lorn, of lamentations by faithful and tirades against faithless

---

[1] Page 14 (*Works*, ed. Grosart, vol. I).
[2] *Works*, ed. R. B. McKerrow, II, 282.

INTRODUCTION

lovers; there are repeated allusions to Troilus and Cressida, to Helen and Paris, to Penelope and Ulysses, to Polyxena and Paris, to Pyramus and Thisbe; and there is an insistence on the imminence of death, the futility of life, the falsity of friends, the misery of love, the changeableness of women, subjects on which originality of expression was hardly possible. But, although the *Gorgeous Gallery* says little that is new, it does reflect faithfully the sentiments and ideas of Tottel's *Miscellany*, the *Handful*, and the *Paradise*. It holds up a mirror to the age that directly preceded Shakespeare. The *Gorgeous Gallery* came ten or fifteen years too late: in 1565, or even in 1576, it would undoubtedly have been a "best seller"; in 1578 it was thrown into a vain competition with the serious, courtly poems of the *Paradise*.

Fortunately its interest for the modern reader does not depend entirely on the merits or the demerits of its poetry. Even as poetry, however, the contents of the *Gorgeous Gallery* deserve some consideration. Of more than ordinary interest is the long "history" of Pyramus and Thisbe, while, among other graceful songs, "The glittering shows of Flora's dames" (page 26) and "Willow, willow, willow" (page 83) call for special praise. Worthy of notice, furthermore, are the surprisingly numerous proverbs and wise saws and the versatility of the metres and rhythms.

Few early Tudor collections of poems run the gamut of so many metrical forms, and in the history of English rhythms this book should have a place of considerable distinction. Of course the influence of Tottel's *Miscellany*, of Gascoigne and Whetstone, and of Turbervile had popularized the poulter's measure. In that jog-trot metre some fifteen of the poems are written.[1] Septenary couplets — the ballad stanza — are used for twelve poems.[2] Poulter's measure and septenary couplets are combined (somewhat awkwardly) in one poem;[3] another is written

---

[1] Pages 9, 13, 16, 21 (twice), 29, 35 (twice), 37, 47, 48, 59, 63, 69, 101.
[2] Pages 7, 34, 42, 49, 52, 56, 59, 74, 77, 78, 103 (in part), 113 (in part).
[3] Page 86.

INTRODUCTION

in octosyllabic anapestic couplets;[1] while three poems are in hexameter couplets[2] and two in irregular heroic verse.[3]

The stanza forms are of various types, some of them important. Quatrains of many metres and rhyming-schemes occur: iambic trimeter in three poems;[4] iambic tetrameter (with occasional irregularities) in five;[5] iambic pentameter, of varying rhyme-schemes, in eleven.[6] The six-line iambic pentameter stanza that Shakespeare adopted for his *Venus and Adonis* is used in six poems (one of them irregular).[7] Rhyme-royal is found twice.[8] Eight-line stanzas are common: the metre is trimeter, rhyming *abababcc*;[9] or tetrameter, rhyming *ababcdcd*;[10] or tetrameter, rhyming *ababcaca*, with the fourth line catalectic and the second quatrain irregular.[11] *Ottava rima*, imperfectly managed, occurs twice.[12] Interesting, too, is the use of a ten-line stanza made up of five octosyllabic couplets;[13] of an elaborate broadside-ballad stanza of eight lines[14] and another of twelve;[15] and of one stanza that resembles the "wheel and bob" of the Middle English alliterative poems.[16] Four of the poems are sonnets,— one of a curious type,[17] and three following strictly the English, or Shakespearean, form that Surrey had introduced.[18] Such metrical versatility — and not all the forms have been mentioned — demands attention.

I am indebted to the Librarian of the Bodleian Library for permission to reprint the Malone copy of the *Gorgeous Gallery* and for other courtesies; to my friend Miss Addie F. Rowe for the painstaking care

---

[1] Page 65.   [2] Pages 46, 51, 52.   [3] Pages 81, 98.
[4] Pages 28, 44, 45.   [5] Pages 31, 33, 55, 88, 116 (in part).
[6] Pages 79, 80, 89, 91, 95, 99, 100, 102, 105 (in part), 108, (in part), 109 (in part).
[7] Pages 68, 72, 73, 82, 94, 116.   [8] Pages 22, 113.
[9] Page 27.   [10] Pages 26, 57.   [11] Page 30.
[12] Pages 53, 61.   [13] Page 96.   [14] Page 83.
[15] Pages 38, 39.   [16] Page 70.   [17] Page 58.
[18] Pages 56, 69, 108. 2–15 (cf. 111. 2–15).

INTRODUCTION

with which she verified the manuscript and assumed the chief burden of the proof-reading; and to Professor George Lyman Kittredge for suggestions, always too numerous to be mentioned specifically, for the betterment of the Notes.

H. E. R.

NEW YORK UNIVERSITY
March 2, 1925

A gorgious Gallery,

of gallant Inuentions.

Garnished and decked with *diuers dayntie deuises, right* delicate and delightfull, to recreate eche modest minde withall.

First framed and fashioned in sundrie formes, by diuers worthy workemen of late dayes: and now, ioyned together and builded up:

By T. P.

¶ Imprinted at London, *for Richard Iones.*
1578.

A. M. Vnto all yong Gentilmen,
in commendacion of this Gallery
and workemen therof.

SEE Gallaunts, see, this Gallery of delightes,
With buyldings braue, imbost of variant hue: 5
With daynties deckt, deuisde by worthy wights,
(Which) as time serude, vnto perfection grew.
By studies toyle with phrases fine they fraught:
This peereles peece, filde full, of pretty pith:
And trimde it, (with) what skill, and learning taught, 10
In hope to please your longing mindes therwith.
Which workemanship, by worthy workemen wrought,
(Perusde) least in obliuion it should ly:
A willing minde, eche part togeather sought,
And termde (the whole) *A gorgious Gallerye:* 15
Wherin you may, to recreate the minde,
Such fyne Inuentions finde, for your delight:
That, for desart, their dooings will you binde,
To yeelde them prayse, so well a worke to wright.

FINIS.   A. M.   20

Owen Roydon to the curious
company of Sycophantes.

THe busie Bees whose paynes doo neuer misse,
But toyle their time the winters want to wielde:
And heape in hiues, the thing that needfull is, 25
To feede their flocke till winter bee exilde:
Somtimes the **Drones** *the Hony combes doo eate,*
And so the Bees must starue for want of meate.

A ii   *The*

To curious Sycophantes.

The drowsie **Drones** *doo neuer take such toyle,*
But lye at lurch, like men of **Momus** *minde:*
Who rudely read and rashly put to foyle,
What worthy workes, so euer they doo finde: 5
  Which workes would please the learned sorte full well,
  But **Sicophantes** *will neuer cease to swell,*
Though (learnedly) themselues be voyde to write,
And haue not knowen the height of **Hellicon**:
Yet, carpingly, they needes must spit their spite,   10
Or els their former force, (they iudge) is gon:
  Who only liue, the seelly Bees t'annoy,
  And eate the meate, wheron the Bees should ioy.
(Depart from hence) that cursed kinde of crew,
And let this Booke, embrace his earned meede: 15
Which was set forth (for others) not for you,
What likes them best, that only for to reade:
  And let the rest, without rebuke to passe,
  And helpe t'amend the thing that blamelesse was.
(APELLES) might suffise, to warne you wel,   20
(who) while hee was a paynting in his Shop:
Came in (a Sowter) who began to swell,
And viewd his Image all from toe to top:
  And scofte at this, and did mislike at that,
  Of many a fault the Champion gan to chat.   25
At length (**Apelles** *) angry with his man,*
Dislyked much and gaue him answere so:
(Talke thou of that, wherin some skill thou can)
Vnto the slipper (Sowter) only go:
  The saucye (Sowter) was abasshed much,   30
  And afterward, his talke was nothing such.
So? (**Momus** *thou) no further then thy marke,*
And talke no more, then skill doth giue thee leaue:
But in thy hart, there is a burning sparke,
And (whiles thou liues) that sickenesse will thee greaue: 35
  But doo thy worst, and doo no more but right,
  The learned route, wil laughe at thy despight.
            FINIS.   O. R.

THE GALLERY
of gallant Inuentions.

To a Gentilwoman that sayd: All men be false,
they thinke not what they say.

Some women fayne that *Paris* was,
The falsest louer that could bee:
Who for his (life) did nothing passe,
As all the world might playnly see:
But ventred life and limmes and all,
  To keepe his freend from *Greekish* thrall:
  With many a broyle hee dearely bought,
  His (*Hellen*) whom hee long had sought.
For first (Dame *Venus*) graunted him,
A gallant gifte of *Beauties* fleece:
Which boldely for to seeke to win,
By surging Seas hee sayld to *Greece*:
  And when hee was arriued theare,
  By earnest sute to win his Deare:
  No greater paynes might man endure,
  Then *Paris* did, for *Hellen* sure.
Besides all this when they were well,
Both hee, and shee, arryu'd at *Troy*:
Kinge *Menelaus* wrath did swell,
And swore, by sword, to rid their ioyes:
  And so hee did for ten yeres space,
  Hee lay before the *Troyans* face:
  With all the hoste that hee could make,
  To bee reueng'd for *Hellens* sake.

         A iij   Loe?

The gorgious Gallery

Loe? thus much did poore *Paris* bide,
Who is accounted most vntrue:
All men bee false it hath bin sayd,
They thinke not what they speake (say you)　　　　5
　Yes *Paris* spoke, and sped with speede,
　As all the heauenly Gods decreed:
　And proou'd himselfe a Louer iust,
　Till stately *Troy* was turnd to dust:
I doo not reade of any man,　　　　10
That so much was vnfaythfull found:
You did vs wrong, t'accuse vs than,
And say our freendship is not sound:
　If any fault bee found at all,
　To womens lot it needes must fall:　　　　15
　If (*Hellen*) had not bin so light,
　Sir *Paris* had not died in fight.
The falsest men I can excuse,
That euer you in stories reade:
Therfore all men for to accuse,　　　　20
Mee thinkes it was not well decreede:
　It is a signe you haue not tride,
　What stedfastnesse in men doth bide:
　But when your time shal try them true,
　This iudgment then, you must renue.　　　　25
I know not euery mans deuise,
But commonly they stedfast are:
Though you doo make them of no price,
They breake their vowes but very rare:
　They will performe theyr promis well,　　　　30
　And specially where loue doth dwell:
　Where freendship doth not iustly frame,
　Then men (forsooth) must beare the blame.

　　　　FINIS.　　O. R.

[6]

of gallant Inuentions.

❧ The lamentable louer abiding in the
bitter bale of direfull doubts towards
his Ladyes loyalty, writeth vnto her as followeth.

HEalth I thee send, if hee may giue, y͠ which himself doth misse: 5
For thy sweet brest, doth harbor whole, my bloody bale or blisse,
I neede no scribe, to scry my care, in restlesse rigor spread:
They that behold, my chaunged cheare, already iudge mee dead.
My baned limmes, haue yeelded vp, their woonted ioy to dye:
My healthles hand, doth nought but wring, & dry my dropping eye,   10
The deadly day, in dole I passe, a thousand times I craue
The noysome night: agayne I wish, the dolefull day to haue.
Eche howre to mee, most hatefull is, eche place doth vrge my wo:
No foode mee feedes, close vp mine eyes, to gastly graue I go.
No Phisickes art, can giue the salue, to heale my paynfull part: 15
Saue only thou, the salue and sore, of this my captiue hart,
Thou art the branch y͠ sweetly springs, whose hart is sound & true
Can only cheare mee wofull wight, or force my want to rue.
Then giue to mee, the sap I thirste, which gift may giue mee ioy,
I mean thy firme, & faythful loue, whose want breeds mine annoy,   20
Remember yet sure freendship had, ypast betweene vs twayne
Forget him not, for loue of thee, who sighes in secret payne.
I oftdoo seeme in company, a gladsome face to beare,
But God thou knowst my inward woes, & cares y͠ rent mee there:
And that I may, gush out my greefe, in secret place alone,   25
I bid my freends farewell in haste, I say I must be gone.
Then haste I fast, with heauy hart, in this my dolefull case:
Where walkes no wight, but I alone, in drowsie desart place,
And there I empt, my laden hart, that sweld in fretting mone:
My sighes and playnts, and panges I tell, vnto my selfe alone.   30
What shall I say? doo aske mee once, why all these sorowes bee?
I answere true, O foe or freend, they all are made for thee,

Once

The gorgious Gallery

Once knit the lynck, that loue may last, then shal my dollors cease
It lyes in thee, and wilt thou not, the yeelding wight release?
O would to God, it lay in mee, to cure such greefe of thine: (mine,
Thou shouldst not long, be voyd of helpe, if twere in power of   5
But I would run, & range in stormes, a thousand miles in payne:
Not fearing foyle, of freends to haue, my coūtenance whole agayn
And wilt thou then, all mercylesse, more longer torment mee?
In drawing backe, sith my good helpe, is only whole in thee?
Then send mee close, ẙ hewing knife, my wider wound to stratch: 10
And thou shalt see, by wofull greefe, of life a cleane dispatch.
When thou shalt say, and prooue it true, my hart entirely lou'd,
Which lost the life, for countnance sweet frõ whõ hee neuer mou'd
Write then vpon my wofull Tombe, these verses grauen aboue,
Heere lyes the hart, his truth to trie, that lost his life in loue.   15
Loe, saue or spill, thou mayst mee now, thou sitst in iudgment hie,
Where I poore man, at Bar doo stand, and lowd, for life doo cry.
Thou wilt not bee, so mercylesse, to slea a louing hart:
Small prayse it is to conquer him, that durst no where to start,
Thou hast the sword, that cut the wound, of my vnholpen payne: 20
Thou canst and art, the only helpe, to heale the same agayne.
Then heale the hart, that loues thee well, vntill the day hee dye:
And firmely fast thy loue on him, thats true continually,
In thee my wealth, in thee my woe, in thee too saue or spill:
In thee mee lyfe, in thee my death, doth rest to worke thy will.   25
Let vertue myxt, with pitty great, and louing mercy saue
Him, who without thy salue, so sicke, that hee must yeeld to graue,
O salue thou then, my secret sore, sith health in thee dooth stay:
And graūt w̃ speed, my iust request, whose want woıks my decay
Then shal I blesse, the pleasāt place, where once I tooke thy gloue,   30
And thanke ẙ God, who giues thee grace, to graūt me loue for loue.

FINIS.

[8]

¶ A louing Epistle, written by *Ruphilus* a 𝔶𝔬𝔫𝔤𝔢 𝔊𝔢𝔫𝔱𝔦𝔩𝔪𝔞𝔫, 𝔱𝔬 𝔥𝔦𝔰 𝔟𝔢𝔰𝔱 𝔟𝔢𝔩𝔬𝔲𝔢𝔡 𝔏𝔞𝔡𝔶
Elriza, as followeth.

Twice hath my quaking hand withdrawen this pen away
And twice againe it gladly would, before I dare beewray   5
The secret shrined thoughts, that in my hart do dwell,
That neuer wight as yet hath wist, nor I desire to tell.
But as the smoothered cole, doth wast and still consume,
And outwardly doth geue no heate, of burnyng blaze or fume:
So hath my hidden harmes, been harbred in my corpce,   10
Till faintyng limmes and life and all, had welnigh lost his force:
Yet stand I halfe in doubt, whiche of these two to choose,
To hide my harmes still to my hurt, or els this thraldome loose.
I will lay feare aside, and so my tale beginne:
Who neuer durst assaile his foe: did neuer conquest win.   15
   Lo here my cause of care to thee vnfolde I will:
Help thou *Minerua*, graunt I pray, some of thy learned skill.
Help all you Muses nine, my wofull Pen to write:
So stuffe my verse with pleasant wordes, as she may haue delight,
With heedyng eares to reade my greeif and great vnrest: 20
Some wordes of plaint may moue perhaps, to pitty my request.
Oft haue I hard complaint, how Cupid beares a sway
In brittle youth, and would commaund: and how they did obay.
When I with skorning eares did all their talke dispise:
But well I see the blinded boy: in lurking den hee lies,   25
To catch the careles sorte: awayting with his Darte:
Hee threw at mee when I vnwares, was wounded to the harte.
To speake and pray for helpe, now loue hath mee constrainde:
And makes mee yeeld to serue the sorte, that lately I disdainde.
Sith beggars haue no choyce: nor neede had euer law   30
The subiecte Oxe doth like his yoke: when hee is driuen to draw.
That *Ruphilus* this wrote: thou wonder wilt I know,
Cause neuer erst in louinge vearse: my labor I bestowe,
Well, woful loue is mine, and weeping lines I wright,
And doubtfull wordes with driery cheere: beseemes a careful wight   35
O thou *Elrisa* fayre, the beuty of thine eyes
Hath bred such bale within my brest, and cau'sde such strife to ryse.

𝔅   As

The gorgious Gallery

As I can not forget: vntill deuouring death
Shal leaue to mee a senceles goast: and rid my longer breath,
Or at the least that thou: doo graunt mee some releefe
To ease the greedy gripes I feele, and end my great mischeefe.   5
As due to mee by right, I can no mercy craue,
Thou hast the power to graunt mee life: refuse not for to saue.
Put to thy helping hand, to salue the wounded sore,
Though thou refuse it for my sake: yet make thine honour more,
Too cruell were the facte: if thou shouldst seeke to kill   10
Thy faythful freend that loues thee so: and doth demaund no ill.
Thy heauenly shape I saw: thy passing bewty bright,
Enforst mee to assay the bayt: where now my bane I bight
I nought repent my loue: nor yet forthinke my facte,
The Gods I know were all agreed: and secretly compacte.   15
To frame a worke of prayse: to show their power deuine
By good aduice this on the earth: aboue the rest to shine.
Whose perfecte shape is such: as *Cupid* feares his fall,
And euery wight that hath her seene, I say (not one) but all
With one consent they cry: lo here dame *Venus* ayer,   20
Not *Danae* nor shee dame *Lede:* was euer halfe so faire.
Though Princes sue for grace: and ech one do thee woo,
Mislyke not this my meane estate: wherwith I can nought doo.
As highest seates wee see: be subiect to most winde,
So base and poore estates we know, be hateful to the minde.   25
The happy meane is mine: which I do haply holde,
Thy honor is to yeeld for loue: and not for heape of golde.
If euer thou hast felte: the bitter panges that stinges
A louers brest: or knowest the cares, that *Cupid* on vs flinges.
Then pitty my request: and wayle my wofull case,   30
Whose life to death with hasty wheeles: doo toumble on apace.
Vouchsafe to ease the paine: that loue on mee doth whelme,
Let not thy freend to shipwracke go: sith thou doost hold his helme.
Who yeeldeth all hee hath: as subiect to thy will,
If thou commaund hee doth obey, and all thy heastes fulfill.   35
But if thou call to minde: when I did part thee fro,
What was the cause of my exile: and why I did forgo
                                                        The

[10]

of gallant Inuentions.

The happy life I held, and lost therewith thy sight,
Well mayst thou wayle thy want of troth: & rue thy great vnright
If thou be found to fayle thy vow that thou hast sworne
Or that one iot of my good will, out of thy minde be worne.   5
Or if my absence long: to thy disgrace hath wrought mee   (mee.
Or hindering tales of my back freends: vnto such state hath brought
I can and will accurse the cause of my ill speede:
But well, I hope, my feare is more: then is the thing indeede.
Yet blame mee not though I doo stand somewhat in feare   10
The cause is great of my exile, which hardly I do beare.
Who hath a sternles ship amidst the trustles Seaes,
Full greedely desires the porte: where hee may ride at ease.
Thy bewty bids mee trust, vnto thy promise past,
My absence longe and not to speake: doth make mee doubt as fast.   15
For as the sommers sonne, doth make eche thing to spring:
Euen so the frosen winters blast, as deadly doth them wring.
Vnsuer thus I liue in dreade I wot not why
Yet was there neuer day so bright, but there be cloudes in sky.
Who hath of puer Golde, a running streame or flud   20
And is restraind for comming nigh, this treasure great and good.
Hee must abide a time: till Fortune graunt him grace,
That hee haue power by force to win: his riche desired place.
I neede not thus to doo: nor yet so much mistrust,
I know no time can change thy minde: or make thee bee vniust.   25
No more then water soft, can stir a stedfast rocke:
Or seely flyes vpon their backes can beare away a blocke.
Eche beast on earth wee see: that liuing breath doth draw,
Bee faythfull found vnto their mates: and keepes of loue the law.
My wretched life to ease: when I doo seke to turne,   30
Thy bewty bright doth kindle mee, in greater flame to burne.
No day, no night, nor time, that geues mee mirth or rest,
Awake, asleape, and at my meales, thou doost torment my brest.
Though weary lothsome lyfe: in care and wo haue clad mee,
Remembrance of thy heauenly face, giues cause again to glad mee.   35
Thus Ioyfull thoughtes a while, doth lessen much my payne
But after calme and fayer tides, the stormes do come agayne.

𝔅 ij   And

The gorgious Gallery

And I in cares doo flame, to thinke of my exile,
That I am barred from thy sight: I curse and ban the while.
Would God I had the craft a Laborinth to frame,
And also had a *Mynotaure:* inclosed in the same: 5
And that our enemies all, might therin take some paine,
Till *Dedales* line I did them bringe, to helpe them out againe.
Then should my sorowes seace, and drowne my deepe dispaire,
Then should my life be blest with Ioyes: and raisde aboue the ayre.
But as the mazed birde, for feare dare skantly fly, 10
When hee hath scapte the Falcons foote: euen so I know should I
Scarse able be to speake, or any word to say,
Least *Argus* wayting ielous eyes, might haply mee bewray
But oh *Elrisa* mine, why doo I stir such war
Within my selfe to thinke of this: and yet thy loue so far? 15
Why rather should not I: giue vp the life I haue
And yeeld my weary wretched corps: vnto the gaping grau
If I hopte not that thou with faith didst binde thy life,
This hand of mine with bloody sworde, should stint my cruel strife.
No length of lingring time: no distance can remooue, 20
The fayth that I haue vowed to thee: nor alter once my loue.
Beleeue this to bee true, that streames shall soner turne,
Or frosen Ice to fier coales, on blasing flame to burne.
Then I will seke to change: or alter once my minde,
All plagues I pray may fall on me, if I be found vnkinde. 25
Or if I meane to swarue while I haue liuing breath
God graunt my end then may be such as *Agamemnons* death.
I wish thy life no harme: but yet I woulde thou knew
The wofull ende that *Cressed* made, because shee was vntrue.
Those angry gods or men, asonder that doo set vs, 30
Shal neuer pearce our mindes in twaine nor eke to loue can let vs.
As well they may deuide the fier from the flame,
And euery beast that now is wilde, as soone shalbe made tame.
Let not this pistle long, my sute with thee deface,
Who pleadeth for his life thou knowest: at large must tel his case. 35
And all these wordes I write, to one effect do tende,
I am all thine, and not mine owne: and herewithal to ende.

I

[12]

of gallant Inuentions.

I pray thee to regarde: thy health and my request,
And that my loue doo neuer fleet out of thy secret brest.
FINIS.

¶ NARSETVS a wofull youth, in his exile writeth
to *Rosana* his beloued mistresse, to assure her of his
faithfull constancie, requiring the like of her.

O stay thy musinge minde: hee did this pistle frame,
That holds the deere, & loues thee most: *Narsetus* is his name
Would God thy frend had brought: y̌ health y̌ here he sendes 10
I should haue seene my lacking ioy, and heale that hart that rendes.
And redy is eche hower: to sunder still in twaine,
Saue now this pistle that I write: doth lessen wel my paine,
And helpes mee to vpholde a lingring lothsome life,
Awaiting still the blisfull hower, when death shall stinte the strife. 15
What dooth it mee preuaile: to haue king *Cresus* wealth,
Or who doth ioy in golden Giues, imprisoned with his health,
I sweare by *Ioue* to thee, whose godhead is aye iust,
These wordes I write are not vntrue: then do mee not mistrust.
Thy selfe shalbe the iudge: and if thou list to vewe, 20
The bared bones, the hollow lookes, the pale and ledy hew,
The stealing strides I draw: the wo and dreadfull feares
The boyling brest with bitter brine, the eyes be sprent with teares
The skant and hungry meales: the seldome slepe I take,
The dainty dames that others ioy, no iest to mee do make 25
These hated hatefull harmes: when I them feele to greeue mee
Remembrance of thy beuty bright, doth straight again releeue mee
And then I cal to minde, thy shape and cumly grace,
Thy heauenly hew thy sugred words, thy sweet entising face
The pleasant passed sportes: that spent the day to ende, 30
The lothsom lookes that liked not to leue so soone thy freend.
Sith froward fortune hath, my Mystresse thus bereft mee,
Perforce I yeeld and am content, to like the lot is left mee.
If *Pyramus* were sad, when hee found *Thisby* slayne,
If *Cresseds* craft and falsing fayth: did *Troylus* turne to payne, 35

B iij *Eneas*

[13]

The gorgious Gallery

Eneas traytor false: oh treason that hee did,   (hath rid
With bloody woundes and murdering sword, Queene *Didos* lyfe
If these haue won by death and end of pyning payne,
And I aliue with torments great in dying deathes remaine.   5
The sound of instruments: or musickes pleasant noyce,
Or riches rule, or proude estate, doth cause mee to reioyce
Or *Venus* damsels deere, do please mee euen as well,
As dying bodies ioy to here, for them a passing bell.
The greefes that gripe my hart, and dayly do mee slay   10
It lessen would much of the smart, if thou vouchsafe to say:
God graunt his weary life: and sorrowes to asswage,
God yeeld him health and happy dayes with honor in his age.
These wordes would win my life, dispaired now to death,
Thou should but saue that is thine own, while I haue liuing breath 15
What heapes of haples hopes, on me shall chance to fall,
So thou doo liue in blisfull state: no force for mee at all.
Amid my greatest greefe, the greatest care I haue,
Is how to wish and will thee good: and most thy honor saue.
Bee faythfull found therfore, bee constant true and iust   20
If thou betray thy louing freend, whom hensforth shall I trust?
When shal I speake with thee? when shal I thee imbrace?   (grace?
When will the gods appease their wrath? when shal I haue sutch
Hath *Ioue* forgotten dame *Lede* for loue: and how hee prayed her,
Transformed like a swan at length: the seely soule hee trayde her. 25
When faire fresh *Danae* was closed vp in tower:
Did hee not raine himselfe a drop, amidst the golden shower
And fell into her lap: from top of chimney hie?
The great delight of his long loue: hee did attaine thereby,
What cruell gods be these? what trespasse haue I doone?   30
That I am banisht thus from thee, what conquest haue they woon?
I know their power deuine: can for a while remooue mee,
But whilste I liue, and after death, my soule shall likewise loue thee
Not *Alcumena* shee, for whom the treble night
Was shaped first, can well compare with thee for bewty bright   35
Not *Troylus* sister too, whom cruell *Pirrhus* slew,
Nor shee, the price of ten yeres wars, whom yet the Grekes do rew
                                                                    Nor

of gallant Inuentions.

Nor shee *Penelope*, whose chastnes wan her fame,
Can match with thee *Rosina* chaste: I see her blush for shame.
The childe of mighty *Ioue*, that bred within his braine
Shall yeeld the palme of filed speche, to thee that doth her staine. 5
And euery wight on earth: that liuing breath do draw,
Lo here your queene sent from aboue, to kepe you all in awe
But nowe I fine my talke, I finde my wits to dull,
There liueth none that can set forth thy vertues at the ful.
Yet this I dare well say, and dare it to auowe, 10
The Gods do feare *Rosinas* shape: and bewty doth alowe.
In *Tantalus* toyle I liue: and want that most I would,
With wishing vowes I speake, I pray: yet lacke the thing I should
I see that I do want: I reach, it runnes mee fro:
I haue and lacke, that I loue most, and lothest to forgo. 15
But oh *Rosanna* dere: since time of my exile   (while
How hast thou done? and doost thou liue: how hast thou spent the
How standeth health with thee? and art thou glad of chere?
God graunt those happy restful dayes, increase may still each yere.
If any greefe or care, do vex thy wofull hart, 20
Then God I pray to giue thee ease, and swagement of thy smart.
Yet this I doo desire, that thou be found to abide
A freend: euen such as shal mislike, with sodaine change to slide.
If pleasure now thou hast, to spend the dreiry day,
Read then this pistle of my hande, to driue the time away. 25
If all thy freendes aliue: would from thy frendship swarue,
A thousand deathes I do desire, in wretched state to starue.
If I amongst the rest, should alter so my minde,
Or thou shouldest charge I promise brake, or els am found vnkinde
Though *Argus* ielus eyes: that daily on vs tend, 30
Forbid vs meat and speech also, or message for to send.
A time will come to passe, and thinke it not to long
That thou and I shall ioyne in ioy, and wreake vs of our wrong.
Which time I would abide: though time too long doth try mee
In hope againe when time shal serue, thou wilt not then deny mee. 35
Thus hope doth mee vpholde: for hope of after blisse,
And lose therby my present ioy, in hoping still for this.
                                                          I do

[15]

The gorgious Gallery

I doo commend to thee: my life and all I haue,
Commaund them both as thee best likes: to lose or els to saue.
I am no more mine owne, but thine to vse at will
The same is thine without desert, if thou mee seke to kill. 5
Bee glad thou litle quere, my mystresse shall thee see
Fall flat to ground before her face: and at her feet doo lie:
Haste not to rise againe, nor doo her not withstand
If of her bounty shee vouchsafe, to rayse thee with her hand.
Say thy maister sent thee, and humbly for mee greete her,   (her. 10
Thou knowest my selfe doth wish full ofte: to be in place to meete
If any worde in this, hath scapte and doo her greeue,
A pardon craue vpon thy knee, and pray her to forgeue
A giltles hand it wrote, thou mayst be bolde to tell:
No minde of malice did mee moue, her self doth know it well. 15
Thou canst and I deserue: make glad my wofull sprite,
I craue no answer to thy payne: nor force thee for to write.
It should suffise if thou: voutchsafe to reade the same,
This pistle then if thou mislyke, condemne it to the flame.
But now there needes no more, I will this pistle ende, 20
Esteeme *Narsetus* alwayes well: that is thy faythfull freend.

FINIS.

The Louer forsaken, writeth to his Lady
a desperate Farwell.

Euen hee that whilome was: thy faithful freend most iust, 25
That thrise three yeeres hath spent & past, reposing all his
In thy bewayling words, that seemed sugar sweet (trust
The selfsame man vnwillingly: doth with these lines thee
I can not speake with thee: and speaking is but paine,   (greet.
To speake and pray and not to speede: too fruitles were the gayne. 30
Inforste therfore I write, and now vnfolde my minde,
I loue, and like as earst I did, I am not yet declinde.
Though time that trieth all, hath turnde the loue you ought,
No changing time could alter mee: or wrest awry my thought.
And

[16]

of gallant Inuentions.

And sure I doo mislyke, that wemen choose to change,
Vngratefull folkes I do detest, as monsters foule and strange.
Sith first I did you know: I neuer spake the thing
That did intend you to beguile, or might repentance bring. 5
Thrise hath my pen falne downe: vpon this paper pale,
And scantly can my hart consent: to write to thee this tale.
Least hasty Iudgmentes might, misdeeme my giltes minde,
To charge that malice moues my speech, or some new frend to finde.
The gods I vouch to ayd: who knowes the troth I ment, 10
To swarue or fleet from that I vowed, was neuer my intent.
But as the Courser fearce, by pearcing spur doth run,
So thy desertes enforce mee now: to see this worke begun.
Would God I had no cause to leaue that I did loue,
Or lothe the thing that likt mee so: nor this mishap to proue. 15
But sith no thing in earth: in one estate can bide,
Why striue I then against the streame, or toyle against the tide?
And haue you now forgot, how many yeeres I sought,
To get your grace with whot good will: how dearly I it bought.
There is no one aliue, that nature euer made 20
That hath such giftes of vertues race, and such vntroth doth shade.
If fayth might haue bin found, within a womans brest,
I did beleeue within thy hart, shee chose her place to rest.
Vnskilful though I bee, and cannot best deserne,
Where craft for troth doth preace in place, yet am I not to learne. 25
And I did thinke you such: that litle knew of guile,
But seemings now be plaste for deedes, and please fulwel the while
Why doo I wunder thus? to thinke this same so strange,
Who hath assayed and knoweth not? that wemen choose to change.
Haue you thus sone forgot, the doutes and dreades you made, 30
Of yongmens loue how litle holde, how sone away they fade.
How hardly you beleeued? how often would you say,
My wordes were spoken of the splene: and I as oft denay.
How oft did you protest with handes vpstretcht to skyes?
How oft with othes vnto the Gods? how oft with weeping eyes? 35
Did you beseech them all, to rid your spending dayes?
When that you thought to leaue your freend: to dy without delayes.

ℭ   My

The gorgious Gallery

Mee thought in heauen I saw: how *Ioue* did laughe to skorne,
To see you sweare so solemly, and ment to be forsworne.
But as the *Sirens* singe, when treason they procure,
So smyling baytes the harmles soules: vnto their bane alure.   5
Thy fawning flattering wordes, which now full falce I finde,
Perswades mee to content my selfe, and turne from *Cressids* kinde.
And all the sorte of those: that vse such craft I wish
A speedy end, or lothsome life, to liue with *Lasars* dish.
Yet pardon I do pray: and if my wordes offend,   10
A crased ship amid the streame, the Marriner must mende.
And I thus tost and turnd: whose life to shipwracke goes
Complaynes of wrongs thou hast mee don, and all my greefe forth
And could your hart consent? and could you gree therto?   (showes.
Thus to betray your faythful freend, and promis to vndo?   15
If nought your wordes could binde, to holde your suer behest,
Nor ought my loue ne othes you sware, could bide within your brest
Yet for the worldly shame, that by this facte might rise,
Or for the losse of your good name, for dealing in this wise.
Or thus to see mee greeu'd: tormented still in payne,   20
Thy gentil hart should haue bin pleasde such murder to refrayne.
But through thy cruell deede: if that vntamed death,
With speedy dart shall rid my life, or leaue my lyuing breath.
The gods then can and will: requite thy bloddy acte,
And them I pray with lowly sute, for to reuenge thy facte.   25
God graunt the earth may bring: nought forth to thy auayle,
Nor any thing thou takest in hand, to purpose may preuayle.
Thy most desired freend, I wish may bee most coy,
Wherin thou doost thee most delite: and takest the greatest ioy.
That same I would might turne: vnto thy most mischeefe,   30
That in thy life thy hart may feele, the smart of others greefe.
But sith no good can come: of thy mishap to mee,
I graunt some blame I doo deserue, that thus desire to see
Thy blisfull life so changde, from weale to wretched state,   34
When freendes do breake the bonde of loue, then is their greatest
Thy deedes do sure deserue, much more reuenging spight,   (hate.
Then hart can thinke or tongue can tel, or this my pen can wright.
                                                            Thy

[18]

of gallant Inuentions.

Thy bewty bright is sutch, that well it would inuade,
A hart more hard then Tigar wilde: and more it can perswade.
Then *Tullyes* cunning tongue: or *Ouids* louing tale,
Well may I curse and ban them both, that so haue brewed my   5
I feare to praise to far: least haply I begin,   (bale.
To kindle fier that well is quencht, and burne mee all within.
For well I may compare: and boldly dare it say,
Thou art the Queene of women kinde, and all they ought obay.
And all for shame doo blush, when thou doost come in place,   10
They curse ech thing that gaue thee life, and more disdain thy face.
Then any liuyng wight: doth hate the Serpent foule,
Or birdes that singe and flies by day, abhors the shrikyng Owle.
Oh that a constant minde: had guided forth thy dayes,
I had not then assayd myshap: nor pen spoke thy disprayse.   15
Decreed sith that thou art, for euer to forsake mee,
In sorrows sweete I wil mee shrine: till death shall list to take mee.
Bewayle O woful eyes, with fluds of flowing teares,
This great mischaunce thy lothsome life, that all ill hap vp beares,
Since parted is your ioy, resigne likewise your sight,   20
I neuer will agree to like, or looke on other wight.
Nor neuer shall my mouth consent to pleasant sound,
But pale and leane with hollow lookes: till death I will bee found.
And you vnhappy handes: with lyking foode that fed mee,
Leaue of to labor more for mee: since sorrow thus hath sped mee.   25
Lament vnlustie legges: bee lame for euer more,
Sith shee is gone for whom you kept: your willing pace in store.
O hatefull heauy hart: bewayle thy great vnrest,
Consume thy selfe or part in twaine: within my blouddy brest.
And yee my sences all: whose helpe was aye at hand,   30
To length the life that lingreth now, and lothsomely doth stand.
Yee sonne, ye moone and starres: that gyues the gladsome light
Forbeare to show your force a while: let all bee irkesome night.
Let neuer soyle bringe forth, agayn the lusty greene
Nor trees that new dispoyled are, with leafe be euer seene.   35
Let neither birde nor beast: posses their wonted minde
Let all the thinges that liues on earth, be turned from their kinde.

                C ij   Let

The gorgious Gallery

Let all the furies forth, that pine in Hell with payne,
Let all their torments come abroad: with lyuing wightes to rayne.
Let peace be turnd to war, let all consume with fier,
Sith I must dye that once did ioy, and lose that I desier.   5
I hate my life and breath, I hate delighting food,
I hate my greefe I hate my death: I hate that doth mee good.
I hate the gentill hart: that rueth on my payne,
I hate the cruell stubborn sorte, that doth my life disdayne.
I hate al sortes of men, that haue their life in price,   10
And those I hate that folow death, esteeming them vnwise
I hate those carefull thoughtes that thinke on my sweet fo,
I hate my selfe then twice as much: if I forget her so.
I hate, what would you more, I wot not what I hate,
I wish her dead and layed in graue: I wish her better state.   15
Come wilde and sauadge beastes, stretch forth your cruell pawes,
Dismember mee, consume my flesh: imbrew your greedy iawes.
Within your entrayles: see a coffin ye prepare,
To tombe this carefull corpes that now, vnwillingly I bare.
Come lingringe slothful death: that doost the wretch deny   20
To show thy force and ridst the riche, that list not for to dye.
Is this the recompence? is this the due reward?
Doth loue thus pay his seruants hier? and doth hee thus regard?
And doth hee vse to set, the harmles soules on fier,
With faire sweet intisinge lookes: to kindle their desier?   25
Fye false loue that hast so decte, with bewty bright,
A Lady faire with such vntroth, to worke such cruell spight.
And ye that doo pursue blinde loue with speedy pace,
Restraine your steps example take, of this my wofull case.
Let this alone suffise, that in few wordes I say,   30
Who can beware by others harmes, thrice blest and happy they.
Beleeue this to bee true: that now too true I proue,
But litle troth in womens breast: and fleeting in their loue.
God graunt each wight on earth, that serues with faythfull minde,
A better hap and that hee may, a truer Mystrisse finde.   35

FINIS.

of gallant Inuentions.

The Louer in distresse exclaymeth agaynst Fortune.

HOw can the criple get, in running race the game?
　Or hee in fight defend himselfe, whose armes are broken lame?
How can th' imprisoned man whose legs be wrapt in chaynes,
Thinke this his life a pleasant time, who knoweth nothing but
So how can I reioyse, that haue no pleasant thing,　　(paines?
That may reuiue my doulfull sprits, or cause mee for to singe.
My legs be lame to goe, mine armes cannot embrace,
My hart is sore, mine eyes bee blinde, for lacke of Fortunes grace.
All this is Fortunes fault, that keepes these sences so,
Shee may aduaunce them if shee list, and rid them of this wo.
It is her cruell will, alwayes on mee to lower,
To kepe frō mee her pleasant giftes, to make mee know her power.
Alas, alas, fie Fortune, fie: why art thou so vnkinde,
To mee that fayne would bee thy sonne, and euer in thy minde?
Now doo I thee beseech, with pleasures mee to frayght,
To temper this my wofull life, or els to kill mee strayght.

FINIS.

An other complaint on Fortune.

IN doubtful dreading thoughts, as I gan call to minde,
This world, and eke the pleasures al, that *Adams* children
A place of pleasant hew appeared to my thought　(finde,
Where I might see the wonderous works which nature
All things of any price, approched to my sight,　(for vs wrought.
And still me thought that each man had, that was his most delight.
The riche man hath his ioy: his riches to imbrace,
So hath the huntesman his desire, to haue the Hart in chace.
And other haue their sporte to see the Falcon flee,
And some also in Princes court: in fauor for to bee.
The warring Knight at will, an horse doth run his race,
And eke the louer, in his armes, his Lady doth embrace.
　　　　　　　　　　　　　　　　　　　　When

The gorgious Gallery

When that I see eche man enioy his whole delite,
Saue I alas poore cursed man whom *Fortune* doth so spite.
I fall straight to the ground, amazed with much griefe,
With blouddy strokes vpon my brest, I striue to rid my lief.
And thus I thinke, how can fayre pictures those delight:
Whom nature from their tender age, defrauded of their sight.

FINIS.

¶ The louer beeing newly cought in Cupids snares, complayneth
on the Gods of loue, and compareth his greefe as followeth.

THe hugie heape of cares, that in this world I finde,
The sodayne sighes that sore molest my hart
The foolish fansies that still run in my minde:
Makes mee to lay all ioy and myrth apart,
Lamenting still the causes of my smart.
  But oh, alas, the more I weepe and wayle,
  The more my greefe to mee seemes to preuayle.

The more I seeke my pinchinge panges to swage,
  By diuers wayes, such as I thinke be best
The more it frets, the more it gins to rage,
  So that my senceles head can take no rest:
Ah seely wretch, what doth thee thus mollest
  Or what doth thus perturbe thy restlesse braynes,
  And from thy harte all worldly ioye detaynes.

Alas what this should bee I can not tell,
  My youthfull yeares can skill of no such change
But if some vgly shape of fury fell:
  Or wicked wight that in this world doth range
Hath witched mee with this disease so strange.
  Or *Cupid* with his force of cruell dart,
  Hath stricken mee and wounded thus my hart.

                                                Hath

of gallant Inuentions.

Hath *Cupid* then sutch power on mortall wightes?
   And strikes the blinded boy his dart so sure?
That no man can auoyd his subtill slightes,
   Nor ought agaynst his fury may indure?   5
Hath *Venus* force men thus for to allure?
   And why then? doth shee not her sonne commaund
   To shoote alike and strike with equall hand?

Is this the guise of powers that raigne aboue,
   Vs seely soules in snares thus for to trap   10
And care they not to yeeld vs death for loue?
   Ioy they in woes our corses for to trap?
And passe they not what vnto vs doth hap?
   Can Gods aboue to man beare any hate,
   Or doo they mocke and iest at our estate?   15

Ah foolish foole? what fancy rules thy head.
   Or what doth cause thee now this talke to moue?
What fury fell doth thee poore wretch now lead?
   To rayle on all the Gods doth it behooue?
Sith it is only *Cupid* God of loue.   20
   That guiltlesse shee with stroke of goulden shafte,
   Hath wounded thus and thee of ioyes berafte.

Euen as the slender Barke that long is tost
   By surging waues cast vp from deepest seas:
And Saylars still in daunger to be lost,   25
   Doo hale and pull in hope to take their ease:
When stormy fluds begin once to appease.
   Euen so fare I beeing in *Cupids* power
   In hope at last to see that happy hower.

Wherin I shall my wished ioyes obtayne,   30
   And placed bee within her gentill hart,
Then shall I take my sorrowes all for gayne.
   When I haue her that causeth now my smart,
                                           Then

The gorgious Gallery

Then farewell *Cupid* with thy cruell darte
And welcome shee that pearst mee with her sight,
Shee is my Ioy, shee is my hartes delight.

FINIS.

    The Louer extolleth, aswell the rare vertues of his Lady
        beloued, as also her incomparable beautie.

Desire hath driuen from mee my will,
Or *Cupids* blase hath bleard mine eyes:
Knowledge mee fayles, my sight is yll:
If kinde or cunning could deuise
Nature to paynt in better plight
To set her forth with red and white:
Or if men had *Apelles* arte,
Who could her mend in any parte?

Her face declares where fauor growes,
And telles vs heere is Beauties grace:
Her eyes hath power to binde and lose,
Her countenance may freendes embrace.
Her cheekes be decte with bloud full fayre,
Her collour cleare as is the ayre:
Her haire, her hand, her foote also,
Hath wonne the praise where euer shee go.

Her lookes doo seeme to speake alone,
When that her lips remooue no whit
Her inwarde vertues may be knowen:
By vsinge of her sober wit.
Her iestures also cumly are,
My tongue lackes skill them to declare:
The rest of her that are vnnamed,
In perfect shapes are lyuely framed.

                      Now

of gallant Inuentions.

Now though that kinde hath set her forthe,
And natures workes shee hath possest,
Theese goodly giftes are litle worth:
If pitty dwelt not in her brest. 5
Oh, God forbid such flowring youth
Should bee mislyked for lacke of ruth,
For I with other might say then:
Lo, this is shee that killeth men.
FINIS. 10

¶ The Louers farewell, at his departure, perswadeth his
beloued to constancie in his absence.

THough Fortune cannot fauor
  According to my will:
The proofe of my behauor: 15
  Shall bee to loue you still.

Entending not to chaunge,
  Whiles that my life doth last:
But still in loue to raunge:
  Till youth and age be past. 20

Though I bee far you fro,
  Yet in my fantacie:
I loue you and no mo:
  Thinke this assuredly. 24

Your owne both true and iuste,
  Alwayes you shall mee finde:
Wherfore of right you must,
  Haue mee likewise in minde.

And doo not mee forsake,
  Though I doo tarry longe: 30
But take mee for your make,
  I will not chaunge my songe.

Though absence now a while,
  Do part vs thus in twayne:
Thinke neither craft nor gyle, 35
  For I will come agayne

The same man that I went,
  Both in my woorde and deede:
Though some men doo relent,
  And grudge that I should speed. 40

But if you doo remayne,
  And do not fro mee starte:
My hart you doo attayne,
  Till death vs two depart.

And thus farewell adew, 45
  And play an honest parte:
And chaunge mee for no new,
  Seeing that you haue my hart.
FINIS.
𝔇.

The gorgious Gallery

A propper Dittie. To the tune of lusty Gallant.

THe glyttering showes of *Floras* dames
 Delightes not so my carefull minde,
Ne gathering of the fragrant flames:
 That ofte in *Floras* Nimphes I finde.
Ne all the noates of Birdes so shryl
 Mellodiously in woods that singe,
Whose solemne Quires the skyes doth fill:
 With noate on noate that heauenly ringe.

The frisking Fish in streames that springe
 And sporte them on the riuers side,
The Hound the Hauke and euery thinge:
 Wherin my ioyes did once abide,
Doth nothinge els but breede my wo
 Sith that I want which I desier,
And death is eke become my fo:
 Denying that I most requier.

But if that Fortunes freendly grace
 Would graunt mine eyes to take the vew,
Of her whose porte and amorous face
 My senses all doth so subdew.
That raunging too and fro to gayne
 The pray that most delighteth mee,
At last I finde that breedes me payne:
 Shee flyes so fast it will not bee.

Then in my selfe with lingering thoughts
 A sodayne strife begins to gro,
I then doo wish such Birdes at noughts:
 That from their louers flyeth so.
At last I see the Fowlars gin,
 Prepared for this Birde and mee
Then wisht I lo his hed therin:
 So that my birde and I were free.
FINIS.

of gallant Inuentions.

¶ The Louer perswadeth his beloued, to beware the
deceites and allurements of strange suters.

BE stedfast to thine owne
  As hee is vnto thee,   5
Regard not men vnknowen
But loue thine owne truly
For oft deceyts are sowen
By them that vnknowen bee
  Wherfore cast of the rest: 10
  And thine own loue thou best.

For though that their false suite
Seeme pleasant in thine eare,
Thou knowst oft times ill fruit
A pleasant tree doth beare. 15
If thou chaunce to repute
A rotten Apple cleare,
  Better to loue thine owne
  And forsake men vnknowne.

Thou doost well vnderstand 20
These wordes not spoken seilde
More suer a birde in hand,
Then twenty in the feild. (band
Thou knowest thine owne sure
And how that it hath helde 25
  Then chaunge it for no new:
  But loue him that is trew.

If suters doo thee moue
Or dayly to thee write,
Yet graunt to them no loue 30
Their paynes for too requite.
But thinke it doth behooue
Thee alwayes to doo right
  Thē must thou loue thine own
  And forsake men vnknowne. 35

This counsayle I thee giue
As farforth as I can,
As I that whiles I liue
Wilbee thine onely man.
For sure it would mee greeue, 40
To see thee out of frame
  Or chaunge at any time:
  Thine owne not to bee thine.

Thus written by thine owne
To thee with all his harte, 45
Disiringe the vnknowen
Of thee may haue no part.
For if sutch chaunge bee sowen
No doubt thou killest my hart
  Wherfore I say beware: 50
  Always the vnknown snare.

FINIS.

The gorgious Gallery

¶ The Lady beloued exclaymeth of the great
vntruth of her louer.

WOuld god I had neuer seen,
   the teares of thy false eyne 5
Or els my eares ful deaf had bin
   That herd those words of thine

Then should I not haue knowne
   Nor chosen to my part:
So many euils in one   10
   To kill my poore true hart.

As now in thee I finde,
   Who bidst mee from thee go:
As false and full vnkinde,
   Alas why doost thou so? 15

Was neuer man so false of othe,
   To none as thou to mee
Was neuer womā of more troth
   Then I haue ben to thee.

And thou to leaue mee so, 20
   And canst no iust cause tell:
But wilt thou spill with wo,
   The hart that loues thee wel.

Mee thinkes that for my part,
   I may speake in the same, 25
I say me thinkes thou art,
   Euen very mutch to blame.

Pardy, it is but litle praise,
   To thee that art a man:

To finde so many crafty wayes, 30
   To fraude a poore woman.

At whom all women smile,
   To see so fonde on thee:
And men although they wayle,
   To see how thou vsest mee. 35

To lure mee to thy fist,
   To ease thy feigned payne:
And euer when thou list,
   To cast mee of agayne. 39
                (his dayes,
The wretched hound ẙ spendes
   And serueth after kinde:
The Horse that tredeth ẙ beaten
   As nature doth him binde (ways

In age yet findes releefe,
   Of them that did him wo: 45
Who in their great mischeefe,
   Disdayne not them to know.

Thus they for wo and smart,
   Had ease vnto their paine:
But I for my true hart, 50
   Get nought but greefe agayne.

The weary and long night
   doth make mee dreame of thee,
And still me thinks with sight,
   I see thee here with mee. 55
                    And

of gallant Inuentions.

And then with open armes,
  I strayne my pillow softe:
And as I close mine armes,
    mee thinkes I kisse thee ofte.   5

But when at last I wake
And finde mee mockte w̃ dremes
Alas, with moone I make
  My teares run down like strea-
                     (mes
All they that here this same,   10
  Wyll spit at thy false deede:

And bid, fie on thy cursed name,
  And on thy false seede.

That shewest so to the eye,
  And bearest so false an hew: 15
And makest all women cry,
  Lo, how ye men be vntrew?

But yet to excuse thee now,
  To them that would thee spot:
Ile say, it was not thou,   20
  It was mine owne poore lot.

FINIS.

¶The Louer declareth his paynfull plight
for his beloued sake.

Since needes ye will mee singe, giue eare vnto the voyce,   25
Of mee pore man your bond seruant, y̓ knoweth not to re-
Consider wel my care, my paine and my vnrest: (ioyce.
Which thou with force of *Cupids* Dart hast grafted in my
Heale, and withdraw from mee, the venim of that Darte   (brest.
Haue pitty, and release this wo, that doth consume my hart: 30
The greatnes of my greefe, doth bid mee seeke release
I seeke to finde to ease my payne, yet doth my care encrease.

I cease not to beholde, that doth augment my payne:
I see my selfe I seeke my wo, yet can I not refrayne.
That should my wo release, doth most encrease the same,   35
The colde that should acquench the heat, doth most enrage the flame.
My pleasure is my payne, my game is most my greefe
My cheefe delite doth worke my wo, my hart is my releefe
Sutch haps doth hap to them, that happeth so to loue,
And hap most harde: so fast to binde, that nothing can remooue.   40

𝔇iij   For

The gorgious Gallery

For when the harme is fixed, and rooted in the hart,
No tongue can tell, nor pen may write, how greuous is the smart
I haue thought loue but play, vntill I felte the sore,
But now I felte a thousand greefes I neuer felt before.   5
To tell what paynes I bide, if that I could deuise,
I tel the truth, beleeue mee wel, the day will not suffise
Graunt now therfore some rest, since thus thou hast mee bound,
To be thine owne, til body mine, lye buried vnder ground.

FINIS.   10

¶The Louer hauing his beloued in suspition
declareth his doutfull minde.

Deeme as ye list vpon good cause
    Yee may, and thinke of this or that,
But what, or why, my selfe best knowes,   15
    Wherby I thinke and feare not.
Wherunto I may wel like
    The doubtful sentence of this clause
I would ye were not as I thinke
    I would I thought it were not so.   20

If that I thought it were not so,
    Though it were so, it greeued mee not,
Vnto my hart it were as tho
    I harkened and I heare not.
At that I see I cannot winke,   25
    Nor for my hart to let it go
I would it were not as I thinke
    I would I thought it were not so.

Lo how my thought might make mee free,
    Of that perchance it needeth not   30
For though no doubt in deede I see,
    I shrinke at that I beare not,
                                      Yet

of gallant Inuentions.

Yet in my hart this worde shall sinke,
   Vntill the proofe may better bee
I would it were not as I thinke,
   I would I thought it were not. 5

FINIS.

¶ An exellent Sonet, Wherin the Louer exclaymeth agaynst
Detraction, beeing the principall cause of all his care.
To the tune, when Cupid scaled first the Fort.

PAsse forth in doulfull dumpes my verse, 10
Thy Masters heauy haps vnfolde:
His grisled greefe eache hart well perce,
Display his woes, feare not, bee bould
   Hid hole in heapes of heauinesse
His dismale dayes are almost spent, 15
For fate, which forgde this ficklenesse
My youthly yeares with teares hath sprent.
   I lothe the lingring life I led
O wished death why stayest thy hand,
Sith gladsome Ioyes away bee fled: 20
And linkte I am in Dollors bande.
   In weltring waues my ship is tost
My shattering sayles away bee shorne,
My Anker from the Stearne is lost
And Tacklings from the Maynyards torne. 25
   Thus driuen with euery gale of winde
My weather beaten Barke doth sayle,
Still hoping harbor once to finde
Which may these passinge perrils quayle.
   But out alas, in vayne I hope 30
Sith Billowes prowd, assault mee still
And skill doth want with Seas to cope
And licour salte my Keele doth fill.

D iiii   A

[31]

The gorgious Gallery

   Yet storme doth cease: but lo at hand
A ship with warlike wightes addrest,
Which seemes to bee some Pyrates band:
With Powder and with Pellets prest.   5
   To sinke or spoyle my brused Barke
Which dangers dread could not a daunt,
And now the shot the ayre doth darke:
And Captayne on the Deke him vaunt.
   Then Ignorance the ouerseear proude   10
Cryes to Suspicion, spare no shot:
And Enuy yelleth out aloude,
Yeeld to Detraction this thy Boate:
   And as it is now Sea mens trade
When might to coole the foe doth lacke,   15
By vayling foretop signe I made
That to their lee I mee did take.
   Then gathering winde to mee they make,
And Treason first on borde doth come
Then followes Fraud like wily Snake: 20
And swift amongst them takes his rome.
   These binde mee Captiue, tane with band
Of carkinge care and fell annoy,
While vnder Hatches yet I stand
Therby quight to abandon ioye.   25
   Then hoysting sayles they homeward hye
And mee present vnto Disdayne,
Who mee beheld with scorning eye
The more for to encrease my payne.
   As Lady shee commaunded strayght   30
That to Dispayre they mee conuay,
And bid with skilfull heed hee wayght,
That Truth bee bard from mee away.
   Madam (quoth I) let due desart
Yet finde remorse for these my woes,   35
Of pitty graunt some ease to smart
Let Troth draw neare to quayle my foes.
                                                                   But

of gallant Inuentions.

 But all for nought I doo complayne
For why the deafe can mone no noyse,
No more can they which doo disdayne:
But will in harte therat reioyce.   5
 Wherfore twixt life and death I stay
Til time with daughter his drawe nye
Which may these furious foes dismay:
Or els in ruthfull plight I dye.

FINIS   10

¶The Louer in bondage looketh for releasement and
longeth for the releefe of his wedding day.

WHen shall reliefe release my wo?
When shall desert, disdayne digest?
When shall my hap, hap to mee so?   15
That my poore hart may come too rest.
  When shall it so? when shall it so?
When shall longe loue bee looked vpon?
When shall tried truth bee homeliest?
When shall hope haue that hope hangeth on?   20
That my poore hart may come to rest.
  When shall it so? &c.
When shall I see shee seethe right?
When shall I heare shee heareth mee best?
When shall I feele, shee feeleth delight?   25
That my poore harte may come to rest.
  When shall it so. &c.
When stinte all stormes that thus agreeue?
When stinte all stayes that wrong hath wrest?
When stinte all strifes right to releeue?   30
That my poore hart may come to rest.
  When shall it so? &c.
        Œ   When

[33]

The gorgious Gallery

When right shall see right time to boste?
When right shall aright vnright oppresse?
When right shall raigne and rule the roste?
Then my poore harte shall come to rest.   5
  Then shall it so. &c.
When shall I watch the time to see?
Now shall I wish the time possest,
Now shall I thinke each day yeeres three
That my poore harte may come to rest.   10
  When shall it so? &c.
Now farewell harte, most smooth most smart,
Now farewell hart with hart hartiest,
And farewell harte, till hart in harte:
By harty harte may come to rest.   15
  God graunt it so. &c.

FINIS.

¶ A fine and freendly Letter, of the Louer to his beloued.

Like as the Hauke is led by lure, to draw from tree to tree,
So is my hart through force of loue, where euer my body bee   20
The Hauke to pray doth double wing, her flight is fled in vayne
I make my flight in waste of winde, my hope receyueth no gayne.
Haukes that be high it hurtes to light, two flightes wᵗout reward
My flight is two, and three againe, alas Mistresse regarde: (foode
The Hauke brought low, is soone made high, by feeding on warme 25
Your mouthes breath settes mee aloft, there is nothing so good.
Good Lady then strain forth ẙ strings, whose tune may mee reuiue
And with straũg tongue do not prolong, my ioyes thus to depriue.
Within your brest my hart is hid, your will and it is one,
Regard my smart, the cure is yours, and losse, when I am gone. 30
Thus all your owne, I recommend mee wholly to your grace,
As seemeth you best for to reward, my plight and wofull case.
Which plight if you do counterpaise, with ioyes, as doth belonge,
My hart for ioy would tune accorde, to singe some pleasant songe.
    FINIS.

of gallant Inuentions.

¶ The Louers fatal farewell at his death.

AL wealth I must forsake, and pleasures eke forgo,
My life to ende in wo and greefe, my desteny is so
For where I had perfixt, with sute to win my ioy, 5
I found I had right speedy death, al welth for to distroy.
Whose Image lo I am, though lyuing I appeare,
Both body and soule be seperate, my heauen it is not here.
My harte I haue bestowed, wheras it is not found
Thou body thē depart thou hence, why pleasurest thou the ground? 10
And Death draw thou mee neare, O Death my dearest freend,
Then with thy dart, shoot through my hart, my sorrows so to ende.
And when that death did heare the thing that I did craue,
Hee weighed mee, euen as I was, a man fit for the graue.
Come follow mee sayth hee, thou man bee not agast, 15
Hee that delighteth in earthly things, shal feele these panges at last
All yee then that list to loue, this lesson learne by mee,
Or yee begin, noate well, the ende, is payne and misery.

FINIS.

¶ The Louer complayneth of his Ladies vnconstancy 20
to the Tune of I lothe that I did loue.

YOu graues of grisly ghosts
   Your charge frō coffins send
Frō roring rout in *Plutoes* costs
   You Furies vp ascend. 25

You trampling steades of Hell
   Come teare a wofull wight,
Whose haples hap no tonge can
   Ne pen can well endight. (tell

I hate this lothsome life 30
   O *Atropos* draw nie,
Vntwist ỹ thred of mortall strife
   Send death and let mee die.

For Beauties taynted trope
   Hath made my cares assay, 35
And ficklenes with her did cope:
   To fordge my whole decaye.

                             E ij   My

The gorgious Gallery

My fayth alas I gaue
  To wight of *Cressids* kinde,
For stedfast loue I loue did craue
  As curtesy doth binde. 5

Shee likewise troth doth plight
  To bee a constant loue,
And proue her self euen maugre
  A faythfull turtle Doue. (spight

But lo a womans minde 10
  Cloakt hole with deepe deceyt
And driuen with euery gale of
  To bite at fresher bayt (winde.

For when bewitch shee had
  My minde that erst was free, 15
And that her cumly beauty bad
  My wounded hart agree.

And fixt on Fancyes lore
  As world can witnesse beare,
No other saynct I did adore: 20
  Or Idole any whear

Ne will, no wo, or smart
  Could minde from purpose fet,
But that I had a *Iasons* harte
  The golden fleese to get. 25

Ne for my part I swere
  By all the Gods aboue,
I neuer thought on other fere
  Or sought for other loue.

In her the like consente 30
  I saw ful oft appear,
If eyes be iudge of that it mente
  Or eares haue power to heare.

Yet woordes bee turnd to winde
  A new found gest hath got 35
The Fort, which once, to vnder
  And win I planted shot (mine

Her freend that ment her well
  Out of conceyt is quite,
While other beares away ye bell 40
  By hitting of the white.

In this our wauering age
  So light are womens mindes,
As Aspen leafe yt stil doth rage
  Though *æole* calme his windes. 45

No place hath due desart
  No place hath constancy (start
In eueri mood their mindes back
  As dayly wee may see.

What paps did giue them food 50
  That weue sutch webs of wo
What beast is of so cruell mood
  That countes his freend for fo:

Yet women doo reward
  With cares the louing wight 55
They constancy no whit regard,
  In change is their delight.
                You

of gallant Inuentions.

You gallant youths therfore
  In time beware by mee
        FINIS.

Take heed of womēs subtil lore,
  Let mee example bee.   5

¶ The Louer, hauing sustayned ouermuch wrong at his
Ladyes hande wisheth speedy death.

TO feeble is the thread
  That holdeth mee in lyfe, 10
That if it bee not succoured
  Short end shal stint the stryfe.

For though the spindle ronne
  To draw the thread on length
Alas therby what hold is wonne
  If it be weake of strength   16

Or how can it haue ayde
  Since rigor is so rife, (thread
In her whose handes to cut the
  Gaue cruelly the knife.   20

Whose edge of Enuy hard
  In *Venus* forge hath wrought,
Wherby his deth is thus preferd
  Whose life offended nought.

But sithe thy cheefe delite,   25
  My cheefe delightfull fo, (spite
Is with such wrong to work the
  With speed come end this wo.

And when my death hath done
  My duty at her will,   30

A greater greefe be not begonne
  To last therafter still.

For after death, if strife
  Should still my life pursue,
What thē doth death but breed a   35
  Of mone & mischeefe new? (life

Wherfore if needes thou wilte
  Thy spindle spin no more,
But $\tilde{y}$ this thred with spoyle bee
  Which led my life before. (spilt   40

Prouide then for the nonce
  Prouide for mee the best,
That I may dye at once
  From all thy mindes vnrest.

And let not presente death   45
  Prefer an after paine,
But let the paines pas with my
  And not reuiue againe. (breath

For thus by this you shall
  Two thinges at once fulfill,   50
I shalbe free that haue bin thrall:
  And you shall haue your will.

        FINIS.

The gorgious Gallery

¶ The Louer exhorteth his Lady to bee
constant. To the Tune of
Attend thee go play thee.

Not light of loue lady,
Though fancy doo prick thee,
Let constancy possesse thy hart:
Well worthy of blamyng:
They bee, and defaming,
From plighted troth which backe do start:
  Deare dame:
Then ficklenésse bannish,
And folly extinguish,
Bee skilfull in guiding,
  And stay thee from slidinge
  And stay thee. &c.

The constant are praysed
Their fame high is raysed
Their worthynesse doth pearce the skye,
The fickle are blamed:
Their lightiloue shamed,
Theyr foolishnesse doth make them dye:
  As well,
Can *Cressid* beare witnesse,
Fordge of her owne distresse,
Whom Leprosy paynted
  And penury taynted:
  And penury. &c.

Still Muses are busie
To tell vs of *Thisbe*
Whom stedfastnesse doth much commend
And *Camma* is placed,
To blame the defaced
That light of loue doo sende.

                                Phedra

of gallant Inuentions.

Phedra,
Is checked most duly
Because that vntruly
Forst therto by loue light
  Shee slayeth Hippolite.
  Shee slayeth. &c.

A spring of annoyance,
And well of disturbance,
New fanglenesse in loue hath bin:
It killeth the Master,
It poysons the taster,
No worldly wight by it doth win.
  Therfore,
Good lady bee constant,
So shall you not bee shent,
But woorthely praysed,
  As you haue deserued,
  As you haue, &c.

FINIS.

The Louer wounded with his Ladies beauty
craueth mercy. To the Tune of
where is the life that late I led.

IF pitty once may mooue thy hart,
  To rew a wofull wight?
If curtesy can force thy minde,
  To vew my doulfull plight?
Sith I cannot deuise
  To quench this raging fier,
With trickling teares I craue of thee
  Attend to my desier:
Whom *Venus* fethered boy
  Hath crasde with deadly dart,

                Sent

The gorgious Gallery

Sent from the rayes of those thy eyes
   Which bread my wo and smart.

In vewing thee I tooke sutch ioy
   As wofull wight in rest   5
Vntill the blinded boy I felte
   Assault my captiue brest.
And since that time alas
   Such pinching payne I taste
That I am now remedilesse   10
   If mercy make not haste.
For hid in deepe dispayre
   My teares are all my ioy,
I burne, I freese, I sinke, I swim
   My wealth is mine annoy.   15

Lyke as the tender turtle Doue
   Doth wayle the losse of mate,
In mourning weed, so spend I tyme
   Lamentinge mine estate.
The night renewes my cares   20
   When weary limmes would rest,
And dreadfull dreames abandon slepe
   Which had my greefes represt.
I drench my couch with teares
   Which flow from gushing eyes,   25
A thousand heapes of hidden thoughtes
   In minde I doo deuise.

Full often times it dooth mee good
   To haunt and vew the place,
Where I receiued my wound, alas   30
   By vewing of thy face.
Full oft it ioyes my hart
   To kisse that clot of clay,

                              From

of gallant Inuentions.

From whence thou shot those louing lookes
    Which bred my whole decay.
O blessed place I cry
    Though woorker of my payne,   5
Render I craue most hartely
    To mee my loue agayne.

Not wofull *Monsier dom Dieg*
    Or *Priams* noble sonne,
Constrayned by loue did euer mone   10
    As I for thee haue donne.
Sir *Romeus* annoy
    But trifle seemes to mine,
Whose hap in winning of his loue
    Did clue of cares vntwine.   15
My sorrowes haue no ende
    My hap no ioy can spie,
The flowing Fountayne of my teares
    Beginneth to waxe drie.

Let pitty then requyte my payne   20
    O woorker of my woe,
Let mercy milde possesse thy harte
    Which art my freendly foe.
Receiue the hart which heare
    I yeeld into her hand,   25
Which made by force a breach in Fort
    Which I could not withstande.
Thou hast in Ballance paysd
    My life and eke my death,
Thy loyalty contaynes my ioy   30
    Disdayne will stop my breath.

If constant loue may reape his hire
    And fayth may haue his due,
                      ff   Good

[41]

The gorgious Gallery

Good hope I haue your gentill hart
  My grislie greefe will rue.
And that at length I shall
  My hartes delight imbrace: 5
When due desart by curtesie,
  Shall purchace mee thy grace.
Vntill which time, my deare
  Shall still increase my payne,
In pensiue thoughtes and heauinesse   10
  Because I shall remayne.

FINIS.

¶ A Caueat to yongmen to shun the snares
of Cupids crafty sleightes.

IF euer wight had cause to mone   15
  or wayle with bitter teares,
His wretched life and wofull plight
  that still in languish weares.
Then haue I cause that late haue lodgde
  such loue within my hart,   20
With greefe, with payne, with pyning panges
  my body boyles in smart.

O earth why doost not thou
  my wofull plight sustayne?
O surging Seas with swallowing gulfe   25
  release mee of this payne.
For languishing loue with dolefull doomes
  hath layd my hart in brine,
O wofull wretch, O wicked wight
  That so for loue doth pine.   30

The Sonne that shines with golden beames
  and dries the dewie flowers,
                              Doth

of gallant Inuentions.

Doth cause mee wretch with blubbering eyes
   to gush forth extreame showers.
The hermony of chirping birdes
   that ioyes with siluer songes,   5
Eche lyuing wight, doth cause my cares
   to fill my hart with thronges.

Eche gladsome ioy of mundaine glee
   That glads the worldly minde,
Doth heape vp cares on carefull corps   10
   agaynst all course of kinde.
And so eche thing that ought delight
   and rid the minde from pause,
Contrariwise agaynst all right
   a thousand cares doth cause.   15

For when that I in sugred sleepe,
   most sweetly should take rest,
Then doo I wring my wofull handes
   and beate my dolefull brest.
And if I chaunce on sleepe to fall,   20
   a thousand dreames I haue:
And doo suppose I her embrace,
   whose want will cause my graue.

And then with gladsome hart I ioy
   thus cleane depriued of wo: 25
But (oh alas) when that I wake,
   I finde it nothing so.
And then my sighes from sobbing harte
   doth reaue my brest in twayne,
And teares that run from blubbered eyes   30
   doth more encrease my payne.

And when I should sustayne my lyfe
   and feeble corps with foode,   Vnsauory

The gorgious Gallery

Vnsauory seemes it vnto mee:
   eache thing should doo mee good

Amidst the nipping frostes I broyle,
   in pearching heate I freese 5
And thus agaynst all course of kinde:
   for loue my life I leese.
Wo woorth the time that first I lodgde
   thy spoyling loue in harte,
You yonge men al bee warnd by mee 10
   And shun blinde *Cupids* Darte.

FINIS.

¶ The aged Louers noate, at length to learne to dye.

WHy askest thou the cause
   Wherfore I am so sad 15
Thou knowst whē age on draws
   No creature can bee glad.

And sith shee hath mee rested
   And threatned mee to die:
Therfore I am sequestred 20
   All mirth for to denie.

And now with feeble age
   The rest of all my dayes,
My coūtenance must be ful sage:
   Since that my life decayes. 25

Like as the harte of Oke
   By time doth rot at last,
Like time doth age prouoke
   With time my hart doth brast.

Lo thus by course of time 30
   My youth is gone and past,
And now the turne is mine
   Of bitter death to taste.

And noate that I haue sayd
   The cause wherof and why, 35
My youthfull partes be playde
   And I must learne to die.

FINIS.

of gallant Inuentions.

¶ The desperate Louer exclaymeth his Ladyes cruelty
and threatneth to kill himselfe.

MY ioyful dayes bee past,
   My pleasant yeres be gone,
My life it may not last
   My graue and I am one.

My mirth, and all is fled
   And I a man in woo,
Desireth to bee dead
   My mischeefe to forgoe.

I burne and am a colde
   I freese in middest of fire,
I see shee dooth with hold
   That most I doo desire.

I see that shee doth see
   And yet shee wilbe blinde,
I see in healpinge mee
   Shee seeketh and wil not finde.

I see how shee doth wrye
   When I begin to mone,
I see when I come nye
   How fayn shee would be gone.

I see shee knoweth my harte
   And how I doo complayne,
I see shee knoweth my smarte
   Shee seeth I doo not fayne.

I see my helpe at hand
   I see my death also,
I see where shee doth stand
   I see my cruell fo.

I see, what would you more?
   Shee would mee gladly kill,
And shee shall see therfore
   That shee shall haue her will.

I cannot liue by stones
   It is to harde a food,
I would be dead at once
   to doo my Lady good.

Shee shall haue her request
   And I will haue mine ende,
Lo heere my blouddy brest
   To please her most vnkinde.
       FINIS.

¶ The Louer beeing blinded with the faythlesse loue of his Lady
is contented to remit her fault vpon promis of amendment.

SInce that thou diddest mee loue
   When lust did thee prouoke,
And that thou doost well proue:
   That I cannot reuoke,
                             My

The gorgious Gallery

My freendship fast, my loue nor my good will,
Shew some releefe, least in dispayre I spill.

How well I was content
Alwayes to follow thee?   5
How well I did assent,
Thy thrall aye for to bee
Thy selfe can iudge to whom I doo appeale,
By sentence lo, to yeeld mee wo or weale.

But if thou mee forsake,   10
As *Cressid* that forgot,
True *Troylus* her make,
And that thy hart is whot   (flie,
On him whom shame did force thee once his fayth to
I see no hope but y͡t hee must yeeld forth himself to die.   15

And though thou thinke that I,
Am loth thee too forgoe,
Yet shall I rather die
Then liue and please my foe:
But hindre him in loue, all others doth refrayne,   20
Whose treasō once did mee purchace thy due disdain

FINIS.

¶ A worthy comparison of Vertue agaynst
all worldly pompe.

WHen that I way with wit, and eke consider now,   25
The tickle stay of her, that Fortunes wheele doth bow
And turne euen at her will, such luck, loe, as shee list,
No thread so surely sponne, but that shee may vntwist.
I can but aye lament, and wayle the lacke of them,
That in her holde doo trust, weighing they are but men.   30
                                                            For

of gallant Inuentions.

For if I were a Lorde, and come of high degree,
And had all thing at will, as best contented mee:
My Prince therwith well pleased, that nothing might offend,
And all my deedes so done, that eche man might commend. 5
My parent of great state, and eke of worthy fame,
That worldly men did wish, the honor of his name:
My friends and mine allyes so worthy in eche presse,
That I neede beare no wrong, that I could not redresse.
Of courage and of strength, so doughty of my hand, 10
That Ladyes might mee loue, that dwell in forrayn land.
And enemyes might mee dread, for feare of ouerthrow,
And that all this were true, eche worldly wight did know.
Yet were I but a man, and mortall in this earth,
For death doth not accept, the worship of my byrth: 15
Since so I holde it best, that eche man should contend,
So to directe himselfe, that after this liues ende,
Yet vertue might remayne, that soundes a Trompet, loe,
A comfort to a freend, a wound vnto a foe.

> As some to simple turne from sage, 20
> And ouerthrow with euery winde,
> Some eke correct with rigorous rage
> Whom wealth could neuer foord good minde,
> Hath wonne in prison such a feelde,
> As liberty could neuer yeelde. 25

FINIS.   *Virtute nulla possessio maior.*

¶ Of a happy wished time.

EChe thing must haue a time, and tyme doth try mens troth,
And troth deserues a special trust, on trust great frenship groth:
And freendship is full fast, where faythfulnesse is found 30
And faythfull thinges be ful of fruicte, and fruitful things be sound
The sound is good in proofe, and proofe is Prince of prayse,
And woorthy prayse is such a pearle, as lightly not decayes.
                                                                All

The gorgious Gallery

All this doth time bring forth, which time I must abide,
How should I boldely credit craue? till time my truth haue tried.
And as a time I found, to fall in Fancies frame,
So doo I wish an happy time, at large to shew the same. 5
If Fortune aunswer hope, and hope may haue her hire,
Then shall my hart possesse in peace, the time that I desire.

FINIS.

¶ The Louer perswadeth him selfe to pacience
agaynst Enuie and slanderous tongues. 10

IF only sight suffise, my hart to loose or binde,
What cause haue I to mooue debate, wherby no peace I finde?
If that my restlesse will, by payne doth still renue,
What force haue I? but shee consent, my fo for to subdue?
To yeeld and suffer then, I thinke it for the best, 15
And by desert as time shall serue, to purchase quiet rest.
Let ielous enuy lowre with browes, and visage bent,
I know the worst, no shameles tongue, shall alter myne intent.
The Dice of Loue are throwen, god speede the doubtfull chaunce
Misdeeme who lyst, so shee at last, my seruice will aduaunce. 20
To aske and to obtayne, that Fortune were so swifte,
Sith trauaill is the ready way, vnto eche noble gyfte.
And feeble is the ioy, that lightly is begonne,
As tender Flaxe can beare no stresse, before that it bee sponne.
Wherfore with sad aduice, in hope my harte shall dwell, 25
And all the tale that I confesse, in silence will I tell
Vnto her selfe alone, whose fauour I require,
None els shall know her name for mee, to constre my desire.

FINIS.

The

[48]

of gallant Inuentions.

¶ The Louer greeuously complayneth agaynst the vniust
dealing of his Lady beloued.

SInce thou vniust, hast caught a lust,
   To plough in barrayne ground:
Who long thee loue, hee shall thee proue,
   Mutch better lost then found.

As brickle clay, in Winters day,
   That in the frost is wrought,
So doo I finde, thy double minde,
   Mutch better solde then bought.

It is as eefe, a broken Syue,
   Should holde the dropping rayne:
As for to binde, thy chaunged minde,
   That nought can doo but fayne.

So may I say, both night and day,
   Cursing the time and place:
Where I profest, to loue thee best,
   Whose troth I finde so scace.

Whose lyinge wordes, and faigned bourdes,
   Did mee so far enchayne:
When thou didst flyt, by chaunged wit,
   That I could not refraine.

But of my hart, to ease the smart,
   The best redresse I know:
Is to vntwinde, my constant minde,
   And let sutch fansies goe.

For thoughe I serue, vntill I sterue,
   I see none other boote

Such

The gorgious Gallery

Such doublenesse, thy hart doth presse,
  And croppes it by the roote.

Yet will I pray, euen as I may,
  That *Cupid* will requite,   5
Thy froward harte, with such a smart,
  As I haue by thy spite.

For to bee fed, with wake a bed,
  And fast at boorde among:
Till thou confesse, ah pittilesse,   10
  That thou hast doone mee wrong.

On bush and brier, may it appeare,
  Wherby most men doo pas,
Thy faygned fayth, how nere my death,
  It hath mee brought alas.   15

That they vncaught, may once bee taught,
  By reason to refrayne:
Their crafty wiles, and subtill smiles:
  That so in loue can fayne.

A due vniust, sith that I must,   20
  Of force declare thee so,
The fault is thine, the payne is mine:
  And thus I let thee go.
         FINIS.

¶ The Louer in great distresse comforteth   25
        himselfe with hope.

O Heauy hart whose harmes be hid,
    Thy healpe is hurte, thy hap is hard,
    If thou shouldest brast, as God forbid:
    Then should I dye without reward.   30
                                    Hope

of gallant Inuentions.

Hope well to haue, hate not sweet thought,
Ofte cruell stormes faire calmes haue brought:
After sharp showres, the sunne shyneth faire,
Hope commeth likewise after dispayre. 5

In hope a Kinge doth go to warre,
In hope the Louer lyues full longe,
In hope the Marchaunt sayles full farre,
In hope most men doo suffer wronge:
In hope the Ploughman soweth much seede, 10
Thus hope helpes thousands in their neede.
Then faynt not hart amonge the rest,
What euer chaunce hope thou the best.

Though wit biddes will to blowe retrayte,
Wyll cannot worke as wit would wish 15
When that the Roche doth taste the bayte:
To late to warne the hungry fishe.
When Cities bren of firy flame,
Great Ryuers scarce will quenche the same.
If Will and Fantasie bee agreed 20
To late for Wyt to bid take heede.

FINIS.

¶ In the commendacion of faythfull loue.

THe faithful cannot flye, nor wander to nor fro,
  Fayth only they holde them bye, though that the fickle go. 25
A Piller of more force, then Marble layd with hand,
With Pickaxe may deuorce, and lay it flat on land.
Th' other so deuine, that no arte can remoue,
Once layd cannot decline, th' only Piller loue,

FINIS.

The gorgious Gallery

¶ The Louer wisheth himselfe an Harte in the Foreste, (as
Acteon was) for his Ladyes sake.

Would I were *Acteon*, whom *Diana* did disguise,
To walke the woods vnknown, wheras my lady lies: 5
A hart of pleasant hew, I wish that I were so,
So that my Lady knew, alone mee, and no mo.

To follow thicke and plaine, by hill and dale alow,
To drinke the water fayne, and feede mee with the sloe:
I would not feare the frost, to lye vpon the ground, 10
Delight should quite the cost, what payne so that I found.

The shaling nuts and mast, that falleth from the tree,
Should serue for my repast, might I my Lady see:
Sometime that I might say, when I saw her alone,
Beholde thy slaue alone, that walkes these woods vnknowen. 15

FINIS.

¶ An Epytaph vpon the death of Arthur
Fletchar of Bangor Gent.

YE grisly ghostes which walke below in black *Cocistus* Lakes,
Mids *Ditis dennes*, *Erebus* Dames, with heare of vgly Snakes 20
Medusa with thy monstrous mates, assist mee now a while,
In dyre wamenting verse to shew, and drierie dolefull stile.
The fayre vntimely fatall ende of *Fletcher*, now by death,
Vnto the Ayre his soule with *Ioue*, resignde his latest breath:
Whose life full due wee must commend, as it deserues the same, 25
And conuersation to eche one, did seldome meryt blame.
A faythfull freend to eche hee was, to none an oppen foe,
Vnto his Prince a subiect true, till fates had lodgd him loe.
His actes did tend to no mans harmes, no Parasite to prayse,
For greedy gayne but still the troth, mayntaynd at all assayes. 30
His

[52]

of gallant Inuentions.

His time hee spent in Vertues lore, as seemd his state full wel,
By serious study what hee could, hee sought for to excel.
But what of al this same? the fates no wight in time wyll spare,
Whē gastly death hath pearst in earth, thē must our bodyes weare 5
In age aswell in youthes, in youthes aswell in age,
No certayne time wee haue to bide, when death with vs wil wage.
No thing can still abide, but comes to nought in ende,
The craggy Rocks the sturdiest okes: starke rotten once is rend.
And so hath *Fletcher*, now to death payd his due, 10
What hee is now wee must bee all, his Funerall then vew.

FINIS.

¶ *A Lady writeth vnto her Louer wherin shee most
earnestly chargeth him with Ingratitude.*

Wretched wight whom hensfoorth may I trust 15
All men both falce and fell I will them painte,
If thou (vnkinde) bee cruell and vniust
Whom I alwayes so faythfull held and quainte:
What cruelty? what trustles treasons iust?
Was euer hard by tragicall complaint? 20
But lesse then this, my merit if I may,
And thy desart in equall ballance lay.

Wherfore (vnkinde) since that on liue?
A worthier wight of prowes ne beauty,
Ne that by much to thee that doth ariue, 25
In cumly porte ne generositie.
Why doost thou not tweene these thy vertues striue,
It may bee sayd thou hast serbillitie:
Then say that who of fayth is holden stable:
There may to him none els bee comparable. 30

𝔉 iii   For

The gorgious Gallery

For write ye not that vertues haue no grace
Wheras this trust and stablenesse doth want,
As other things, though much of cumly face:
Cannot be seene, where gladsome light is skant. 5
A mayd to false for thee, an easie case,
Whose Idol, Lord & God thou werst most puisant
Whom with thy wordes it easly had bin donne,
To make beleue both colde and darke the sonne.

Cruell, what offence hast thou for to bewayle, 10
The killing of thy loue if thou not repent?
If yee accompte so light of fayth to fayle:
What other sinne can make thy harte lament?
How treate you foes, if mee ye doo assayle?
That loues thee so, with such cruell torment: 15
The heauens iustles, I will say to bee:
In case they shew the iust reuenge of mee.

If of offences all, that monstrous vice
Ingratitude, do most a man offend,
And if for that, an Angell of great price, 20
Was forced to Hell, from heauen to dissend:
If great offence, great chastisment entice
When to reforme, the hart doth not him bend,
Take heed sharp skourge that God on thee not send
Thou art to mee vnkinde, and doost not mend. 25

If these also, besides some other spot
I haue (vnkinde) wherof thee to accuse,
That thou my hart with holdst, I meane it not,
I speake of thee that madest thee myne by lot,
And robbest mee since, against reasō which I must 30
Restore (vnkinde) for well thou wottest it playne,
They shalbe damned that others goods retaine.
                                        Vnkinde

[54]

of gallant Inuentions.

Vnkinde, thou hast forsaken mee, but I will
Not will thee willingly for none assayes
Yet this hard hap, and trouble for to flie,
I can and will, ende these my wofull dayes:
In onely way, in thy disgrace to dye,
For if the Gods had graunted by their payes
My death, geuen then, when I stoode in thy grace,
No wight had dyed in halfe so happy a case.

FINIS.

¶ The Louer vnto his Lady beloued,
of her disdaynfulnesse toward him.

         (might,
FOr beauties sake though loue doth dread thy
 And *Venus* thinks, by sute to proue thy dame:
Though *Pallas* striues, by hope of equall right,
For *Wisdoms* watch, as daughter thee to claime.
Though *Mercury* would entitled be thy Syre,
For thy sweet talke, so sweetly blazed forth:
Though all the Gods, do burne in like desire,
Thy graces rare, in heauen so much worth:
Yet lo, thy proofe I know, the trusty waight,
Of Tygars milke, thou fostred wert from molde,
And *Cipres* Well with dainful chaung of fraight.
Gaue thee to drinke infected poyson colde.
But yet beware, least loue renew in thee,
The dreadfull flame *Narcissus* whylom felt,
With eger moode, and sight to feede thine eye.
Of thine owne, from others flame to swell:
For loue doth loue with hot reuenge to wreake,
The ruthles Iron hart, that will not breake.

FINIS.

The gorgious Gallery

The Louer in the prayse of his beloued and comparison of her beauty.

NOt shee for whom prowde *Troy* did fall and burne,
The *Greekes* eke slaine, that bluddy race did runne: 5
Nor shee for spight that did *Acteon* turne,
Into an Hart her beauty coye did shunne:
Nor shee whose blud vpon *Achilles* Tombe,
Whose face would tame a Tygars harte:
Nor shee that wan by wise of Paris dome. 10
Th'apple of Golde for Beauty to her parte:
Nor shee whose eyes did pearce true *Troylus* brest,
And made him yeeld, that knew in loue no law,
Might bee compared to the fayrest and the best,
Whom Nature made to keepe the rest in awe: 15
For Beauties sake, sent downe from *Ioue* aboue,
Thrise happy is hee, that can attayne her loue.

FINIS.

¶ In the prayse of a beautifull and vertuous Virgin, whose name begins with M. 20

(do leade
BEhold you Dames y̌ raigne in fames, whose lookes mens harts
And triumph in the spoyle of those, vpō whose brests you trede.
A myrror make of *M*, whose molde, Dame Nature in disdayne,
To please her self, & spight her foes, in beauty raysd to raigne:
Whose sunny beames & starry eyes, presents a heauenlyke face, 25
And shewes the world a wonderous worke, sutch are her giftes of
In forhed, feature beareth, brunt in face doth fauor guyde, (grace
In lookes is life, in shape is shame, in cheekes doth coulor hyde:
In boddy seemelynesse doth shew, in wordes doth wisdome shade,
All partes of her doth prayse deserue, in temprance is her trade. 30
In humble porte is honor plaste, in face is maydens smyles
Her life is grafte with Golden giftes, her deedes deuoyd of gyles.
And

of gallant Inuentions.

And as the Star to Marriners, is guyde vnto the Port,
So is this *M*, a heauenly ioy, to Louers that resort:
Who run and rome with inward wounds, & folded armes acrosse,   4
And hide their harms with clokes of care, & feed their hope w̌ losse.
Her lookes doth lift aboue the skyes, her frowns to Hel doth throw
All sues to her, shee seekes on none, that daily proofe doth show:
Wherfore her saying late set forth, shee burnt and could not flee,
Though ment in prayse, yet far amis, I take it written bee.
Shee is none such as if shee would, that any would disdayne: 10
But for the smartes of others greefes, of pitty shee did playne,
As one most lothe of any lyfe, for loue of her bee loste,
Or that with blud or cruell deedes, men write her beauties boste:
For mercy is in *M*, her brest, and modest is her life,
A courtuous mayd, and like to prooue, a constant worthy wife.   15

FINIS.

¶ The Louer deceyued by his Ladyes vnconstancy,
writeth vnto her as foloweth.

T He heat is past that did mee fret,
The fier is out that nature wrought   20
The plantes of youth that I did set,
Are dry and dead within my thought
The Frost hath slayne the kindly sap,
That kept the hart in liuely state:
The sodayne storme and thunder clap: 25
Hath turned loue, to mortall hate.

The myst is gon that bleard mine eyes,
The lowring cloudes I see appeare,
Though that the blinde eate many flyes,
I would you knew, my sight is cleare: 30
Your sweete deceyuing flattryng face
Did make mee thinke that you were white:

I

[57]

The gorgious Gallery

I muse how you had such a grace:
To seeme a Hauke, and bee a kyte.

Where precious ware is to be solde,
They shall it haue, that giueth most:
All things wee see, are woon with Golde,
Few things is had, where is no cost.
And so it fareth now by mee,
Because I preace to giue no gyftes:
Shee takes my sute vnthankfully,
And driues mee of with many dryftes.

Is this th' end of all my sute,
For my good will, to haue a skorne?
Is this of all my paynes the frute,
To haue the chaffe in steade of corne?
Let them that lyst, posses such drosse,
For I deserue a better gayne:
Yet had I rather leaue with losse,
Then serue and sue, and all in vayne.

FINIS.

¶ A true description of Loue.

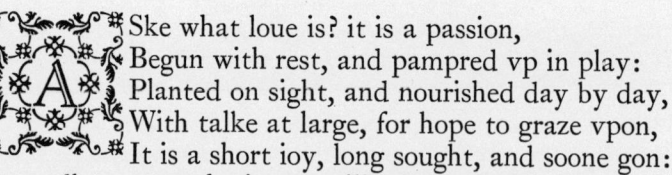

Ske what loue is? it is a passion,
Begun with rest, and pampred vp in play:
Planted on sight, and nourished day by day,
With talke at large, for hope to graze vpon,
It is a short ioy, long sought, and soone gon:
An endles maze, wherin our willes doo stray:
A gylefull gaine, repentance is the pay.
A great fier bred of small occasion,
A plague to make, our fraylty to vs knowen,
Where wee therby, are subiecte to their lay:
Whose fraylty ought, to leaue vntill our stay,

In

of gallant Inuentions.

In case our selues, this custome had not knowen.
Of hope and health, such creatures for to pray,
Whose glory resteth cheefly on denaye.

FINIS. 5

¶ The Louer to his beloued, by the name
of fayre, and false.

O Cruell hart with falsehood infecte, of force I must complayne,
  Whose poyson hid, I may detect, as cause doth mee constrayn:
Thy name I shryne within my brest, thy deedes though I doo tell, 10
No minde of malice I protest, thy selfe doth know it well.
If thy deserts then bids mee write, I cannot well reuoke it,
I shall not spare to shew thy spite, I will no longer cloake it:
As *Troylus* truth shall bee my sheeld, to kepe my pen from blame,
So *Cressids* crafte shall kepe the feeld, for to resound thy shame. 15
Vlisses wife shall mate the sore, whose wishly troth doth shine,
Well Fayre and False, I can no more, thou art of *Helens* lyne:
And daughter to *Diana* eke, with pale and deadly cheare,   yeare.
Whose often chaunge I may well like, two moonthes within the

FINIS. 20

¶ The Louer describeth his paynfull plight, and
requireth speedy redresse, or present death.

The slaue of seruile sort, that borne is bond by kinde,
Doth not remayne in hope, w̃ such vnquiet minde:
Ne tossed crasid Ship, with yrksome surging seas, 25
So greedely the quiet Port, doth thirst to ride at ease.
As I thy short returne, with wishing vowes require,
In hope that of my hatefull harmes, the date will then expire:
But time with stealing steps, and driery dayes doth driue,
And thou remaynst then bound to come, if that thou bee aliue. 30
𝔥 ij   O

[59]

The gorgious Gallery

O cruell Tygars whelpe, who had thy hand in holde?
When y̆ with flattering pen thou wrotst, thy help at hand behold?
Beleeue it to bee true, I come without delay,
A foole and silly simple soule, yet doost thou still betray:　　　5
Whose mooueles loue and trust, doth reason far surmount,
Whom *Cupids* trumpe, to fatall death hath sommond to accompt
My fayth and former life: fed with such frendly fier,
Haue not of thee by iust reward, deserued such falts hyer:
I promesse thee not mine, but thy case I bewayle,　　　10
What infamy may greater bee, then of thy fayth to fayle?
How ofte with humble sute? haue I besought the sonne,(to ronne?
That hee would spur his Coursers fearce, their race more swifte
To th'end with quicker speed, might come the promised day,
The day which I with louing lookes, and weary will did pray.　　　15
But thou art sure disposde to glory in my death,
Wherfore to feede thy fancy fond, loe, here I ende my breath.
I can not sighe nor sob, away by playnt I pine:
I see my fatall fainting file, ye Sisters doo vntwine,
The Feriman I finde, prest at the Riuer side:　　　20
To take mee in his restles Boate, therin with him to ride.
And yet although I sterue, through thy dispitous fault:
Yet craue I not in my reuenge, that harme should thee assault,
But rather that thy fame, eternally may shine:
And that eche to thine auayle, aboundantly encline.　　　25
That eche thine enterprise, hath luckye lot and chaunce,
And stable fortune, thine estate, from day to day aduaunce,
That Sun, that Moone, that starres, and eke the plannets all,
The fier, the water, and the earth, may freendly to thee fal.
That many quiet yeres, thou number may with rest:　　　30
Voyd of all annoyes and greeues, as may content thee best,
And if that foraine loue, torment and vexe thy harte:
God yeeld thy weary wanting wish, and swagement of thy smart.
With froward flearing face, at mee if Fortune frowne,
Thou doost reioyce and I not so, but ioy thy good renowne:　　　35
And if I thee offend, for that I doo thee loue,
Forgiue it mee: for force it is, I can it not remoue.
　　　　　　　　　　　　　　　　　　　　　For

[60]

of gallant Inuentions.

For I in secret sort, these lines to thee did I write,
My weakned wearied hand hensforth, shall sease for to endyte:
That letters to receiue from mee, thou neede not muse:
The messenger that next of all, of mee shal bring the newes,   5
Dissolued from the corps, shalbe my dolefull spright: (sight,
That first (vnsheathd) shal passe to thee, when hee hath vewd thy
Contented hee shall go vnto the heauens aboue,
In case that ioyed rested place, may gayne it any loue.
And now for that my death, thy name may spot and stayne: 10
If that the flying fame therof, to others eares attayne,
I will not it were red, or knowen by other wayes:
That thou art only cause, I thus in ruthe doo ende my dayes.
Wherfore this Letter red, condemne it to the flame:
And if thou doo thy honnor forse, I know thou wilt the same,   15
And if in lingring time, vnwares they chaunce to come:
Wherin the entrayles of the earth, shall hap to bee my tombe.
At least yet graunt mee this, it is a small request:
O happy wythered pyned corps, God send thy soule good rest.

FINIS.   20

¶ *The Lady beloued, assureth her Louer to bee his
owne, and not to change, while life doth last.*

DEare hart as earst I was, so will I stil remayne,
Till I am dead, and more if more may bee:
Howsoeuer loue do yeeld mee ioy or payne,   25
Or Fortune lyst to smyle or frowne on mee
No chaunging chaunce my fast fayth may constrayne,
No more then Waues, or beating of the Sea
May stir the stedfast rocke, that will not ply,
For fayre nor fowle one inche, no more will I.   30
A file or knife of lead, shall sooner carue
The Diamant vnto what forme you will:
Ere Fortunes dynte, compell mee for to swarue,
Or the ire of Loue, to breake my constant will,

𝕳iij   Yee

[61]

The gorgious Gallery

Yee sooner shall, the law of nature starue,
When Ryuers take their course agaynst the hill,
Ere sodayne hap, for better or for worse,
Disturne my thoughts, to take a better course.   5

With hartes consent, my loue you doo possesse,
A surer holde may chaunce, then many weene:
The fayth by othe, that subiectes doo confesse,
To their new prince, is seldome stronger seene:
No fyrmer state than that, which loue doth sure expresse,   10
Of Kinge, ne Keyser hitherto hath been:
So that you neede not fortifie your hould,
With Towre or Ditch, least others win it should.

For though you set, no Souldiers for defence,
For all assaults, this one may yet suffise: 15
It is not goods can alter my pretence,
No gentle hart, yeeldes to so vile a prise.
Though crowne and septier, few would dispise,
Not beauty meete, to moue a wauering minde,
Yet more then yours, I wot not where to finde.   20

And feare you not, what forme my hart once tooke,
Least any new print, shall the same deface:
So deepe therin, ingraued is your looke,
As neuer may bee wyped from that place:
My hart like Waxe, so lightly did not brooke,   25
More then one stroke, ere *Cupid* brought to passe
One splint of skale, therof to take away,
The best reserued, your Image to pourtray.

That like as what stone, it selfe best desendeth,
And hardiest is with toole to bee graue: 30
Doth sooner breake in peeces, then it bendeth,
To looze the stampe, afore my hand it gaue:
Euen so the nature, of my hart contendeth,
As hard is this, as any stone you haue:

                                                                Though

of gallant Inuentions.

Though forse do breake it, vnto peeces small,
Those peeces somewhat, you resemble shall.

FINIS.

¶ In the prayse of the rare beauty, and manifolde 5
vertues of Mistres D. as followeth.

IF *Chawcer* yet did lyue, whose English tongue did passe,
Who sucked dry *Pernassus* spring, and raste the Iuice there was:
If *Surrey* had not scalde, the height of *Ioue* his Throne,
Vnto whose head a pillow softe, became Mount *Helycon:* 10
They with their Muses could, not haue pronounst the fame,
Of *D.* faire Dame, lo, a staming stock, the cheefe of natures frame.
They would but haue eclipsed, her beauties golden blast,
Nor *Ouid* yet of Poets Prince, whose wits all others past.
Olde *Nestor* with his tongue, and flowing dew so sweete, 15
Would rather haue berefte her right, then pend her praises meete
In *Helens* heauenly face, whose grace the *Greekes* bought deare,
For whose defence prowd *Troy* did fal, such forme did not appeare.
In *Hectors* sister loe: who *Pirhus* Father rapte,
Did not abound sutch beauty bright, as now to *D,* hath hapt: 20
For *D,* doth passe as far, Dame *Venus* with her prise,
As *Venus* did the other two, by doome of Paris wise.
If shee had present been, within the walles of *Ide,*
They would not had such discord then, nor Paris iudgd that side.
In minde all voyd of doubt, they straight agreed would, 25
That *D,* should of good right, the Aple haue of Golde.
Whom as I must beleeue, that nature did create,
To rob the hartes of noble Kings, and courage stoute to mate:
Her forhead seemely spaste, wherin doo shine her eyes,
No whit vnlike to starres by night, or beame when *Phebus* ryse. 30
Her haire that shines like golde, her shoulders couer whight.
To which no snow on Mountayne highe, may be compared right:
Her mouth well compast small, in smylings vtters forth
A treasure riche of Orient Pearle, therto no Golde more worth,
I

[63]

The gorgious Gallery

I feare much *Promethius* fall, dare no further wade,
Whom loue embraced with the shape, that hee so finely made:
Yet this I dare presume, one thought of her may draw,
A harte of Iron, and it subdue, vnto blinde *Cupids* law.   5
I sorrow to recite, the bitter teares that flow:
Within the eyes of other Dames, that beauty know.
I weepe to wayle in minde, the burning slights that flame:
In troubled hartes of Natures case in spreading of her fame,
They all doo curse themselues, of Nature makes complaynt,   10
That shee on them had smal regard, that did her thus depaynt.
Of her doth nobles spring, and sutors sue for grace,   (place,
And Fountaines eke of sugred speech, where voice can take no
Here *Pallas* should haue lost her prayse, for wisdome great,
Who gendred was of *Ioue* his braines, wher wisdom toke his seat.   15
Here wise *Vlisses* wyfe, whose chastnesse brued her fame:
Should matched bee, ye mated eke, in ventring of the same.
Prowde *Tarquin* with his force, which *Lucresse* did defile:
Could not haue spoyled faire D. so, with neither sound nor gyle.
This Dame I thinke bee such, that heauen can vndermine,   20
And lifte the earth vnto the skyes, eche stone a star to shine.
If passed time (alas) might now returne agayne,
And all the wittes that euer was, would herein take the payne:
They could not at the ful, no due giftes expresse,
A wight vnfit to bee in earth, in heauen no such goddesse.   25
Whose name shall floorish still, though *Atropos* with spight:
In running from her deuelish Den, bereaue vs of this light,
Though *Thesiphon* do cut, her time of life away:
Her cankred Swoord cannot assayle, her fame for to decay.
For wee in these our dayes, our selues may better quight: 30
To geue to her the cheefest prayse, then *Paris* which did right.
Lesse hatred cannot want, though power for to reuenge:
Our stately house as they did *Troy*, their force doth faile to senge.
Their might if it were like, these verses wee should rew,
With no lesse payne then *Ouid* did, whose greefe by Muses grew.   35

FINIS.

[64]

of gallant Inuentions.

Prety parables, and Prouerbes of Loue.

I Spake when I ment not, in speeding to gayne,
I sought, when I sped not, but trauaild in vayne:
I found where I feard not, would writh w̃ the wind,   5
I loste where I lou'd not, nor forsid to finde.
Nothing in which, truth is not trustie,
But double is such, and beauty but rustie:
I coole with the colde, I leue that I like not,
I know not the olde, that rotteth and ripes not.   10
I sauor no such, that fondly doth fauor,
I care not to much, for such sory sauor:
I taste or I try, in parte or in all,
I care not a flye, the losse is but small.
I labor at leasure, I pricke without payne,   15
In vsing for pleasure, beates in my brayne:
I spare not in byrding, to beat well the bush,
Nor leaue not in stryking, as long as they rush.
I try ere I trust, nought wasting but winde,
Before I finde iust, they know not my minde: 20
I iet not with *Geminie*, nor tarry not with *Tawre*
In bluttring who bleares mee? I leaue them with *Lawre*.
For fier who fyndeth, in burning to bight,
The wise man hee warneth, to leape from the light:
Forseeing the weede, and losing from bandes,   25
The plowing in Sea, and sowing in Sandes.

FINIS.

The gorgious Gallery

Of patience.
A Soueraygne salue there is for eche disease:
   The cheefe reuenge for cruell ire
Is pacience, the cheefe and present ease,
   For to delay eche yll desire.

Of lawlesse lust.
AN euerlasting bondage doth hee choose,
   That can not tell a litle how to vse:
Hee scant ynough for shame puruayes,
   That all alone to lust obayes.

Of will, and reason.
I Count this conquest great,
   That can by reasons skill:
Subdue affections heate,
   And vanquish wanton will.

Of three things to be shunned.
THree thinges, who seekes for prayse, must flye,
   To please the taste with wine
Is one: another, for to lye
   Full softe on fethers fine.
The thirde and hardest for to shunne,
   And cheefest to eschew,
Is lickerous lust, which once begun,
   Repentance doth ensue.

Of beauty, and chastity.
CHastity a vertue rare,
   Is seldome knowen to run her race:
Where cumly shape and beauty faire,
   Are seene to haue a byding place.

Of wisdome.
WHo seeketh the renowne to haue,
   And eke the prayse of Vertues name:
Of Wisdome rare hee ought to craue,
   With gladsome will to worke the same.

                                       Of

of gallant Inuentions.

Of a pure conscience.
A Conscience pure withouten spot,
  That knoweth it selfe for to bee free:
Of slaunders lothsome reketh not,
  A brazen wall full well may bee.

Of frendship founde by chaunce.
THe frendship found by chaunce is such,
  As often chaunce is seene to chaunge:
And therfore trust it not to much,
Ne make therof a gaine to straunge:
For proofe hath taught by hap is had,
Sometime as well the good as bad.

Of good will got by due desert.
BUt I suppose the same good will,
  That once by good desart is got:
That fancy findes by reasons skill,
And time shall try withouten spot,
Is such as harde is to bee gayned,
And woorthy got to bee retayned.

Of flatterers and faythfull friendes.
THe finest tongue can tel the smoothest tale,
  The hottest fiers haue ofte the highest smoke:
The hardiest knightes the soonest will assaile,
The strongest armes can giue the sturdest stroke
The wysest men be thought of greatest skill,
And poorest freendes be found of most goodwill.

Of a vertuous, life, age, and death.
GOd wot my freend our life full soone decayes,
  And vertue voydes no wrinkels from the face:
Approching age by no entreatie stayes,
And death vntamed, will graunt no man grace.

FINIS.
A proper Posie for a Handkercher.

Fancy is fearce, Desire is bolde,
Will is wilfull, but Reason is colde.

Iij   ¶ The

The gorgious Gallery

¶ The Louer beeing ouermuch weryed with seruile
lyfe, compareth it to a Laborinth.

With speedy winges, my fethered woes pursues,
My wretched life, made olde by weary dayes:
But as the fire of *Ethna* stil renues,
And breedes as much, by flame as it decayes:
My heauy cares, that once I thought would ende mee,
Prolongs my life, the more mishap to lende mee.

Oh haples will, with such vnwary eyes,
About mishap that hast thy selfe bewrethed:
Thy trust of weale, my wailfull proofe denyes,
To wofull state wherby I am bequethed:
And into such a Laborinth betake,
As *Dedalus* for *Minotaure* did make.

With helples search, wheras it were assinde,
Without reuoke, I tread these endles Mayes:
Where more I walke, the more my selfe I winde.
Without a guyde, in Torments tyring wayes:
In hope I dread, where to and fro I rome,
By death ne life, and findes no better home.

But sithe I see, that sorrow cannot ende,
These haples howres, the lines of my mischance:
And that my hope, can nought a whit amend,
My bitter dayes, nor better hap aduance:
I shall shake of, both doubtfull hope and dreede,
And so bee pleased, as God is best agreede.

FINIS.

of gallant Inuentions.

How to choose a faythfull freende.

Hough that my yeares, full far doo stande aloofe,
From counsell sage, or Wisdomes good aduice:
What I doo know by soone repenting proofe, 5
I shall you tell, and learne if you be wise.
From fined wits, that telles the smoothest tale,
Beware, their tongues doo flatter oft a wry:
A modest loke shall well set forth your sale,
Trust not to much, before somewhat you try: 10
So guyde your selfe in worde, and eke in deede,
As bad and good may prayse your sober name:
Assay your freend, before your greatest neede,
And to conclude, when I may doo that same,
That may you please, and best content your minde, 15
Assure your selfe, a faythfull freend to finde.

FINIS.

The Louer beeing accused of suspicion of flattery, pleadeth not gyltie, and yet is wrongfully condemned.

TO seeme for to reuenge, eche wrong in hastie wise, 20
By proofe wee see of gyltlesse men, it hath not bin the guise:
In slaunders lothsome brute, when they condemned bee,
With rageles moodes they suffer wronge, when truth shall try
These are the pacient panges, y̌ pas within the brest (them free:
Of those that feele their case by mine, where wrong hath right 25
I know how by suspect, I haue been iudged awry, (opprest:
And graunted gyltie in the thing, that clearly I denye.
My fayth may mee defende, if I might leuid bee,
God iudge mee so, as from that gylte I know mee to bee free:
I wrought but for my freend, the greefe was all mine owne, 30
As if the troth were truely tryde, by prooft it might be knowne.
Yet are there such that say, they can my meaning deeme,
Without respect to this olde troth: things proue not as they seeme:
Wherby

The gorgious Gallery

Wherby it may befall, in iudgment to bee quicke,
To make them be suspecte therwith, that needeth not to kicke:
Yet in resisting wrong, I would not haue it thought,
I doo accuse as though I knew, by whom it may be wrought: 5
If any such there bee, that herewithall be vext,
It were their vertue to beware, and deeme mee better nexte.

FINIS.

The Louer describeth the daungerous state of Ambition. 10

Beholde these high and mighty men,
Their chaunging state and tell mee then:
Where they or wee, best dayes doo see,
Though wee seeme not and they to bee
    In wealth. 15
Their pleasant course straung traces hath,
On tops of trees that groundles path:
    Full waueringly.
For bee it calme they tread not fast,
Blow roughe, blow soft, all helpe is past: 20
    Appearingly.
With vs, ye see, it is not so,
That clime not vp, but kepe below:
In calmes our course is faire and playne,
Huge hilles defendes from stormy rayne: 25
    For why?
The raging winde and stormy shower,
On mountaynes high it hath most power
    Naturally.
But wee that in lowe valleis lye, 30
Beholde may such as wander hye:
    So slydingly:
Then what is hee that will aspire,
To heape such woe to please desire:
                   That

of gallant Inuentions.

That may in wealth by staying still,
Spend well his dayes and fly from yll:
    To good.
By hauing his recourse to God
To loue his lawes to feare his rod:
    Vnfaynedly.
To doo that in his worde wee finde,
To helpe the poore, the sicke, the blinde:
    Accordingly.
But though gaynsayd this can not bee,
Deeme men by deedes, and yee shall see:
That these low valleies they can not bide,
But vp will clyme, though downe they slyde:
    Agayne.
The poore the riche mans place doth craue,
The riche would fayne hyer places haue:
    Ambiciously.
The Squyre, the Knight, a Lorde would bee,
The Lorde, the Erle would hyer then hee:
    Full dangerously.
When these attayne to their desire,
Then meaner men are set on fire:
To haue the roomes which they in were,
So that ye see all times some there:
    In hart.
When one is gon, another is come,
The third catching the secondes roome:
    Full speedely.
Thus clyming one to others tayle,
The bowes either breake, or footing fayle:
    Full totteringly.
For when the top they haue attaynd,
And got is all they would haue gaynd:
Then downe they come wit sodayne fall,
In doubtfull case of life and all.
    And thus,

            Jiiii   Ambition

The gorgious Gallery

Ambition reapeth worthy hyre,
Because hee would such sporte aspyre
      Vnequally.
And there his bragge is layd full low,
That thought on hie, himself to show,
      Deseruedly.

FINIS.

The paynfull plight of a Louer remayning in doubtfull
hope of his Ladyes fauour.

THe bitter sweete, that straynes my yeelded harte,
  The carelesse count, which doth the same imbrace:
The doubtfull hope, to reape my due dezart,
The pensiue pathe, that guides my restles race:
Are at such war, within my wounded brest,
As doth bereaue, my ioy and eke my rest.

My greedy will, which seekes the golden gayne,
My luckles lot, doth always take in worth:
My matched minde, that dreades my sutes in vayne,
My pittious playnt, doth helpe for to set forth:
So that betwixt, two waues of raging Seas,
I driue my dayes, in troubles and disease.

My wofull eyes, doo take their cheefe delight,
To feede their fill, vpon their pleasant maze:
My hidden harmes, that grow in mee by sight,
With pyning panges, doo driue mee from the gaze:
And to my hap, I reape none other hire,
But burne my selfe, and I to blow the fire.

FINIS.

of gallant Inuentions.

*The Louer recounteth his faythfull diligence towarde
his beloued, with the rewardes that
hee reapeth therof.*

MY fancy feedes, vpon the sugred gaule,
My witlesse will, vnwillingly workes my woe:
My carefull choyse, doth choose to keepe mee thraule,
My franticke folly, fawns vpon my foe:
My lust alluers, my lickering lyppes to taste,
The bayte wherin, the subtill hooke is plaste.

My hungry hope, doth heape my heauy hap,
My sundry sutes, procure my more disdayne:
My steadfast steppes, yet slyde into the trap,
My tryed truth, entangleth mee in trayne:
I spye the snare, and will not backward go,
My reason yeeldes, and yet sayth euer, no.

In pleasant plat, I tread vpon the snake,
My flamyng thirst, I quench with venomd Wine:
In dayntie dish, I doo the poyson take,
My hunger biddes mee, rather eate then pine:
I sow, I set, yet fruit, ne flowre I finde,
I pricke my hand, yet leaue the Rose behinde.

FINIS.

𝕶   ¶ A letter

The gorgious Gallery

¶ A Letter written by a yonge gentilwoman and sent to her husband vnawares (by a freend of hers) into Italy.

IMagine when these blurred lines, thus scribled out of frame,
Shall come before thy careles eyes, for thee to read the same: 5
To bee through no default of pen, or els through prowd disdayne,
But only through surpassing greefe, which did the Author payne
Whose quiuring hand could haue no stay, this carful bil to write
Through flushing teares distilling fast, whilst shee did it indite:
Which teares perhaps may haue some force (if thou no tigre bee, 10
And mollifie thy stony hart, to haue remorse on mee.
Ah periurde wight reclaime thy selfe, and saue thy louing mate,
Whom thou hast left beclogged now, in most vnhappy state:
(Ay mee poore wench) what luckles star? what frowning god aboue
What hellish hag? what furious fate hath changd our former loue? 15
Are wee debard our wonted ioyes? shall wee no more embrace?
Wilt thou my deare in country strang, ensue *Eneas* race:
Italians send my louer home, hee is no *Germayne* borne,
Vnles ye welcome him because hee leaues mee thus forlorne.
As earst ye did *Anchises* sonne, the founder of your soyle, 20
Who falsely fled from Carthage Queene, releeuer of his toyle:
Oh send·him to *Bryttannia* Coastes, vnto his trusty feere,
That shee may vew his cumly corps, whom shee estemes so deere:
Where wee may once againe renue, our late surpassed dayes,
Which then were spent with kisses sweet, & other wanton playes: 25
But all in vayne (forgiue thy thrall, if shee do iudge awrong)
Thou canst not want of dainty Trulles *Italian* Dames among.
This only now I speake by gesse, but if it happen true,
Suppose that thou hast seene the sword, that mee thy Louer slue:
Perchance through time so merrily with dallying damsels spent, 30
Thou standst in doubt & wilte enquire frō whom these lines were
If so, remember first of all, if thou hast any spowse,   (sent:
Remember when, to whom and why, thou earst hast plited vowes,
Remember who esteemes thee best, and who bewayles thy flight,
Minde her to whom for loyalty thou falshood doost requight. 35
                                                      Remember

of gallant Inuentions.

Remember Heauen, forget not Hell, and way thyne owne estate,
Reuoke to minde whom thou hast left, in shamefull blame & hate:
Yea minde her well who did submit, into thine onely powre,
Both hart and life, and therwithall, a ritch and wealthy dowre: 5
And last of all which greeues mee most, that I was so begylde,
Remember most forgetfull man, thy pretty tatling childe:
The least of these surnamed things, I hope may well suffise,
To shew to thee the wretched Dame, that did this bill deuise.
I speake in vayne, thou hast thy will, and now sayth *Aesons* sonne, 10
Medea may packe vp her pypes, the golden Fleese is wonne:
If so, be sure *Medea* I will, shew forth my selfe in deede,
Yet gods defend though death I taste, I should distroy thy seede:
Agayne, if that I should enquire, wherfore thou doost soiurne,
No answere fitly mayst thou make, I know to serue thy turne: 15
Thou canst not say but that I haue, obseru'd my loue to thee,
Thou canst not say, but that I haue, of life vnchast bin free. (bound
Thou canst not cloak (through want) thy flight, since riches did a-
Thou needes not shame of mee thy spouse, whose byrth not low is
As for my beauty, thou thy self, earwhile didst it commend (found, 20
And to conclude I know no thing, wherin I dyd offend:
Retier with speed, I long to see, thy barke in wished bay,
The Seas are calmer to returne, then earst to fly away.
Beholde the gentill windes doo serue, so that a frendly gayle,
Would soone conuay to happy Porte, thy most desired sayle: 25
Return would make amends for all, and bannish former wronge,
Oh that I had for to entice, a *Scyrens* flattering songe.
But out alas, I haue no shift, or cunning to entreat,
It may suffise for absence thine, that I my grieefes repeate
Demaund not how I did disgest, at first thy sodayne flight, 30
For ten dayes space I tooke no rest, by day nor yet by night:
But like to *Baccus* beldame Nonne, I sent and rangde apace,
To see if that I mought thee finde, in some frequented place:
Now here, now there, now vp, now down, my fancy so was fed,
Vntill at length I knew of troth, that thou from mee wert fled. 35
Then was I fully bent with blade, to stab my vexed harte,
Yet hope that thou wouldst come agayn, my purpose did conuart:

K ij   And

The gorgious Gallery

And so ere since I liu'd in hope bemixt with dreadful feare,
My smeared face through endles teares, vnpleasant doth appeare:
My slepes vnsound with vgly dreams, my meats are vayn of taste
My gorgious rayment is dispisde, my tresses rudly plaste. 5
And to bee breefe: I bouldly speake, there doth remayne no care:
But that therof in amplest wise, I doo possesse a share:
Lyke as the tender sprig doth bend, with euery blast of winde,
Or as the guidelesse Ship on Seas, no certaine Porte may finde.
So I now subiecte vnto hope, now thrall to carefull dread, 10
Amids the Rocks, tween hope and feare, as fancy mooues, am led:
Alas returne, my deare returne, returne and take thy rest,
God graunt my wordes may haue the force, to penytrat thy brest.
What doost thou thinke in *Italy*, some great exployt to win?
No, no, it is not *Italy*, as sometimes it hath bin: 15
Or doost thou loue to gad abroad, the forrain costes to vew,
If so, thou hadst not doone amisse, to bid mee first adew:
But what hath bin the cause, I neede not descant longe,
For sure I am, meane while poore wench, I only suffer wrong.
Wel thus I leaue, yet more could say: but least thou shouldst refuse, 20
Through tediousnesse to reede my lines, the rest I will excuse:
Vntill such time as mighty *Ioue* doth send such luckye grace,
As wee therof in freendly wise, may reason face to face.
Till then farwell, and hee thee keepe, who only knowes my smart
And with this bill I send to thee, a trusty Louers harte. 25

By mee, to thee, not mine, but thine,
   Since Loue doth moue the same,
Thy mate, though late, doth wright, her plight,
   Thou well, canst tell, her name.

of gallant Inuentions.

¶ A Letter sent from beyond the Seaes to his Louer, perswading
her to continew her loue towardes him.

TO thee I write whose life and death, thy faith may saue or spil:
Which fayth obserue, I liue in ioy, if not, your freend you kill: 5
Suspecte not that I doo misdoubt, your loyalty at all:
But ponder how that louers are, vnto suspicion thrall.
Which thraldome breedeth furth thrall, if woonted fayth doo fayle:
Agaynst the Louer thus forlorne, do thousand Cares preuayle:
It litle helpes to haue begun, and there to set a stay,   10
They win more fame, that fight it out: then those that run away.
Like as the willing hound that doth, pursue the Deare in Chace:
Will not omit vnto the ende, his paynfull weary race:
So Loue (if loue it bee indeed) will stedfast still remayne:
What so betide, good hap or yll, and not reuoult agayne.   15
Such fayth of you, sweet hart I aske, such fayth: why sayd I so?
What neede I to demaund the thing, I haue had long ago:
Your fayth you gaue, the case is playn, you may not seeme to start:
And I in earnest of the match did leaue with you my hart.
But now perhaps you may alleage, long distance may procure,   20
A cause wherby our former loue, no longer may endure:
If so you Iudge to far amisse, although that sayle and winde,
Conuay my corps to cuntry strange, my hart remaynes behinde.
Examples many could I shew, but needles is that payne,
Mine owne example shall suffise, when I returne agayne: 25
Meane while although to swim I want, *Leanders* cunning art,
In all things els (except the same) Ile play *Leanders* part.
In hope that thou wilt shew thy selfe, to mee an *Hero* true,
And so although loth to depart, I say sweete hart adue.

A Ringe I sende, wherin is pende, a Posie (if you reede)   30
Wherby you may, perceaue alway, of what I most haue neede.
By mee your frende, vnto the ende, if you therto agree,
Although not so, your louing foe, I still perforce must bee.

FINIS.

𝔏iii   Another

The gorgious Gallery

An other louing Letter.

BEcause my hart is not mine owne, but resteth now with thee,
I greet thee well of hartinesse, thy selfe mayst Caruer bee:
Muse not hereat but like hereof, first read and then excuse, 5
I wish to you a plyant hart, when you these lines peruse.
Hope bids me speak, fear stayes my tongue, but *Cupid* makes mee (boulde,
And Fancy harps of good successe, when that my playnt is tould:
Thus Hope doth prick, & feare doth kicke, & fancy feeds my brayn,
In you alone doth now consist, the salue to ease my payne. 10
You are my Paradice of ioy, the heauen of my delight,
And therwithall (which thing is strang) the worker of my spight:
Which spight I seeke not to reuenge, but meekely to subdue,
Not as a foe, but as a freend, I do your loue pursue.
I yeeld my selfe vnto your power, and will not you relente? 15
In humble wise I mercy craue, and is your mercy spente?
No sure, as nature outwardly, hath shewde in you her skill,
I doubt not but that inwardly, the like shee doth fulfill.
So good a face, so trim a grace, as doth in you remayne:
A *Cressids* cruell stony harte, I know may not retayne: 20
Wherfore to ratefie my wordes, let deedes apparant bee:
Then may you vaunt and proue it true, you freedom gaue to mee.
Consider of my restles care, and way blinde *Cupids* ire:
Then shal you finde my paynful loue, doth claym but earned hire.
Requite not this my curtesy, and freendship with disdaine, 25
But as I loue vnfainedly, so yeeld like loue againe.
Allow hereof as for the rest, that doth belong to loue:
My selfe therof will take the care, as time, in time shall proue.
Meane while, I wish a *Thisbies* hart, in you there may endure:
Then doubt not, but a *Pyramus*, of mee you shall procure. 30

Yours at your will,
To saue or spill.

FINIS.

Pretie pamphlets, by T. Proctor.

Proctors Precepts.

Leaue vading plumes, no more vaunt, gallant youth,
Thy masking weeds forsake, take collours sage:
Shun vicious steps, consider what ensueth,
Time lewdly spent, when on coms crooked age.
When beauty braue shall vade, as doth the flower,
When manly might, shall yeeld to auncient time:
When yonge delightes shall dye, and ages bower,
Shall lodge thy corps, bemoning idle prime.
Learne of the Ant, for stormy blastes to get
Prouision, least vntimely want do cum,
And mooues thee mone such time, so lewd neglect
From vertues lore, where worthy honors wun.
Thinke how vncertayne here, thou liust a guest,
Amid such vice, thats irksome to beholde:
Thinke whence thou camst, and where thy corps shall rest,
When breathing breath, shall leaue thy carkasse colde.
When dreadfull death, shall daunt thy hauty minde,
When fearfull flesh, shall shrowd in clammy clay:
When pamperd plumes shall vade, and dreads shall finde,
Deseruings due, for erring lewd astray.
Run not to rash, least triall make the mone,
In auncient yeres thy greene vnbridled time:
Olde Age is lothd, with folly ouer grown,
Yonge yeres dispisde, cut of in sprowting prime.
Experience learne, let elder lyues thee lead,
In lyuely yeres, thy fickle steps to guide:
Least vnawares, such vncoth paths thou tread,
Which filthy be thought, pleasant to be eyde.
In calmest Seas, the deepest Whorepooles bee,
In greenest Grasse, the lurking Adder lyes:
With eger sting, the sugerest sap wee see,
Smooth wordes deceiue, learne therfore to bee wise.

FINIS.

The gorgious Gallery

Inuidus alterius rebus macrescit opimis.

THe greedy man, whose hart with hate doth swell,
Because hee sees his neyghbors good estate:
Liues vncontent, with what might serue him well, 5
And eftsoones seemes to blame sufficient fate:
This grudging gluton glut, with goulden gayne,
To serue his vse, although hee hath enough:
Repines at that, which others get with payne,
So that himselfe therby, hee doth abuse: 10
Hee thinkes that much, which passeth by his claw,
And findes a fault for it through luckles hap:
Although the matter valueth scarce a straw,
Hee deemes it small of gaine, that giues no sap.
Hee thinkes his store, shall serue his senclesse corse, 15
Or that no death at all, hee deemes there bee:
Els would hee to his conscience haue remorse,
And seeke to liue content with his degree:
For what auayles, to horde vp heapes of drosse,
Or seeke to please vnsaciate fond desire: 20
Considering that, tis subiect vnto losse,
And wee (therby yll got) deserues Hell fire:
From which O Lord conduct vs with thy hand,
And giue vs grace to liue vnto thy prayse:
Preserue our Queene his subiects and her land, 25
And graunt in peace, shee raigne here *Nestors* dayes.

FINIS.

of gallant Inuentions.

The reward of Whoredome by the fall of Helen.

From Limbo Lake, where dismall feendes do lye,
Where *Pluto* raignes, perpend *Helenas* cry:
Where firy flames, where pittious howlings bee,   5
Where bodyes burne: from thence giue eare to mee.
I am *Helena* shee, for whose vilde filthy fact,
The stately Towers of *Troy*, the hauty *Grecians* sacte:
High *Troy*, whose pompe, throughout the world did sound,
In Cinders low, through mee was layd on ground.   10
Kinge *Priamus* through mee, did end his life:
And *Troians* all almost, I was the cause of strife.
I am that Dame, whose beauty passing braue,
Dame *Venus* praysde, the golden Pome to haue:
Whose feature forste, Sir *Paris* boyling brest,   15
To leaue his land, and seeke to be my guest.
That trull which tost, the surging Seas a maine,
From Grecian shoare, to *Troy* vnto my paine.
That flurt, whose gallant sproutinge prime,
Through vilde abuse, was scorcht ere auncient time: 20
I vertue shund, I lothd a modest mynde,
I wayd not fame, my beauty made mee blinde.
Each braue delight, my masking minde allurde,
My fancy deemed, my beauties gloze assurde:
Such worthy fame, did sound of *Helens* hue,   25
Although my deedes, reapt shame, and guerdon due.
In gorgious plumes, I maskt, puft vp with pride,
In braue delights I liu'd, my fancy was my guide:
But fie of filth, your world is all but vayne,
Your pomp consumes, your deeds shall guerdon gaine: 30
See here by mee, whose beauty might haue boast,
For splendant hue, throughout each forrain coast.
But what preuayles, to vaunt of beauties glose,
Or brag of pride, wheron dishonor growes:
If I had vsde my gifts in vertues lore,   35
And modest liud, my prayse had bin the more.

𝕷   Where

The gorgious Gallery

Where now too late, I lothe my life lewd spent,
And wish I had, with vertue bin content.

FINIS.   T. P.

A Louers lyfe.   5

THe tedious toyle, the cares which Louers taste, (feare:
The troubled thoughts, which moues their mindes to
The pinching pangs, the dole which seemes to waste,
Their lothsome life, deepe plungd in gulfes of care:
    Would mooue ech shun, such snares of vayne delight,   10
    Which irksome be, though pleasant to the sight.
The minde full fraught, with care enioyes no ease,
A boyling brest, desires vnlawfull lust:
The hart would haue, what best the minde doth please,
And fancy craues, the thing which is vniust.   15
    Beside eche frown, which eftsoones moues them deeme,
    They abiect are, if sad their Louers seeme.
Or if occasion shun, their vsuall sight,
Not seene, they thinke themselues vnminded bee:
And then in dumps, as mazd they leaue delight,   20
And yeeld to greefe, till one, eche others see:
    So that with feare, their mindes are alwayes fraught,
    That liue in loue, experience some hath taught.
Eche lowring frown, from mirth doth moue the minde,
One iesting worde, procures a thousand woes: 25
So that lyke greefe or more, through sight they finde,
Then absence sure, such cares fro fancy flowes:
    Such goring gripes, such heapes of hideous harmes,
    Such sorowing sobs, from daunted louers swarmes.
Rosamond a spowsed Dame, her husbands death procurde,   30
For speaking but a worde in iest:
Itrascus too, full thyrty yeares indurde,
The panges of loue, within his boyling brest: (care,
    So that in greefe they harbor, still their mindes are cloyd with
    They diue in dole, they plunge in payne, & liue in cruell feare.   35
                                                       And

of gallant Inuentions.

And diuers moe, as *Axeres* whose beauty passing faire,
So *Iphis* hart, and boyling brest allurde:
That for her sake, hee liude in extreame care,
And cruell greefe, while breathing breath indurde: 5
   But at the length, disdayne vpon a tree,
   Hee honge himselfe, where shee his corps might see.

FINIS.

   ¶ A Louer approuing his Lady vnkinde.
    Is forsed vnwilling to vtter his minde. 10

Willow willow willow, singe all of greene willow,
Sing all of greene willow, shall bee my Garland.

MY loue, what mislyking in mee do you finde,
   Sing all of greene willow:
That on such a soddayn, you alter your minde, 15
   Sing willow willow willow:
What cause doth compell you, so fickle to bee?
   Willow willow willow willow:
In hart which you plighted, most loyall to mee,
   Willow willow willow willow. 20

I faythfully fixed, my fayth to remayne,
   Sing all of greene willow:
In hope I as constant, should finde you agayne,
   Sing willow willow willow:
But periurde as *Iason*, you faythlesse I finde, 25
Which makes mee vnwilling, to vtter my minde:
   Willow willow willow, singe all of greene willow,
   Sing all of greene willow shall bee my Garland.

Your beauty braue decked, with showes gallant gay,
   Sing all of greene willow: 30
Allured my fancy, I could not say nay,
   Sing willow willow willow.

L ij   Your

The gorgious Gallery

Your phrases fine philed, did force mee agree,
   Willow willow willow willow:
In hope as you promis'd, you loyall would bee,
   Willow willow willow willow.   5

But now you be frisking, you list not abide,
   Sing all of greene willow:
Your vow most vnconstant, and faythlesse is tride,
   Sing willow, willow willow:
Your wordes are vncertayne, not trusty you stand,   10
Which makes mee to weare, the willow Garland:
    Willow willow willow, sing all of greene willow,
    Sing all of greene willow, shall bee my Garland.

Hath Light of loue luld you, so softe in her lap?
   Sing all of greene willow: 15
Hath fancy prouokte you? did loue you intrap?
   Sing willow willow willow:
That now you be flurting, and will not abide.
   Willow willow willow willow:
To mee which most trusty, in time should haue tride,   20
   Willow willow willow willow.

Is modest demeanure, thus turnd to vntrust?
   Sing all of greene willow:
Are fayth and troth fixed, approoued vniust?
   Sing willow, willow will: 25
Are you shee which constant, for euer would stand?
And yet will you giue mee, the willow Garland?
    Willow willow willow, singe all of greene willow,
    Sing all of greene willow, shall bee my Garland.

What motion hath moude you, to maske in delight,   30
   Sing all of greene willow,
What toy haue you taken, why seeme you to spight
   Sing willow willow willow,
                                            Your

of gallant Inuentions.

Your loue which was ready for aye to indure,
 Willow willow willow willow:
According to promise most constant and sure,
 Willow willow willow willow.   5

What gallant you conquerd, what youth mooude your minde,
 Sing all of greene willow:
To leaue your olde Louer, and bee so vnkinde,
 Singe willow willow willow:
To him which you plighted both fayth, troth and hand,   10
For euer: yet giues mee the willow Garland?
 Willow willow willow, singe all of greene willow,
 Sing all of greene willow, shall bee my Garland.

Hath wealth you allured, the which I doo want,
 Sing all of greene willow: 15
Hath pleasant deuises, compeld you recant,
 Sing willow willow willow:
Hath feature forste you, your words to deny?
 Willow willow willow willow:
Or is it your fashion to cog, and to lye,   20
 Willow willow willow willow?

What are your sweet smiles, quite turnd into lowres,
 Sing all of greene willow:
Or is it your order, to change them by howres,
 Sing willow willow willow: 25
What haue you sufficient, thinke you in your hand,
To pay for the making, of my willow Garland:
 Willow willow willow, singe all of greene willow,
 Sing all of greene willow, shall bee my Garland.

Farewell then most fickle, vntrue and vniust,   30
 Sing all of greene willow:
Thy deedes are yll dealings, in thee is no trust,
 Willow willow willow willow.

L iii   Thy

[85]

The gorgious Gallery

Thy vowes are vncertayne, thy wordes are but winde,
   Willow willow willow willow.
God graunt thy new louer, more trusty thee finde,
   Willow willow willow willow?   5

Be warned then gallants, by proofe I vnfolde,
   Sing willow willow willow,
Mayds loue is vncertayne, soone hot, and soone colde,
   Sing willow willow willow:
They turne as the reed, not trusty they stand,   10
Which makes mee to weare the willow Garland:
    Willow willow willow, singe all of greene willow,
    Sing all of greene willow, shall bee my Garland.

FINIS.

A gloze of fawning freendship.   15

NOw cease to sing your *Syren* songes, I leaue ech braue delight
   Attempt no more the wounded corps, which late felt fortunes
But rather helpe to rue, with sorowing sobs come mone, (spight:
My lucklesse losse from wealth to woe, by fickle fortune throwne.
I once had freends good store, for loue, (no drosse I tryde)   20
For hauing lost my goods on Seas, my freends would not abide,
Yet hauing neede I went to one, of all I trusted moste:
To get releefe, hee answerd thus, go packe thou peuish poste.
His wordes did pearce my tender brest, and I as mazde did stand
Requesting him with pitteous plaints, to giue his helping hand: 25
Content thy selfe (quoth hee) to serue my owne estate,
I haue not I, yet am I greeu'd to see thy lucklesse fate.
Ah fie of fawning freends, whose eyes attentiue bee,
To watch and warde for lukers sake, with cap and bended knee:
Would God I had not knowne, their sweet and sugered speach,   30
Then had my greefe the lesser bin, experience mee doth teach.

FINIS.

of gallant Inuentions.

A Maze of Maydens.

Ho goes to gaze of euery gallant girle,
And castes his eyes at euery glauncing gloze:
Whose masking minde, with euery motion moou'd,   5
In fine shall finde, his fancy fraught with woes.

For pleasure spent, is but a wishing vayne,
By crooked chaunce, depriude of braue delight:
Cut of by care, a heape of hurtfull harmes,
Our gaze vngaynd, which whilome pleasde our sight.   10

Our vaunts doo vade, our pleasures passe away,
Our sugerest sweetes, reapes sorowing sobs in fine:
Our braggest boast, of beauties brauest blaze,
To sorowed browes, doth at the length resigne.

Our foolish fancy filde, with filthy vice,   15
Pursues his hurt, vnto anothers harmes:
A houering hart, with euery gloze enticed,
gaynes lothsome loue, whence nought but sorow swarmes.

Leaue then to gaze, of euery glauncing gloze,
Contemne the sleights, of beauties sugerest bate: 20
Whose outward sheath, with colours braue imbost,
Shuns cruell craft, and enuious hurtfull hate.

FINIS.

The gorgious Gallery

A short Epistle written in the behalfe of N. B. to M. H.

DEare Lady deckt with cumlynesse,
    To counteruayle my clemency:
Bee prest, I pray, in readynesse,
    To yeeld your courteous curtesie.

Let mee you finde *Penelope*,
    In minde, and loyall hart:
So shall I, your *Vlisses* bee,
    Till breathing lyfe depart.

Yelde loue for loue, to him who lykes,
    To liue in lynckes of loyalty:
And graunt him grace, who nothing seekes,
    For his good will, but curtesy.

Let mee your bondman, fauour finde,
    To gratefie my willing harte:
Whom no attempt, to please your minde,
    Shall hynder mee, to play my parte.

Permit mee not, in lingring sorte,
    To labour in a barrayn soyle:
Ne giue occasion to reporte,
    How loytryng loue, reapes troubled toyle.

But let mee say, my hart obtaynd,
    The gloze, which pleas'd my glauncing eyes:
And that I haue for guerdon gaynd,
    The best that in my Lady lyes.

So shall I boast of that, which best
    Doth please the prime of my desire:
And glory in a gayned rest,
    Which through your fauour I aspire.
        FINIS.

of gallant Inuentions.

A vew of vayn glory.

WHat motion more, may mooue a man to minde
    His owne estate, then proofe, whose dayes vnsure,
Accounted are vnto a puffe of winde,
A breathing blast, whose force can not endure:
Whose lyuely showes consumes, whose pompe decayes,
Whose glory dyes, whose pleasures soone be spent:
Whose stoutest strength, to weakenes subiect stayes,
Whose thoughts bee vaine, and vade as though vnment.
What haue wee then to vaunt, or glory in?
Sith all is vayne, wherin wee take delight:
Why should wee boast or brag, sith nought wee win
In fine, but death? to whom yeeldes euery wight.
To equall state, hee bringeth each degree,
Hee feareth none, all subiects yeeldes to death:
To dankish dust, hee driueth all wee see,
Which in the world, enioyeth any breath:
Why vaunt wee then, in that wee see is vayne,
Or take delight, in that wee proue but drosse?
Why glory wee, or seeke for golden gayne?
Sith at the length, wee reape therof but losse.
Wee lothe to leaue, our hutches filde with golde:
Our annual rents, it greeues vs to forgo,
Our buildings braue, which glads vs to beholde:
Our pleasant sport, it greeues vs to forgo.
Wee nothing brought, ne ought shall carry hence,
Lyfe lost, behinde goods, mony, land, wee leaue:
And naked shall returne, assured whence
Before wee came, when death doth life bereaue:
Liue then, to leaue thy life in euery hower,
Learne how to lead thy minde, from vayne desire,
Of filthy drosse, whose sugerest sweet is sower,
When dreadfull death, shall yeeld our earthly hire.
What is our world but vayne, fraught full of vice,
Wherin wee liue, allured by disceat:
                M   Which

The gorgious Gallery

Which vs in youth, to error doth entice,
And sturs vs vp, inflamed by follyes heat.
Our mindes are mooued, with euery fond desire,
Wee gloze in that, the which wee see vnsure:
Wee vsuall seeke great honor to aspire,
Whose greatest pompe, doth but a while endure:
For proofe the flower, bedect with gorgious hew,
As soone with heate, of scorching sun doth fade:
As doth the weede, the which vnseemly grew,
And showes it selfe, vncouerd with the shade.
The stately ship, which floates on foming fluds,
With waue is tost, as soone to surging Seas:
Doth yeeld his pompe, though fraught with store of goods,
As vessell weake, whose force the streame assayes:
Our selues may show, the state of eche degree,
As *Sampson* stout, whose force *Philistians* felt:
For wealth, let *Diues*, glut with golde our Mirror bee,
Marke *Nemrods* fall, whose hart with pride was swelt.
And diuers mo, whose preter pathes may learne,
Our future steps, our vayn vnsteady stay:
Whose elder lyues, already past may warne,
Vs shun such snares, which leades vs to decay.

FINIS.   T. P.

of gallant Inuentions.

The fall of folly, exampled by needy Age.

BEhold mee here whose youth, to withered yeres,
Doth bow and bend, compeld by crooked age:
See here my lyms, whose strength benumbde weres,   5
Whose pleasure spent, gray heares, bids to bee sage.

But loe to late I lothe my life lewd spent,
And wish in vayne, I had foreseene in youth:
These drowsie dayes, which mooues mee to lament
My idle youth prou'd, what therof ensueth.   10

Vnstorde olde yeres, must serue for lusty prime,
These feebled ioynts, must seeke to serue their want:
With tedious toyle, because I vsde not time,
Loe thus I liue, suffisde perforce to scant.

In flaunting yeres, I flaunting florisht forth,   15
Amid delight, puft vp, with puffing pryde:
Meane garments then, I deemed nothing worth,
Nay, scace the best, might serue, my flesh to hide.

I thought them foes, which tolde mee of my fault,
And iudgd them speake, of rigor, not good will: 20
Who toulde of gayne, mee thought for hire did hault,
Then loe, I lothde what now I wish by skill.

Experience mooues mee mone, the more my greefe,
In lyuely yeres, because I did not shun
Such idle steps, least voyd of such releefe,   25
As might haue helpt my age, now youth is dun.

But what preuayles to wish I would I had,
Sith time delayd, may not bee calde agayne:
A guerdon iust, (for such as youth too bad
Consumes, (it is) in time therfore take payne.   30

Seeke

The gorgious Gallery

Seeke how in youth to serue contented age,
Learne, how to lead, your life in vertues lore:
Beholde you mee, attacht with death his page,
Constraynd through want, my lewdnes to deplore.

What greefe more great, vnto a hauty hart,
Then is distresse, by folly forste to fall:
What care more cruell or lothsom, (to depart
From wealth to want) it greeues vs to the gall.

But what auayles to boast, or vaunt of vayne?
What profit ist, to prayse a passed pryde?
Sith it consum'd, is but a pinching payne,
A heape of harmes, whose hurt I wretch haue tryde.

A direfull dreed, a surge of sorowing sobs,
A carking care, a mount of mestiue mone:
A sacke of sin, coucht full of cankered knobs,
A wauering weed, whose force is soone orethrone.

For proofe behold, the boast of breathing breath,
See see how soone, his valiaunst vaunt doth vade:
Our pleasant prime, is subiect vnto death,
By vices vrgde, in waues of wo to wade.

I know the state, and trust of euery tyme,
I see the shame, wherto eche vice doth cum:
Therfore (by mee) learne how to leaue such crime,
Fœlix quem faciunt, aliena pericula cautum.

Let mee your Mirror, learne you leaue whats lewd,
My fall forepassed, let teach you to beware:
My aunciency yeres with tryall tript, haue vewd,
The vaunt of vice, to be but carking care.

FINIS.   T. P.

of gallant Inuentions.

¶ A proper Sonet, how time consumeth all
earthly thinges.

AY mee, ay mee, I sighe to see, the Sythe a fielde,
Downe goeth the Grasse, soone wrought to withered Hay:		5
Ay mee alas, ay mee alas, that beauty needes must yeeld,
And Princes passe, as Grasse doth fade away.

Ay mee, ay mee, that life cannot haue lasting leaue,
Nor Golde, take holde, of euerlasting ioy:
Ay mee alas, ay mee alas, that time hath talents to receyue,		10
And yet no time, can make a suer stay.

Ay mee, ay mee, that wit can not haue wished choyce,
Nor wish can win, that will desires to see:
Ay mee alas, ay mee alas, that mirth can promis no reioyce,
Nor study tell, what afterward shalbee.		15

Ay mee, ay mee, that no sure staffe, is giuen to age,
Nor age can giue, sure wit, that youth will take:
Ay mee alas, ay mee alas, that no counsell wise and sage,
Will shun the show, that all doth marre and make.

Ay mee, ay mee, come time, sheare on, and shake thy Hay,		20
It is no boote, to baulke thy bitter blowes:
Ay mee alas, ay mee alas, come time, take euery thing away,
For all is thine, bee it good or bad that growes.

FINIS.

𝔐 iii			A

The gorgious Gallery

A Mirror of Mortallity.

SHall clammy clay, shrowd such a gallant gloze,
Must beauty braue, be shrinde in dankish earth:
Shall crawling wormes, deuoure such liuely showes,
                                  (of yong delights.
When valyant corps, shall yeeld the latter breath,
   Shall pleasure vade, must puffing pride decay:
   Shall flesh consume, must thought resigne to clay.
Shall haughty hart, haue hire to his desart,
Must deepe desire die, drenchd in direfull dread:
Shall deeds lewd dun, in fine reape bitter smart,
Must each vade, when life shall leaue vs dead:
   Shall Lands remayne? must wealth be left behinde?
   Is sence depriu'd? when flesh in earth is shrinde.
Seeke then to shun, the snares of vayne delight,
Which moues the minde, in youth from vertues lore:
Leaue of the vaunt of pride, and manly might,
Sith all must yeeld, when death the flesh shall gore:
   And way these wordes, as soone for to be solde,
   To Market cums, the yonge sheepe as the olde.
No trust in time, our dayes vncertayne bee,
Like as the flower, bedect with splendant hue:
Whose gallant show, soone dride with heat wee see,
Of scorching beames, though late it brauely grew:
   Wee all must yeeld, the best shall not denye,
   Vnsure is death, yet certayn wee shall dye.
Although a while, we vaunt in youthful yeares,
In yonge delightes, wee seeme to liue at rest:
Wee subiect bee, to griefe eche horror feares,
The valiaunst harts, when death doth daunt the brest:
   Then vse thy talent here vnto thee lent,
   That thou mayst well account how it is spent.

              FINIS.   T. P.

of gallant Inuentions.

A briefe dialogue between sicknesse
and worldly desire.
¶ Sicknesse.

O darkesome caue, where crawling wormes remayn, 5
Thou worldly wretch, resigne thy boasting breath:
Yeeld vp thy pompe, thy corps must passe agayn,
From whence it came, compeld by dreadfull death.
¶ Worldly desire.
Oh sicknesse sore, thy paines doo pearce my hart, 10
Thou messenger of death, whose goryng gripes mee greue:
Permit a while, mee loth yet to depart
From freends and goods, which I behinde must leaue.
¶ Sicknesse.
Ah silly soule, entis'de with worldly vayne, 15
As well as thou, thy freends must yeeld to death:
Though after thee, a while they doo remayne,
They shall not still, continue on the earth.
¶ Worldly desire.
What must I then neede, shrine in gastly graue? 20
And leaue what long, I got with tedious toyle:
Prolong mee yet, and let mee licence haue,
Till elder yeeres, to put your Brutes to foyle.
¶ Sicknesse.
O foolish man, allurde by lewd delight, 25
Thy labors lost, these goods they are not thine:
But as (thou hadst) so others haue like right,
(Of them) when thou, shalt vp thy breath resigne.
¶ Worldly desire.
Then farewell world, the Nurse of wicked vice, 30
Adue vile drosse which mooues mens mindes to ill:
Farewell delights, which did my youth entice,
To serue as slaue, vnto vnsatiate will.

FINIS.   T. P.

The gorgious Gallery

Aeger Diues habet Nummos, sed
non habet ipsum.

THe wealthy chuffe, for all his wealth,
Cannot redeeme therby his health:
But must to Graue, for all his store,
Death spareth neither riche nor poore:
Not *Cressus* wealth, nor *Mydas* Golde,
The stroke of careles death may holde:
Hee feares no foe, hee spares no freend,
Of euery thing hee is the ende:
Though *Diues* had great store of pealfe,
Yet still the wretch, did want him selfe.

No Phisickes art, or cunning cure,
May any man of life assure:
No highe estate or beauty braue,
May keepe vs from our carefull graue:
No hauty minde or valyant harte,
Agaynst pale Death, may take our parte:
No curious speach, or witty tale,
Our dyinge corps may counteruayle:
No force, no gyle, no powre or strength,
But death doth ouercome at length.

The riche man trusteth in his Gould,
And thinkes that life, is bought and sould:
The sight therof so bleares, his eye,
That hee remembreth not to dye:
Hee hath enough and liues in ioye,
Who dares (thinkes hee) worke mee annoy:
Thus is hee made, to pleasure thrall,
And thinkes that death will neuer call:
Who vnawares with stealing pace,
Doth ende in payne his pleasant race.

The

[96]

of gallant Inuentions.

The greedy Marchant will not spare,
For lukers sake, to lye and sware:
The simple sorte hee can by slight,
Make to beleeue the Crow is white: 5
No science now, or arte is free,
But that some gyle therin wee see:
Thus euery man for greedy gayne,
Vnto himselfe encreaseth payne:
And thinkes the crime to bee but small, 10
When that they loose both soule and all.

Who lyueth here, that is content,
With such estate as God hath sent:
The hungry Churle, and wealthy Chuffe,
Doth neuer thinke, hee hath enough: 15
Fortune to many, giues to much,
But few or none, shee maketh riche:
Thus euery man, doth scrape and catch,
And neuer more, for death doo watch:
Who still is present at their side, 20
And cuts them of, amids their pride.

Such is the world, such is the time,
That eche man striues alofte to clyme:
But when they are in top of all,
In torments great they hedlong fall: 25
Where they do giue accompt at large,
How they their tallent did discharge:
There no man takes their golden fee,
To plead their case, and set them free:
Then too too late they doo begin, 30
For to repent their former sinne:

Wherfore I wish that eche degree,
With lotted chaunce contented bee:
𝔑   Let

[97]

The gorgious Gallery

Let not thy treasure make thee prowde,
Nor pouerty bee disalowde:
Remember who doth giue and take,
One God both riche and poore doth make: 5
Wee nothing had or ought shall haue,
To beare with vs vnto our graue:
But vertuous life which here wee leade,
On our behalfe for grace to plead.

Therfore I say thy lust refrayne, 10
And seeke not after brickle gayne:
But seeke that wealth, the which will last,
When that this mortall life is past:
In heauen is ioy and pleasure still,
This world is vayne and full of yll: 15
Vse not so lewd thy worldly pelfe,
So that thou doost forget thy selfe:
Liue in this world as dead in sinne,
And dye in Christ, true life to win.

FINIS. 20

Win fame, and keepe it.

WHo sees the yll, and seekes to shun the same,
Shall doutlesse win at length immortal fame:
For wisdome, vice and vertue doth perceaue,
Shee vertue takes, but vice shee seekes to leaue. 25
A wise man knowes the state of each degree,
The good be praysde, the euill dishonord bee:
Hee sees the good, the euill hee doth espye,
Hee takes the good, the euill hee doth denye:
Hee folowes good, the euill hee dooth eschue, 30
Hee leapes the lake, when others stay to vew.
His honor stands, his fame doth euer last,
Vpon the earth when breathing breath is past:
                                            As

[98]

of gallant Inuentions.

As *Solomon* whose wisdome recht vnto the lofty skye,
And *Dauid* King, theyr prayses liue (though bodies tombed lye)
They saw the good, the euill they did eschue,
Their honor liues, the proofe affirmes it true: 5
Then sithe examples playnly, showes the same,
Their prayses liue, who seekes to merit fame.
finis   T. P.

    Respice finem.

LO here the state of euery mortall wight,   10
See here, the fine, of all their gallant ioyes:
Beholde their pompe, their beauty and delight,
Wherof they vaunt, as safe from all annoyes:
To earth the stout, the prowd, the ritch shall yeeld,
The weake, the meeke, the poore, shall shrowded lye   15
In dampish mould, the stout with Speare and Sheeld
Cannot defend, himselfe when hee shal dye.
The prowdest wight, for all his lyuely showes,
Shall leaue his pompe, cut of by dreadfull death:
The ritch, whose Hutch, with golden Ruddocks flowes,   20
At lenght shall rest, vncoynd in dampish earth:
By Natures law, wee all are borne to dye,
But where or when, the best vncertayne bee:
No time prefixt, no goods our life shall buye,
Of dreadfull death, no freends shall set vs free.   25
Wee subiect bee, a thousand wayes to death,
Small sicknesse moues the valiaunts hart to feare:
A litle push bereaues your breathing breath,
Of braue delights, wherto you subiect are:
Your world is vayne, no trust in earth you finde,   30
Your valyaunst prime, is but a brytle glasse:
Your pleasures vade, your thoughts a puffe of winde,
Your aunicent yeres, are but a withered grasse.

Mors omnibus communis.   finis   T. P.

The gorgious Gallery

A briefe Caueat, to shun fawning friends.

TRy, ere thou trust, vnto a fawning freend,
Giue no regard, vnto his sugered wordes,
Make your account to leese, what you him lend,
For collourd craft, the smoothest speech affordes.

My selfe haue tried, the trust of tatling tungs
Who paynt their prates, as though they would performe:
(The more my greefe) for they (which) whilome clungs,
Like Bees (goods lost) sole left mee in the storme,

Where I was fayne, in worldly woes to waue,
And seeke releefe, of former freends, no fie:
Perforce constraynd, to seeke my selfe to saue,
Or els vnhelp'd, sance succor still to lye.

I made my mone, the greater was my greefe,
To him which was, as seruant to my state:
But what preuayld, by proofe I found him cheefe,
Who not of mee, but on my wealth did wate.

Donec eris fœlix, multos numerabis amicos,
Tempora si fuerint nubila, solus eris.

FINIS.   T. P.

of gallant Inuentions.

Beauty is a pleasant pathe to distruction.

THrough beauties sugered baites,
 Our mindes seduced are:
To filthy lustes to wicked vice,
 Whence issueth nought but care.

  For hauing tride the troth
   And seen the end of it:
  What wayle we more with greater greefe,
   Then want of better wit,

  Because so lewd wee luld,
   In that wee see is vayne:
  And follow that, the which to late,
   Compels vs to complayne.

  The boast of Beauties brags,
   And gloze of louing lookes:
  Seduce mens mindes as fishes are,
   Intic'd with bayted hookes.

  Who simply thinking too,
   Obtayne the pleasant pray:
  Doth snatch at it, and witlesse so,
   Deuoures her owne decay.

  Euen like the mindes of men,
   Allurde with beauties bayt:
  To heapes of harmes, to carking care,
   Are brought, by such decaite.

  Lo thus by proofe it proou'd,
   Perforce I needes must say:
  That beauty vnto ruinous end,
   Is as a pleasant way.
     FINIS. T. P.

The gorgious Gallery

T. P. his Farewell vnto his faythfull
and prooued freend. F. S.

FArewell my freend, whom fortune forste to fly,
I greeue to here, the lucklesse hap thou hast:
But what preuayles, if so it helpe might I,
I would be prest, therof be bold thou maste.

Yet sith time past, may not be calde agayne,
Content thy selfe, let reason thee perswade:
And hope for ease, to counteruayle thy payne,
Thou art not first, that hath a trespasse made.

Mourne not to much, but rather ioy, because
God hath cut of thy will, ere greater crime:
Wherby thou might, the more incur the lawes,
And beare worse Brutes, seduc'd by wicked prime.

Take heede, my woordes let teach thee to be wise,
And learne thee shun, that leades thy minde to ill:
Least beeing warnd, when as experience tries,
Thou waylst to late, the woes, of wicked will.

FINIS. T. P.

The History of *Pyramus* and *Thisbie*
truely translated.

IN *Babilon* a stately seate, of high and mighty Kinges,   (ringes:
Whose famous voice of ancient rule, through all the world yet
Two great estates did whilom dwell: and places ioyned so,   5
As but one wall eche princely place, deuided other fro: (sought,
  These Nobles two, two children had, for whom Dame Nature
The deepest of her secret skill, or shee their byrth had wrought:
For as their yeares in one agreed, and beauty equall shone,
In bounty and lyke vertues all, so were they there all one.   10
And as it pleased Nature then, the one a sonne to frame,
So did the glad olde Father like him *Pyramus* to name:
Th'other a maide, the mother would that shee then *Thisbie* hight,
With no smal blisse of parents al, who came to ioy the sight:
I ouerslip what sodaine frights, how often feare there was,   15
And what the care each creature had, ere they did ouerpas:
What paynes ensue, & what the stormes in pearced harts y̆ᵗ dwel,
And therfore know, what babe & mother whose chast, & subtil brād
No earthly hart, ne when they lust, no God hath yet withstand,
Ere seuen yeres these infants harts, they haue with loue opprest: 20
Though litle know their tender age, what causeth their vnrest,
Yet they poore fooles vntaught to loue, or how to lesse their payne:
With well contented mindes receiue, and prime of loue sustayne.
No pastime can they elswhere finde, but twayn themselues alone
For other playfeares sport, God wot, with them is reckend none: 25
Ioy were to here their pretty wordes, and sweet mamtam to see,
And how all day they passe the time, till darknes dimmes the skye:
But then the heauy cheare they make, when forst is their farwell
Declares such greefe as none would thinke, in so yong brests could
Ye looke how long, y̆ any let, doth kepe them two a sunder, (dwell: 30
Their mourning harts no ioy may glad, y̆ heuens y̆ᵗ passeth vnder
And when agayn, they efte repayre, and ioyfull meeting make,
Yet know they not the cause therof, ne why their sorowes slake.
𝔑 iiij   With

[103]

The gorgious Gallery

With sight they feede their fancies then, and more it still desire,
Ye more they haue, nor want they finde of sight they so require:
And thus in tender impe spronge vp, this loue vpstarteth still,
For more their yeres, much more ỹ flame, ỹ doth their fancies fill. 5
And where before their infants age, gaue no suspect at all.
Now needefull is, with weary eye, to watchfull minde they call:
Their whole estate, & it to guide, in such wise orderly,
As of their secret sweete desires, ill tongues no light espy.
And so they did, but hard God wot, are flames of fire to hide 10
Much more to cause a louers hart, within it bounds to finde:
For neither colde, their mindes consent so quench of loue the rage
Nor they at yeres, the least twise seuen, their passions so aswage
But ỹ to *Thisbes* Mothers eares, some spark therof were blowen,
Let Mothers iudg her pacience now, til shee ỹ whole haue knowẽ. 15
And so by wily wayes shee wrought, to her no litle care,   (snare:
That forth shee found, their whole deuise, and how they were in
Great is her greefe, though smal the cause, if other cause ne were,
For why a meeter match then they, might hap no other where:
But now tween Fathers, though the cause, mine Auctor nothing 20
Such inward rancor risen is, and so it daily swels.   (tels,
As hope of freendship to be had, is none (alas) the while,
Ne any loueday to be made, their mallice to begyle: (chere,
Wherfore straight charge, straight giuen is w̃ fathers frowning
That message worde, ne token els, what euer that it were: 25
Should frõ their foe to *Thisbee* passe, & *Pyramus* freends likewise,
No lesse expresse commaundement, doo for their sonne deuise.
And yet not thus content alas, eche Father doth ordayne,
A secret watch and bounde a point, wherin they shall remayne:
Sight is forbid, restrained are wordes, for scalde is all deuise, 30
That should their poore afflicted mindes, reioyce in any wise:
Though pyning loue, gaue cause before of many carefull yll,
Yet dayly sithe amended all, at least well pleased them still:
But now what depth of deepe distresse, may they indrowned bee,
That now in dayes twise twenty tolde, eche other once shall see. 35
Curst is their face, so cry they ofte, and happy death they call,
Come death come wished death at once, and rid vs life and all.
                                                                And

of gallant Inuentions.

And where before (Dame Kinde) her selfe, did wonder to beholde
Her highe bequests within their shape, Dame Beauty did vnfold:
Now doth shee maruel much and say, how faded is that red?
And how is spent that white so pure, it wont to ouerspred. 5
For now late lusty *Piramus*, more fresh then flower in May,
As one forlorne with constant minde, doth seeke his ending day:
Since *Thisbe* mine is lost sayth hee, I haue no more to lose,
Wherfore make speed, thou happy hand, these eyes of mine shall
Abasid is his princely port, cast of his regall weede, (close. 10
Forsaken are assemblies all, and lothed the foming steed:
No ioy may pearce his pensiue mynde, vnlesse a wofull brest
May ioyed bee, with swarmes of care, in haples hart that rest:
And thus poore *Piramus* distrest, of humaine succor all,
Deuoyd to *Venus* Temple goes, and prostrate downe doth fal: 15
And there of her, with hart I korue, and sore tormented mindes,
Thus askes hee ayd, and of his woes, the Fardell thus vnbindes.

O Great Goddesse, of whose immortal fire,
  Vertue in Erbe, might neuer quench the flame:
Ne mortall sence, yet to such skill aspire, 20
As for loues hurt a medecine once to name:
With what deare price, my carefull pyned ghost,
Hath tried this true, and ouer true alas:
My greefeful eyes, that sight hath almost lost,
And brest through darted, with thy golden Mace. 25
Full well declare, though all that mee beholde,
Are iudges, and wonders of my deadly wo:
But thou alone, mayst helpe therfore vnfolde,
Els helples (Lady) streight will knap in two
The feeble thread, yet stayes my lingering life. 30
Wherfore, if loue, thy sacred Goddes brest?
Did euer presse, or if most dreadly griefe,
And causeles not thy inward soule opprest:
When crooked *Vulcane*, to your common shame,
Bewrayed of stolen ioyes, thy sweet delight: 35

If

[105]

The gorgious Gallery

If then I say the feare of further blame,
Caus'd you refrayne your Louers wished sight:
And forst restraynt did equall then impart,
And cause you taste, what payne in loue may bee: 5
When absence driues, assured hartes to part.
Thy pitty then (O Queene) now not denye
To mee poore wretch, who feeles no lesse a payne:
If humayne brests, so much as heauenly may:
Haue ruthe on him, who doth to thee complayne, 10
And onely helpe of thee, doth lowly pray:
Graunt Goddesse mine, thou mayst it vndertake,
At least wise (Lady) ere this life decay:
Graunt I beseeche so happy mee to make,
That yet by worde, I may to her bewray 15
My wonderous woes: and then if yee so please,
Looke when you lust, let death my body ease. (man,
THus praying fast, ful fraught with cares, I leaue this wofull
And turne I will to greater greefe, then minde immagin can:
But who now shall them writ since wit, denayeth the some to 20
Confusedly in *Thisbies* brest, that flow aboue the brinke? (thinke,
Not, I for though of mine owne store, I want no woes to write,
Yet lacke I termes and cunning both, them aptly to recite.
For Cūnings clyffe I neuer clombe, nor dranke of Science spring
Ne slept vpon the happy hill, frō whence Dame *Rhetorique* rings. 25
And therfore all, I doo omit, and wholy them resigne,
To iudgment of such wofull Dames, as in like case hath bin.
  This will I tel how *Thisbie* thus, opprest with dollors all,
Doth finde none ease but day and night, her *Pyramus* to call:
For lost is slepe and banisht is, all gladsome lightes delight, 30
In short of ease and euery helpe, eche meane shee hath in spight:
In langor long, this life shee led, till hap as fortune pleased,
To further fates that fast ensue, with her own thought her eased:
For this shee thinkes, what distance may, or mansions bee between
Or where now stands so cruell wall, to part them as is seene 35
O feeble wit forduld with woe, awake thy wandering thought,
Seeke out, thou shalt assured finde, shall bring thy cares to nought.
                                                              With

of gallant Inuentions.

With this some hope, nay, as it were a new reuiued minde,
Did promis straight her pensiue hart, immediate helpe to finde:
And forth she steres, w̃ swifted pace, ech place she seeks throughout
No stay may let her hasty foote, till all be vewed about. 5
Wherby at length from all the rest, a wall aloofe that lyes,
And cornerwise did buyldings part, with ioyful eye shee spyes:
And scarcely then her pearcing looke, one blinke therof had got,
But that firme hope of good successe, within her fancy shot:
Then fast her eye shee roules about, and fast shee seekes to see, 10
If any meane may there bee found, her comfort for to bee:
And as her carefull looke shee cast, and euery part aright
Had vewed wel, a litle rifte appeared to her sight,
Which (as it seemed) through the wall, the course the issue had:
Wherwith shee sayd (O happy wall) mayst thou so blist be made, 15
That yet sometimes within thy bandes, my dere hart *Pyramus:*
Thou doost possesse if hap so worke, I will assay thee thus.
And from about the heauenly shape, her midle did present
Shee did vnlose heer girdle riche, and pendent therof hent.
And with her fingers long and small, on tipto so shee wrought, 20
That through the wall to open sight, she hath the pendant brought.
That doone shee stayes, and to the wall she closely layes her eare,
To vnderstand if any wight, on th' other side yet were:
And whiles to harken thus shee stands, a wonderous thing behold
Poore *Pyramus* in *Venus* Church, that all his minde had tolde. 25
Performed his vowes and prayers eke, now ended all and dun,
Doth to his Chamber fast returne, with hart right wo begun:
Euen to the same where *Thisbie* stayd, to see if fortune please,
To smooth her browes and her distresse, with any helpe to ease:
Hee as his woonted vsage was, the Chamber once within, 30
Lockes fast the doore with fresh complaynts, new sorrow to begin.
But euen lo as his backe hee turned vnto the closed dore,
A glimpse of light the pendant gaue, his visage iust before:
Let in his face, with speedy pace, and as hee nearer drew,
With wel contented minde forthwith, his *Thisbies* signe he knew 35
And when his trembling hand for ioy, the same receyued had,
And hee ten hundreth times it kist, then thus to it hee sayd.

Though

The gorgious Gallery

*T*Hough many tokens ioyful newes haue set,
   And blisse redust, to carefull pyned ghost:
Yet mayst thou sweare, that neuer lyued hee yet,
Who halfe such ease, receiued in pleasure most:
As thou sweete pendant, now in wofull brest
Impersid hast, O happy *Pyramus*,
Nay beeing a Lady, in whom such ruthe can rest:
Most blisfull Lady, most mighty *Venus*,
And mighty *Thisbie* (yea) *Venus* not displeased,
My Goddesse cheefe, my loue, my life and all:
For who but *Thisbie* would, nay could haue eased,
A hart remedyles, abandon thrall:
Wherfore since thus ye please, to show your might,
Make mee whole happy, with gladnesse of your sight.

*W*Hiles *Pyramus* all clad in ioy, thus talkes within the wall,
   No lesse content, doth *Thisbie* stand without and heareth al:
And w̃t those gladsom lightes, where loue doth sightly ioy to play,
And vanquish harts her loue shee vewes in minde somwhat to say
But maydēly feare plucks backe ẽy word, dread stops her trimbling
A rossy hew inflames her face, with staine of red among. (tongue,
Yet lo at length her minde shee stayes, her sences doo awake,
And with a sweet soft sounding voyce, this answer doth she make.

  Loue *Pyramus*, more deare to mee then lyfe,
Euen as I first this way, for speech haue found:
Of present death, so let the dreadfull knyfe,
At this instant for euer mee confound:
If ioyfull thought my passing pensiue harte,
Did euer pearse, since parents cruell dome.
Pronounst the sentence, of our common smart,
No deare hart mine, for how alasse may blome:
The fading tree, whose sap deuided is,
Ye, further sweet, I dare with you presume:
Your passed woes, but pastimes ware I wis,
In their respect, that did mee whole consume.
But now sharpe sighes, so stop my willing speeche,
Such streames of teares, doo dim my troubled sight:

                                          And

of gallant Inuentions.

And inward feare, of parents wrath is such,
Least longer talke, should giue them any light
Of our repayre, that further to recyte,
My heaped yls I neuer dare ne may,   5
Yet oftenly, wee wisely heare may meete:
At chosen times which shall vs not bewray,
And this for short, thy *Thisbie* shalt thou see:
With morning light, here present eft to bee,
To this full fayne would *Pyramus*, replyed haue agayne,   10
But part as neede, inforst they must, & as they did ordayne:
Ere mornings dawne they doo arise & straight repayre they then
Vnto the fore appoynted place, *Pyrame* thus began.
    MYne entyer soule, what prison dollours?
What hard distresse, and rare deuysed woes?   15
Of mee thine owne, thy captiue *Pyramus*,
Haue so sought, this life from boddy to vnlose:
Hard were to tell the tenth, that haue it strained,
With thought hereof, great wonders mee amaze:
How my poore lyfe, the halfe may haue sustayned,   20
O *Thisbie* mine owne, whom it only stayes.
And at whose will the fates doo lend mee breath,
Yet may I not the fatall stroke eschew:
Ne scape the dinte of fast pursuing death,
Onles your bounty, present mercy shew: 25
And this I trust, there may no ielous thought,
Haue any place within my *Thisbies* brest:
To cause her deeme, I am or may be caught.
With loue but hers wheron my life doth rest,
No bee assured, for yours I onely taste: 30
Yours was the first, and shall bee first and last,
    Why my most sweet (quoth *Thisbie*) then agayne:
I doubt not I, but know ye are all true,
Or how may cause of your vndoubted payne:
With her be hyd, who hourely as it grew,   35
None other felt, but euen what yee haue had:
Yet thinke not sweet, I taste your greefes alone,

Oiii   Or

The gorgious Gallery

Or make esteeme, as yee of mee haue made,
But ten times more, if that more wo begone,
Might euer bee a wretched maydens brest,
Where neuer yet, one iot of ioy might rest.   5
Well then my ioy, (quoth *Pyrame*) since yee please,
With so greater loue, to guerdon my good will:
Safe am I now, but great were mine ease,
If more at full, I might my fancy fill:
With nearer sight, of your most pleasant face,   10
Or if I might, your dayntie fingers straine:
Or as I woont, your body once embrace,
What say I ease? nay heauen then were my gayne.
Howbeit in vayne, in vayne (ay mee) I waste,
Both worde and winde, woes mee (alas) therfore: 15
For neuer shall my hart, O *Thisbie* taste,
So great an hap, nor neuer shall wee more:
In folded armes, as woont were to bewray,
Eche others state, ne neuer get the grace:
Of any ioy, vnlesse wee doo assay,   20
To finde some meane for other meeting place.
Beholde (alas) this wicked cruell wall,
Whose cursed scyte, denayeth vs perfect sight:
Much more the hap, of other ease at all.
What if I should by force, as well one might: 25
And yet deserues, it batter flat to ground,
And open so, an issue large to make:
Yet feare I sore, this sooner will redownde,
To our reproche, if it I vndertake:
As glad I would, then vs to helpe or ayde,   30
Sweet hart (quoth shee) wherwith shee stopt his tale:
This standes full yll: to purpose to be made,
And time it askes, too long for to preuayle:
Without suspect, to flat or batter euen,
Naythlesse, yee this, or what ye can deuise: 35
For our repayre, by thought that may be driuen,
Say but the meane, I will none otherwise.
           Yee

[110]

of gallant Inuentions.

Yee *Thisbie* mine, in sooth, and say you so
(Quoth *Pyramus*) well then I doo you know:
Where King *Minus*, lyes buried long ago,
Whose aunciеnt Tombe aboue, doth ouergrow 5
A Mulbery, with braunches making shade,
Of pleasant show, the place right large about:
There if yee please, when slepe hath ouerlade,
And with his might, the Cittie seas'de throughout:
At the same Well, whose siluer streames then runne, 10
And softe as silke, conserue the tender greene:
With hue so fresh, as springtied spent and dunne,
No winters weede, hath power to bee seene:
Without suspect, or feare of foule report,
There goddesse mine, wee salfely may resort. 15
TO this shee said, what shee best thought, and oft and oft agayne,
Was talke renued, but yet at last, for ease of euery payne:
And death to eschue by other meane, who will them not forsake,
At *Minus* Tombe, euen y̑ same night, they do their meeting make
And so depart, but sore God wot, that day doth them offend, 20
And though but short his long abode, the feare will neuer end.
And sooner doth not cloake of night, alofte his shadow cast,
But *Thisbie* mindefull of her loue, and promis lately past
Of fresh new loue, far fiercer flames, that erst her hart opprest,
Shee feelth the force, and this (alas) deuorced stil from rest: 25
Shee passeth forth in carefull watch, till time haue shapen so,
That slepe w̑ sweet, soft stealing steps his customd vsage do
And when shee seeth both house and all drownd therin fast & deepe,
With fearful pace & trimbling hand, shee forwards gins to creepe:
Shee gaines the doore, out goeth she then, & neyther far ne neare, 30
Appeareth wyght saue *Phebe* fayre, with gladsom seeming cheare
Sole *Thisbie* ioyfull of this guyde, doth say I trust it bee,
Good lucke thy presence doth import, and bring at last to mee:
More hardyer then before shee did, prouoke her foote to hast,
No obiect giues her cause of let, till shee the towne haue past: 35
And when shee seeth the pleasant fields in safetie to haue gayned,
Then ioy therof all dread deuoures, which erst her only payned.
                                                      What

The gorgious Gallery

What wil ye more, th' appointed place at length she doth attayne,
Till Fortune please her loue to send, there minding to remayne:
And whiles shee doth the foūtayn cleare, w̃ thoughtful hope behold
And euery let, her loue may stay, vnto her selfe vnfolde.   5
A dreadfull Lyon downe desendes, from Mountaine huge therby,
With thundring pace, whose sodain sight, whē *Thisbie* can espy:
No maruel was though terror then, & straungenes of the sight,
Within a simple maydens brest, all counsayle put to flight.
Howbeit, though counsayle fayld, yet feare so did ẙ place possesse, 10
That as the tender brest, whose age no feare did yet oppresse:
Now seeth his foe, with rauening Iaw, him ready to receaue,
Sets winges vnto his littell legs, himselfe poore foole to saue.
Euen so this Mayd, her enemy flees, vnto a hollow tree:
For succor flyes, whose ruthful mone, did succor not denye: (wilde, 15
But close her keepes. The Liones fearce, that in the Mountayne
Deuoured had, new slaughtred beastes, & empty belly filde:
With moossell all embrude with blood, drawes to the cristal Well,
Hee dranke, and in his backe returne, this fatall hap befell.
   Amid this way a kercheife white, which frighted *Thisbie* had   20
Let fall by chaunce, as feare and haste, vnto the tree her lad:
This Lion findes, and with his mouth, yet smoaking all in gore,
And armid pawes it staynes with blood, and all in sunder tore.
That doone away hee windes, as fier of Hell, or *Vulcans* thunder
Blew in his tayle, or as his corps it seas'd to teare a sunder: 25
   Now *Pyramus* who could not earst, the wrathfull house forgo,
Hath past the towne, and as hee drew the Fountayn neare vnto:
The cloth hee spies, which when (alas) all stained so hee saw,
In sunder tore, the ground about, full traste with Lyons paw:
The Siluer streames with strekes of blood, besprent and troubled   30
And there again ẙ cursed trace, the woful print to shew: (new,
A sure beleefe did straight inuade, his ouerlyuing minde,
That there the fatall ende (alas) of *Thisbie* was assinde:
And that her dainty flesh, of beastes a pray vnmeet was made,
Wherwith distrest with woodlike rage, the words he out abrade.   35
¶ The

of gallant Inuentions.

The lamentacion of Piramus, for the losse of his Loue Thisbie.

This is the day wherin my irksome life,
And I of lyuely breath, the last shall spend: 5
Nor death I dread, for fled is feare, care, strife,
Daunger and all, wheron they did depend:
Thisbie is dead, and *Pirame* at his ende,
For neuer shall reporte hereafter say:
That *Pyrame* lyu'de, his Lady tane away. 10
O soueraigne God, what straung outragious woe,
Presents (alas) this corsiue to my hart:
Ah sauage beaste, how durst thy spight vndoe,
Or seeke (woes mee) so perfect loue to part:
O *Thisbie* mine, that was, and only art, 15
My liues defence, and I the cause alone:
Of thy decay, and mine eternall mone.
Come Lyon thou, whose rage here only shew,
Aduaunce with speede, and doo mee eke deuoure:
For ruthlesse fact, so shalt thou pitty shew, 20
And mee (too) heere, within thy brest restore:
Where wee shall rest, togeather euermore.
Ah, since thy corps, thou graues within thy wombe,
Denye mee not sweet beast, the selfesame tombe.
(Alas my ioy) thou parted art from mee, 25
By far more cruell meane, then woonted fine:
Or common law, of nature doth decree,
And that encreaseth, for woe, this greefe of mine:
Of that beautie only, which was deuine,
And soueraigne most, of all that liued here: 30
No litle signe, may found be any where,
If the dead corps (alas, did yet remayne:
O great cruelty, O rage of fortune spight,
More greeuous far, then any tongue may fayne:
To reue her life, and in my more despight, 35
Mee to defraude of that my last delight:

P   Her

[113]

The gorgious Gallery

Her once t'embrace, or yet her visage pale,
To kisse full ofte, and as I should bewayle.
But since from mee thou hast the meane outchast,
Of this poore ioy, thy might I heere defie: 5
For maugre thee, and all the power thou hast,
In *Plutœs* raigne togeather will wee bee:
And you my loue, since you are dead for mee,
Good reason is, that I for you agayne:
Receiue no lesse but euen the selfsame payne. 10
Ah Mulberie, thou witnes of our woe,
Right vnder thee assigned was, the place
Of all our ioy, but thou our common foo,
Consented hast, vnto her death alas:
Of beauty all, that had alone the grace, 15
And therfore as the cheefe of others all,
Let men *the Tree of deadly woe* thee call.
Graunt our great God, for honor of thy name,
A guerdon of the woe, wee shall here haue:
For I nill liue, shee dead that rulde the same, 20
Pronounce (O *Pluto*) from thy hollow Caue:
Where stayes thy raigne, and let this tree receiue,
Such sentence iust, as may a witnesse bee,
Of dollour most, to all that shall it see.

And with those wordes, his naked blade hee fiersly frō his side 25
Out drew, & through his brest, it forst w̄ᵗ mortal woūd to glide,
The streames of gory blood out glush, but hee w̄ᵗ manly hart,
Careles, of death and euery payne, that death could them imparte.
His *Thisbies* kercheefe hard hee straines, & kist with stedfast chere
And harder strainde, and ofter kist, as death him drew more nere 30
The Mulberies whose hue before, had euer white lo beene,
To blackish collour straight transformed, & black ay since are seen.
And *Thisbie* then who all that while, had kept the hollow tree,
Least hap her Louers long aboad, may seeme him mockt to bee.
Shakes of all feare, and passeth foorth in hope her loue to tell, 35
What terror great shee late was in, and wonderous case her fel:
                                                              But

[114]

But whē she doth approche yͤ tree, whose fruits trāsformed were
Abasht she stands, & musing much, how black they should appere.
Her *Pyramus* with sights profound, and broken voyce yͭ plained,
Shee hard: and him a kerchefe saw, how hee hit kist and strained:
Shee neuer drew, but whē the sword, and gaping wound she saw,
The anguish great, shee had therof, her caus'd to ouerthrow
In deadly swoone, and to her selfe shee beeing come agayne,
With pittious playnts, and deadly dole, her loue shee did cōplayne
That doone, shee did her body leane, and on him softly lay,
She kist his face, whose collour fresh, is spent and falne away:
Then to yͤ sword these woords she sayth: thou sword of bitter gall,
Thou hast bereaued mee my Loue, my comfort ioy and all.
With that deare blood (woes me) of his thy cursed blade doth shine
Wherfore thinke not thou canst be free, to shed the same of mine,
In life no meane, though wee it sought, vs to assemble could,
Death shall, who hath already his, & mine shall straight vnfolde.
And you O Gods, this last request, for ruthe yet graunt it mee,
That as one death wee should receiue, one Tombe our graue may
With yͭ agayn she oft him kist, & then shee speaketh thus: (bee,
O Louer mine, beholde thy loue (alas) my *Pyramus*.
Yet ere I dye beholde mee once, that comfort not denye,
To her with thee that liu'd and lou'd, and eke with thee will dye.
The Gentilman with this, and as the lastest throwes of death,
Did pearce full fast at that same stroke, to end both life and breath
The voice hee knows, & euen therwith, castes vp his heauy eyes,
And sees his loue, hee striues to speake, but death at hand denyes.
Yet loue whose might, not thē was quēcht in spite of death gaue
And causde frō bottō of his hart, these words to pas at lēgth (strēgth
(Alas my loue) and liue ye yet, did not your life define,
By Lyones rage the foe therof, and caus'd that this of mine
Is spent and past, or as I thinke, it is your soule so deare,
That seekes to ioy and honor both, my last aduenture heare.
Euen with that woord, a profound sighe, from bottom of his hart,
Out cast his corps and spirit of life, in sunder did depart:
Then *Thisbie* efte, with shrike so shrill as dynned in the skye,
Swaps down in swoone, shee eft reuiues, & hents yͤ sword hereby.
P ii Wherwith

The gorgious Gallery

Wherwith beneath her pap (alas) into her brest shee strake,
Saying thus will I die for him, that thus dyed for my sake:
The purple Skarlet streames downe ran, & shee her close doth lay
Vnto her loue him kissing still, as life did pyne away. 5

Lo thus they lou'd and died, and dead, one tombe thē graued there,
And Mulberies in signe of woe, from white to blacke turnde were.

FINIS.

The lamentacion of a Gentilwoman
vpon the death of her late deceased frend 10
William Gruffith Gent.

A doutfull, dying, dolefull, Dame,
Not fearing death, nor forcing life:
Nor caring ought for flitting fame,
Emongst such sturdy stormes of strife: 15
Here doth shee mourne and write her will,
Vpon her liked Louers ende:
Graunt (Muses nyne) your sacred skill,
Helpe to assist your mournfull freend:
Embouldned with your Nimphish ayde, 20
Shee will not cease, but seeke to singe:
And eke employ her willing head,
Her Gruffithes prayse, with ruthe to ringe.

WIth Poets pen, I doo not preace to write,
Mineruæs mate, I doo not boast to bee: 25
Parnassus Mount (I speake it for no spite)
Can cure my cursed cares, I playnly see:
    For why? my hart contaynes as many woes
    As euer *Hector* did amongst his foes.
                                Eche

of gallant Inuentions.

Eche man doth mone, when faythfull freends bee dead,
And paynt them out, as well as wits doo serue:
But I, a Mayde, am forst to vse my head,
To wayle my freend (whose fayth) did prayse deserue: 5
    Wit wants to will: alas? no skill I haue,
    Yet must I needes deplore my *Gruffithes* graue:
For *William*, white: for *Gruffith*, greene: I wore,
And red, longe since did serue to please my minde:
Now, blacke, I weare, of mee, not vs'd before, 10
In liew of loue, alas? this losse I finde:
    Now must I leaue, both, White, and Greene, and Red,
    And wayle my freend, who is but lately dead.
Yet hurtfull eyes, doo bid mee cast away,
In open show, this carefull blacke attyre: 15
Because it would, my secret loue bewray,
And pay my pate, with hatred for my hyre:
    Though outwardly, I dare not weare the same,
    Yet in my hart, a web of blacke I frame.
You Ladyes all, that passe not for no payne, 20
But haue your louers lodged in your laps:
I craue your aydes, to helpe mee mourne amayne,
Perhaps your selues, shall feele such carefull claps:
    Which (God forbid) that any Lady taste,
    Who shall by mee but only learne to waste. 25
My wits be weake an Epitaphe to write,
Because it doth require a grauer stile:
My phrase doth serue but rudely to recite,
How Louers losse doth pinch mee all this while:
    Who was as prest to dye for *Gruffithes* sake, 30
    As *Damon*, did for *Pithias* vndertake.
But *William* had a worldly freend in store,
Who writ his end to small effect (God knowes)
But *I*. and *H*. his name did show no more,
Rime Ruffe it is, the common sentence goes, 35
    It hangs at Pawles as euery man goes by,
    One ryme too low, an other rampes too hye.

𝔓iii   Hee

The gorgious Gallery

Hee prays'd him out as worldly freends doo vse,
And vttered all the skill that God had sent:
But I? am shee that neuer will refuse,
But as I am, so will I still bee bent: 5
  No blastes shall blow, my lincked loue awry,
  Oh? would the Gods, with *Gruffith* I might dye.
Then had it been that I poore silly Dame,
Had, had no neede to blot this scratched scroule:
Then Virgins fist, had not set forth the same, 10
How God hath gripte, my *Gruffithes* sacred soule:
  But woe is mee, I liue in pinching payne,
  No wight doth know, what sorowes I sustayne.
Vnhappy may that drowsie day bee nam'd,
Wherin I first, possest my vitall breath: 15
And eke I wish, that day that I was fram'd,
In stead of life I had receiued death:
  Then with these woes, I needed not to waste,
  Which now (alas) in euery vayne I taste.
Some *Zoylus* sot, will thinke it lightly doone, 20
Because I mone, my mate, and louer, so
Some *Momus* match, this scroule will ouerronne,
But loue is lawlesse, euery wight doth know:
  Sith loue doth lend mee such a freendly scope,
  Disdaynfull dogs I may despise (I hope) 25
Wherfore I doo, attempt so much the more,
By this good hope, to shew my slender arte:
And mourne I must (who) neuer marckt before,
What fretting force doo holde eche heauy hart:
  But now I see that *Gruffithes* greedy graue, 30
  Doth make mee feele, the fits which louers haue.
My mournfull Muse, (good Ladyes) take in worth,
And spare to speake the worst, but iudge the best:
For this is all, that I dare publish forth,
The rest recorded is, within my brest: 35
  And there is lodg'd, for euer to remayne,
  Till God doth graunt (by death) to ease my payne.
                                                    And

of gallant Inuentions.

And when that death is come to pay her due,
With all the paynes, that shee can well inuent:
Yet to my *Gruffith*, will I still be true,
Hap death, holde life, my minde is fully bent: 5
   Before I will our secret loue disclose,
     To *Tantals* paynes, my body I dispose.
So liue I shall, when death hath spit her spight,
And Lady (*Fame*) will spread my prayse I know:
And *Cupids* Knights, will neuer cease to write, 10
And cause my name, through (*Europe*) for to flow:
   And they that know what (*Cupid*) can preuayle,
     Will blesse the ship, that floates with such a sayle.
If I had part of *Pallas* learned skill,
Or if (*Caliope*) would lend her ayde: 15
By tracte of time, great volumes I would fill,
My *Gruffithes* prayse in wayling verse to spread:
   But (I poore I) as I haue sayd before,
     Doo wayle, to want, *Mineruæs* learned lore.
By helpe (I hope) these ragged rymes shall goe, 20
Entituled as louers lyues should bee:
And scape the chyding chaps of euery foe,
To prayse that man, who was best likte of mee:
   Though death hath shapte, his most vntimely end,
     Yet for his prayse, my tristiue tunes I send. 25
In hope, the Gods who guide the heauens aboue,
His buryed corps, aliue agayne will make:
And haue remorce of Ladyes lincked loue,
As once they did for good *Admetus* sake:
   Or change him els, into some flower to weare, 30
     As erst they did, transforme *Narscissus* fayre.
So should I then, possesse my former freend,
Restor'd to lyfe, as *Alcest* was from Hell,
Or els the Gods, some flagrant flower would send,
Which for his sake, I might both weare and smell: 35
   Which flower, out of my hand shall neuer passe,
     But in my harte, shall haue a sticking place.

But

The gorgious Gallery

But wo is mee, my wishes are in vayne,
Adue delight? come, crooked cursed care:
To bluntish blockes (I see) I doo complayne,
And reape but onely sorrow for my share:
   For wel I know that Gods nor sprites can cure,
   The paynes that I for *Gruffith* doo endure.
Since wayling, no way can remedy mee,
To make an ende, I therfore iudge it best:
And drinke vp all, my sorrow secretly,
And as I can, I will abide the rest:
   And sith I dare not mourne, to open showe,
   With secret sighes and teares, my hart shall flow.
Some busie brayne, perhaps will aske my name,
Disposed much, some tidings for to marke:
That dare I not? for feare of flying fame,
And eke I feare least byting bugs will barke:
   Therfore farewell, and aske no more of mee,
   For (as I am) a Louer will I dye.

FINIS.

MISPRINTS AND VARIANT READINGS

MISPRINTS AND VARIANT READINGS

THE following list aims to give (1) every obvious misprint (except those of punctuation, which are retained in the present text) in the original issue of *The Gorgeous Gallery of Gallant Inventions* (*G*); (2) every variation from *G* in the reprints made by J. P. Collier (*C*) and by the Roxburghe Club (*R*), with the readings in Park's edition (*P*) in most of the cases where *C* and *R* vary from *G*. *R* purports to be an exact reprint, except that it always omits the ornaments and paragraph-marks, substitutes large capitals of uniform size for the initial block-letters and smaller capitals of *G*, and never prints runover lines as such; but the following list shows how far it fails in exactness. *C* also pretends to be an exact reprint, except that it does not keep the pagination of *G*, and hence omits headlines, signature-marks, and key-words. Furthermore, it does not follow the variations in typography that distinguish *G*, while it expands such contractions as $\bar{o}$ and uses neither the initial block-letters and ornaments of *G* nor the large initial capitals of *R*. In the list given below, then, these variations in typography and pagination in *C* and *R* are not noted. *C* is a far from accurate reprint, and its fairly close correspondence to *R* suggests that at times Collier may have verified his copy from *R* itself rather than from the original text. *P*, like all of Park's work, is too inaccurate to deserve much attention here. It ignores the pagination, spelling, punctuation, and typography of *G* throughout, omits two entire pages, and falls into strange errors of transcription too often to be worthy of a complete collation.

Perhaps attention should be called to the facts that there are no keywords on twenty-seven pages of *G* (namely, pages 4, 6, 8, 20, 25, 26, 34, 37, 44, 51, 55, 64, 68, 72, 76, 78, 79, 80, 86, 87, 88, 90, 92, 94, 95, 100, 102), — but in each of these cases a new poem begins on the following page, — and that the key-words on seven pages (namely, 15, 17, 31, 48, 77, 101, 112) are incorrect. Emendations of the text of *G* are not given here but are suggested in the Notes.

    3. 2 commendacion] commendation *C*
          4 In *G* the block-initial is upside down
          6 deuisde] deuised *R*

MISPRINTS AND VARIANT READINGS

3. 10 it,] it *C*
   13 obliuion] oblivion *R*.   Perusde] Parusde *C*
   17 Inuentions] Inventions *C*
   22 Sycophantes.] *R* has a comma
   27 In *G* the initial *D* is in wrong font (roman). Cf. 4. 2, 3, etc.   doo] do *C*
4. 2, 3, 7, 9, 26, 32] In *G* the initial of each of the italic proper names in these lines is in wrong font (roman)
   4–6, 12, 16, 17] The initial *W*'s in *G* are here, as in similar cases throughout, consistently of a different font from the other capitals
   11 force,] force *C*
   19 was.] was *R*
   21 who] Who *P, R, C*
   28 The initial *T* is either in wrong font or imperfect.   can)] In *G* there may be an imperfect comma before the parenthesis
   35 greaue:] In *G* the colon is blurred beyond recognition; *P* has a period
5. 2 Jnuentions] Inuentions *R, C*
   17 hee *P*] he *R, C*.   arriued] arrived *R*
   24 to] te *C*
   29 A iij] A.iij. *R* (and occasionally *R* has a period elsewhere, though subsequent instances are not noted here)
6. 4 bee] be *P, C*
   26 deuise] devise *R*
7. 6 blisse,] blisse. *C*
   8 behold *P*] beholde *R, C*
   21 betweene] between *R*
   25 secret] sacret *C*
   32 thee,] thee. *P, R, C*. In *G* the comma may be a blurred period
8. 4 O *P*] I *C*
   13 mou'd] mou'd. *R*
   14 these verses] One word in *C*
   22 dye:] dye *R*
   24 too] to *P, C*
   25 lyfe] life *C*

[124]

MISPRINTS AND VARIANT READINGS

8. 27 without] withont *C*
   29 decay] decay. *R*
9. 1 ¶] Either in wrong font or defective; so also in several other cases, — on pages 22, 27, 31, 33, 38, 44, 45, 46, 47, 48, 52 (twice), 53, 57, 58, 61, 73
   5 againe] again *R*.   beewray] bewray *C*
   18 wofull] woful *R*
   20 vnrest] vnr est *G, as in* 19.28
   22 haue] have *C*
   29 yeeld *P*] yeelde *R, C*
   34 loue] love *C*
   35 doubtfull] doubtful *R*.   wight] wight. *R, C, P*
   37 cau'sde *P, C*] causde *R*.   ryse.] ryse, *C, P*. The period in *G* may be a blurred comma
10. 3 senceles] sencelesse *C*
    13 bight] bight. *R*
    15 compacte.] compacte *R*; compacte, *C, P*
    23 doo.] In *G* the period may be a bad comma
    27 yeeld *P*] yeelde *R, C*
    29 vs] us *C*
    31 doo *P*] do *C*
    33 hold *P*] holde *R, C*
    34 hee hath:] he hath, *P, C*
11. 3 vnright] vnright. *P, R, C*
    8 accurse] accuse *C*
    21 good.] The period may be a broken comma (*P, R, C*)
    24 mistrust] mist rust *G, as in* 13.19
    25 vniust] uniust *C*
    28 wee *P*] we *R, C*
    36 Ioyfull] Joyfull *C*
    37 agayne.] agayne, *R, C*; agayne: *P*
12. 5 the same] *One word in G*
    9 Ioyes] Joyes *C*
    10 skantly *P, R, C*] skautly *G*
    13 bewray] Possibly *G* has a period, as in *R, C, P*
    17 grau] graue. *R, C;* grave, *P*
    21 haue *R, C*] haue haue *G;* have *P*

[125]

MISPRINTS AND VARIANT READINGS

12. 23 burne.] burne, *R, C, P*
    31 vs.] The period is uncertain in *G*
    33 shalbe] shal be *P, R;* shall be *C*
13. 4 FINIS] In *G* the *F* is either in wrong font or broken, as in many other places throughout
    6 Rosana] In *G* the initial is in wrong font (roman). Cf. 4. 2, 3, etc.
    9 the *P*] thee *R, C*
   10 ẙ (*first one*)] ẙ *C.*   ẙ (*second one*) *C, P*] y *R.*   After *sendes* there may be a period in *G*, but the text is blurred badly
  11 rendes. *P*] rendes, *R, C*
  19 mistrust] mist rust *G, as in* 11.24
  25 ioy] joy *C*
  26 mee] mee, *R, C, P.* In *G* an indistinct dot may be meant for a comma or a period
  27 mee *R, C*] mee. *P.*   Possibly a period was intended in *G*
  31 lothsom *P*] lothsome *R, C.*   lookes *P, R, C*] loekes *G*
  35 Cresseds *P*] Cressids *R, C*
14. 3 rid] rid. *P, R, C*
    4 and] an *P*
    5 remaine] remaiue *G*
    7 reioyce] reioyce, *R, C;* reioyce; *P*
    9 bell. *P*] bell, *R, C*
  10 mee slay *P*] me flay *R;* me slay *C*
  15 breath] breath. *P, R, C*
  16 me *P*] mee *R, C*
  17 blisfull] blissfull *P, C*
  19 honor *P*] honour *R, C*
  21 louing] loving *C*
  22 imbrace] embrace *P, R, C*
  29 hee] he *C*
  33 soule *P*] soul, *R, C.*   thee] thee. *P, R, C*
  37 yeres *P*] yeeres *R, C.*   Grekes *P*] Greekes *R, C.*   rew *P*] rew, *R, C*
15. 5 speche] speeche *C*
    9 liueth] liuith *R*
  13 should] Possibly *G* has a period (like *P, R, C*)
  17 while] while? *P, R, C*

MISPRINTS AND VARIANT READINGS

15. 21 thy] the *C*
    29 vnkinde] Possibly *G* has a period (like *R, C*); *P* has a comma
    30 ielus *P*] ielous *R, C*
    31 send.] send, *R, C*; send; *P*
    34 mee] mee. *R, C*; mee, *P*
    35 mee.] The period (*P, R, C*) is uncertain in *G*
16. 5 The same] *One word in G*
    6 litle *P*] little *R, C*
    10 mee *P*] me *R, C*
    13 to] too *R*
    18 suffise *P*] suffice *R, C*
    21 freend. *P, R, C*] *G* probably has a comma
    26 &] and *P, R, C*
    27 words *P*] wordes *R, C*
    32 earst *P*] erst *R, C*
17. 2 mislyke *P*] myslike *R*; mislike *C*
    8 Iudgmentes] Judgmentes *C*
    9 finde. *P*] finde *R, C*. In *G* the period is blurred
    21 race] rare *C*
    22 found *P*] founde *R, C*
    27 while] while. *R, P*
    32 beleeued? *R, C*] The *?* is broken in *G*, resembling a colon; *P* has a comma
    37 delayes.] In *G* the period is badly blurred
18. 2 skorne,] The *e* and the comma are broken in *G*
    12 tost] to st *G*
    17 brest] brest, *R, C*. There may be a period in *G*; *P* has a colon
    24 bloddy] bloody *C*
    27 any thing *P*] *One word in R, C*
    28 bee] be *C*
19. 3 perswade.] perswade, *R*
    11 face.] face, *R, C*; *P* has no mark
    17 shrine] shriue *C*
    19 beares,] beares. *P, R, C*
    21 wight.] wight, *R*
    26 bee] be *C*
    28 vnrest] vnr est *G, as in* 9.20

[127]

MISPRINTS AND VARIANT READINGS

19. 30 yee] see *C*
    35 new] now *C*
20. 5 lose *P*] loose *R, C*
     9 disdayne.] disdayne *C*
    10 al] all *C*
    17 mee *P*] me *R, C*
    24 hee] he *C*
    27 cruell *P*] cruel *R, C*
    33 litle] little *C*
21. 8 mee] me *C*
    13 mee] me *C*
    14 mee know] me know *P, C*.   power.] The period is very doubtful in *G*
    21 doubtful] doubtfull *C*
    26 had, *P*] had *R, C*
    29 And *P*] An *R, C*
    33 *R* supplies the signature-mark C iii, which is not in *G*
22. 8 FINIS] The *F* is either in wrong font or broken. See 13. 4
     9 cought *P*] caught *R, C*
    21 senceles *P*] senceless *R;* sencelesse *C*
    24 harte] hart *C*
23. 12 Ioy] Joy *C*
    16 head.] head, *R;* head? *P*
    21 goulden] golden *C*
    22 thus] thus, *C, P*
    32 gayne.] gayne, *P, R, C*
    33 smart,] smart. *C, P*
    34 Ciiij] Ciiii *R* (and so throughout)
24. 4 Ioy] Joy *C*
    18 lose] In *G* the *o* apparently surrounds a period
    20 bloud] blond *G possibly*
    26 inwarde] inward *C*
    30 her] hir *C*
25. 2 forthe] forth e *G*
     4 litle *P*] little *R, C*
     5 dwelt] dwell *C*
     7 ruth] rut h *G*

[128]

MISPRINTS AND VARIANT READINGS

25. 34 Do *P*] Doo *R, C.*   part vs] vs part *C*
    37 went. *R*] went, *P, C, and perhaps G*
    43 hart] harte *R*
26. 8 woods] woodes *R*
    10 noate (*second one*)] *G may have* uoate
    18 requier. *P, R, C*] *G may have a broken comma*
    25 me] my *C*
27. 4 BE] Bee *R*
     5 hee] he *C*
     6 vnknowen *P, R, C*] vn knowen *G*
    10 rest:] rest *C*
    11 best] be st *G*
    16 chaunce *P*] chance *R, C*
    32 behooue] behoue *C*
    35 vnknowne.] vnknowne *C*
    36 counsayle] couusayle *C*
    37 farforth] *Two words in R*
    40 greeue] greene *G*
    43 thine] t hine *G*
    46 Disiringe] Desiringe *P, C;* Disiring *R*
28. 4 god] God *P, R*
     5 the] The *P, R, C*
    12 finde,] finde *C*
    24 thinkes that] *One word in G*
    30 wayes,] wayes *C*. In *G there seem to be two commas, or a comma and a period*
    31 woman.] woman *C*
    36 mee] me *C*
    40 y̆] that *C*
    41 serueth] serveth *C*
    42 tredeth *P*] treadeth *R, C*
    47 know.] know *C*
    50 hart] *The h is badly broken in G; P calls it* d
    53 doth] Doth *P, R, C*
    54 still] stiil *R*
29. 5 mee] Mee *P, R, C*
    25 *In G the block-initial is upside down*

[129]

MISPRINTS AND VARIANT READINGS

29. 36 flame. *P, R*] flame *C*. The period is doubtful (blurred) in *G*
    41 Diij] Diii *R*
30. 3 smart] smart. *P, R*
     4 thought] thou ght *G*
     7 suffise] suffise. *P, R, C*
    10 FINIS] The *F* is either in wrong font or broken. Cf. 13. 4
    17 Wherunto] Wher vnto *C*
    30 needeth] reedeth *C*
    32 not,] not. *P, R, C*
31. 2 sinke] sin ke *G*
     7 exellent *R*] excellent *P, C*. Wherin] For the *W* cf. 4. 4–6, etc. *R* has a lower-case letter here, but capitals in all similar cases
    13 bould] bould. *P, R, C*
    20 Ioyes] Joyes *C*
    25 Maynyards torne] Maynyard storne *G, R*
    31 mee] me *C, P*
    34 A] Yet *R*. (See the note on this line)
32. 14 Sea mens] *One word in P* (l. c.) *and R*
    23 carkinge] carking *C*
    28 scorning] scorni ng *R*
33. 3 mone] moue *C*. (See the note on this line)
    10 FINIS] FINIS. *P, R, C*
    18 longe] long *C*
    27 so.] so? *P, R, C*
    28–30 stinte] stint *P*
34. 6 so.] so? *P, R, C*
    17 FINIS] The *F* is either in wrong font or broken. Cf. 13. 4
    20 through] throngh *G*
    25 Hauke] hauke *C*; hawke *P*
35. 2 fatal *P*] fata *G, R*; fata[l] *C*
     5 perfixt] prefixt *C*
     6 al] all *C*
     8 seperate,] seperate. *C*
     9 harte] hart *R*
    13 heare] Possibly a blurred comma in *G*.   craue,] craue *C*
    22 You *P*] Yyou *G, R, C*
    33 death] death, *P, C*

MISPRINTS AND VARIANT READINGS

35. 37 decaye. *P*] decaye, *R*; decaye *C*
36. 10 lo] in *C*
    12 winde.] winde, *R, C*; winde *P*
    13 bayt] bayt. *P, R, C*
    18 lore] lore, *P, C*
    23 fet] set *R*
    32 it] is *C*
    34 woordes] wordes *R*.   bee] be *C*
    37 shot] shot. *P, R, C*
    40 other] others *C*
    43 mindes,]   In *G* the comma is badly blurred
    54 doo] do *R*
37. 7 hauing] having *R*
    10 lyfe] life *C*
    12 stryfe] strife *C*
    14 length] length, *C, P*
    25 delite,] delite *P, R, C*
    45 presente] pres ente *G*
    53 *R* supplies the signature-mark Eiii
38. 26 paynted] painted *C*
    32 placed,] placed *C, P*
39. 3 Is] I *C*
    13 it doth] *One word in G*
    14 Therfore *P*] Therefore *R, C*
    30 thee] the e *G*
40. 4 vewing *P*] viewing *R, C*
    22 slepe] sleepe *C*
    33 clay,] clay *C*
42. 7 purchace] purchase *C*
    12 FINIS] The *F* is either in wrong font or broken. Cf. 13. 4
    30 That] that *P, C*
    31 golden] golde n *G*
44. 2 mee] m ee *G*
    3 good] good. *P, R, C*
    11 Darte.] The period is very doubtful in *G*
    18 sith] since *C*
    35 why,] why *P, R, C*

[131]

MISPRINTS AND VARIANT READINGS

44. 39 *R* supplies the missing key-word
45. 5 pleasant *P*] plasant *G, R;* plesant *C*
    35 will.] will *R*
    39 to] To *P, R, C*
    43 vnkinde.] vnkind. *R, C;* unkinde! *P*
    47 The block-initial is upside down in *G*
    51 *R* supplies F iii
46. 8 Thy selfe] But in *G* the space is very slight
    21 disdain] disdain. *P, R, C*
    30 men. *P*] men *R, C*
47. 20–25 In *G* each line of this italic verse begins with a roman capital. Cf. 4. 2, 3, etc.
    22 Some] *G* apparently has s*ome*, but the roman *s* may be a capital
    23 Whom] For the *W* cf. 4. 4-6, etc.
    26 Virtute] In *G* the *V* is in wrong font (roman). Cf. 4. 2, 3, etc.
    31 sound] sound. *R, C;* sound: *P*
48. 3 till *P*] til *R, C*
    11 or binde] *One word in R*
49. 23 refraine *P*] refrayne *R, C*
50. 15 mee] me *C*
    24 FINIS] The *F* is either in wrong font or broken. Cf. 13. 4
    28 hard,] hard. *R;* hard; *P*
    29 forbid:] forbid, *R, C;* forbid! *P*
51. 4 faire] fair e *G*
    15 cannot *P*] canot *R, C*
    19 the same] *One word in G*
    23 faythfull] fayth full *R*
    29 loue,] loue. *R, C;* Love! *P*
52. 4 Would] would *C*
    13 Lady *P*] lady *R, C*
53. 2 hee] he *C*
     4 al] all *P, C*
     5 bodyes] bodies *C*
     7 wil *P*] will *R, C*
    15 Wretched] wretched *C*
    26 genorositie] generositie *P, R, C*
    27 striue] st riue *G*

[132]

MISPRINTS AND VARIANT READINGS

53. 31 F iii] G iii *R*. (See the note on this line)
54. 12 fayth] fay th *R*
    16 bee:] bee, *P, R, C*
    17 shew *P*] show *R, C*
55. 16 Wisdoms] For the *W* cf. 4. 4–6, etc.
    23 dainful] dainfull *C*.   fraight.] fraight, *P, C*
56. 10 dome.] dome, *P, R, C*
    17 her] his *C*
    26 shewes] shew es *G*
    30 temprance *P*] temperance *R, C*
    31 smyles] smyles, *P, R, C*
57. 5 losse. *P*] losse *R, C*
58. 10 sute] su te *G*
    16 posses] possesse *C*
59. 2 our selues] *One word in C*
    26 greedely] greedily *C*
60. 3 When] When, *C*
    13 hee] he *C*
    28 starres, *P*] starres *R, C*
61. 3 sease] cease *C*
    5 newes,] newes. *P, R, C*. The mark in *G* is imperfect
    7 hee] he *C*
    8 shall *P*] shal *R, C*.   go] go, *P, R, C*
    15 the same] *One word in G perhaps*
    18 graunt] In *G* the blurred *u* may be an *n*
    34 will,] will. *C*; will; *P*
62. 9 stronger] str o nger *G*
    11 Kinge,] Kinge *R, C*; kinge *P*
    29 what stone] what-stone *P*.   desendeth] defendeth *P, R, C*
63. 7 lyue] liue *C*
    8 Pernassus] *G apparently has* Pernaslus.   raste *P, R*] rafte *C*
       (see the note on this line).   Iuice] Juice *C*; juice *P*
    11 Muses] Muses, *P, C*
    16 meete] meete. *P, R, C*
    20 abound *P*] abounde *R, C*
    24 Paris] *R* prints this word in roman type, which is the equivalent of italics in the present reprint

[133]

MISPRINTS AND VARIANT READINGS

63. 28 stoute *P*] stout *R, C*
    29 forhead *P*] forehead *R, C*
    31 whight.] whight, *P, R, C*
64. 8 slights *P*] flights *R, C*
    12 grace, *P*] grace *R, C*
    17 the same] *One word in* G
    19 haue] have *C*.   neither] n either *G*
    28 away] *Two words in* G
    33 faile] fayle *C*
65. 3 Spake] spake *C*
    6 forsid] forsed *P*
    21 tarry not] tarry *C*
    22 Lawre.] The period is doubtful in *G*
    25 Forseeing *P*] For seeing *R, C*
66. 13 Count] count *C*
    15 affections] affectious *G*
    19 wine *P, R, C*] *G* may have a period
67. 3 Conscience] conscience *C*
    24 soonest] sooneth *P*
    29 soone *P*] soon *R, C*
    35–36 In *G* each capitalized word of this italic verse begins with a roman letter. Cf. 4. 2, 3, etc.
    36 Will] For the *W* cf. 4. 4–6, etc.
    37 *R* omits I ij and (as usual) the ¶ before the key-word
68. 4 WIth speedy] WI thspeedy *G*
    7 And] Ind *G* (or else a broken *A*).   decayes] *Possibly* docayes *in G*
    8 My heauy] Myh eauy *G*
    18 winde.] winde, *P, R, C*
    19 tyring *P*] trying *R, C*
69. 6 learne] learue *G*
    14 that] the *C*
    30 all mine] *One word in* R.   owne,] owne *C*
    31 prooft] proofe *P, C*
    34 *R* supplies I iii
70. 6 bee,] In *G* the mark is blurred and somewhat out of position
71. 3 fly from] *One word in* G

[134]

MISPRINTS AND VARIANT READINGS

71. 12 yee] In *G* the second *e* is defective, or else it is *c*.   shall] The second *l* is so broken that it looks something like *t*
    35 wit] wit [h] *C*; with *P*
    37 *R* omits I iiii
72. 6 show, *P*] show. *R, C*
    7 Deseruedly] Deser uedly *G*
    9 doubtfull *P*] doubtful *R, C*
    12 count,] count *P, R, C*
    13 doubtfull *P*] doubtful *R, C*
    22 disease.] In *G* the period is at the top of the *e* instead of at the bottom
73. 8 foe:] foe, *P, R, C*
    9 lust *P*] luste *R, C*
    13 steadfast] stedfast *R*
    17 snake,] The comma is badly broken in *G*
    20 hunger] In *G* either the lower part of the *h* is broken off or the letter is *b*
    22 Rose behinde] *One word in G*
    23 FINIS] The *F* is either in wrong font or broken. Cf. 13. 4
74. 8 carful] careful *C*
    10 if] ,if *P, R, C*
    14 aboue] aboue, *P, C*
    20 ye *P*] yee *R, C*
    26 do] doo *P, R, C*
    33 earst] erst *C*.   hast] has *P*
75. 5 therwithall] ther withall *C*
    14 soiurne] soiourne *R*
    16 obseru'd] observ'd *C*
    20 found,] found. *P, C*
    29 repeate] repeate. *P, C*
    32 apace, *P*] apace: *R, C*
    35 fled] fl ed *G*
    36 harte] har te *G*
    38 *R* omits K ij
76. 2 dreadful] dreadfull *C*
    6 breefe] briefe *C*
    8 of] The *o* is very imperfect in *G*

[135]

MISPRINTS AND VARIANT READINGS

76. 9 Seas] Scas *G*
    10 subiecte] subiect *C*
    17 mee] me *C*.   adew:] a dew: *R, C, and possibly G;* a dew! *P*
    20 yet more] *One word in G*
    22 Vntill] Vntil *R, C*
    26 mee,] mee *P, C*
77. 7 ponder] The *o* in *G* looks more like *e*
    8 furth] furth[er] *P*
    10 litle *P*] little *R, C*.   haue] have *C*
    13 Will] Wil *C*
    14 Loue] loue *R, C;* love *P*
    16 sayd *P*] said *R, C*
    22 Iudge to] Judge so *C;* judge to *P*
    27 the same] *One word in G, C*.   part.] part *C;* part; *P*
    28 shew] shcw *C*
    29 depart] dep art *G*
    31 Wherby] For the *W* cf. 4. 4–6, etc.
    35 L iii] K iii *R*. (See the note on this line)
78. 8 harps] har ps *G*
    15 vnto] into *C*
    24 paynful] paynfull *C*
    26 vnfainedly] vnfaiuedly *G*
    28 proue. *P*] proue, *R, C*
79. 1 Proctor] In *G* the *P* is in wrong font (italic)
    23 the *P*] thee *R, C*
    27 learne,] learne *R, C;* learne; *P*
80. 14 gaine *P*] game *R, C*
    17 haue] have *C*
81. 2 Whoredome] For the *W* cf. 4. 4–6, etc.
    22 blinde. *P*] blinde, *R, C*
    26 due.] due, *C*
    30 pomp] pompe *C*.   consumes] cousumes *G*
    32 splendant] splendaut *G*
82. 7 thoughts] throughts *C*
    18 vsuall] usuall *C*
    20 dumps] dnmps *C*

[136]

MISPRINTS AND VARIANT READINGS

82. 22 So that with *P, R*] So with that *C*.   fraught,] The comma is badly blurred in *G*
    32 thyrty] thirty *R*
83. 9 vnkinde. *P*] vnkinde, *R, C*
    11 Willow willow willow] In *P* and *C* the three words are separated by commas; so *P* throughout
    16 Sing willow] *C* has a comma; so *P* throughout
    32 willow.] In *G* the period is so blurred as to look almost like a comma
84. 4 promis'd,] promis'd *P, C*
    9 Sing *P*] Singe *R, C*.   Sing willow,] No comma in *C*
    18 abide.] abide, *P, R, C*
    19 *C* omits the fourth *willow*
    25 Sing willow,] No comma in *C*.   will *R, C*] willow *P*
    32 why] wh y *G*.   spight] spight, *R, C*; spight? *P*
85. 6 minde] min de *R*
    7 greene] green *C*
    9 Singe *P*] Sing *R, C*
    10 troth] troth, *P, C*
    24 change] cha nge *G*
    25 *C* has *willow* four times
    32 in] iu *G*
86. 2 winde, *P*] winde *C, R*. In *G* the comma is badly blurred
    5 willow?] willow. *P, R, C*
    7 Between *Sing* and *willow* a printer's lead shows distinctly in *G*
    18 sorowing] sorrowing *R*
    27 fate.] fate, *C*
87. 18 gaynes] Gaynes *P, R, C*
    19 euery] enery *G*
    21 outward] inward *C*
    23 FINIS] The *F* appears to be either in wrong font or broken; it is badly blurred.   Cf. 13. 4
88. 4 counteruayle] countervayle *C*
    8 minde,] minde *P, C*
    9 I,] I *P, C*
    19 not,] not *P, C*
    20 To] So *R*

[137]

MISPRINTS AND VARIANT READINGS

88. 24 pleas'd *R, P*] pleasd' *G, C*
89. 15 hee] he *C*
    26 pleasant] pleasaut *R*
90. 3 inflamed *P*] in flamed *G, R, C*
    15 vessell] vesse ll *G*
    18 wealth,] wealth *C*
91. 9 drowsie] drowste *R*
    24 shun *P*] shun, *R, C*
92. 10 auayles] avayles *C*
    13 tryde] tryd e *R*
93. 4 fielde,] The comma is doubtful; *R* and *C* have periods, *P* a semicolon
    20 thy] the *P, C*
94. 3 Shall *P, R, C*] Ssall *G*, where the initial is upside down
    16 Between *moues* and *the* a printer's lead shows distinctly in *G*
    23 wee *P*] we *R, C*
    24 grew:] grew. *P, C*
    27 youthful *P*] youthfull *R, C*
95. 5 darkesome] darksome *C*
96. 9 holde: *P*] holde *R, C*
    10 freend, *P*] freend *R, C*
    22 strength] stength *G*
    23 ouercome] onercome *G*
    29 annoy:] annoy *C*; annoy? *P*
    30 hee] he *C*
97. 3 sake, *P*] sake *R, C*
    33 contented] content ed *G*
98. 8 wee] we *C*
    21 Win] For the *W* cf. 4. 4–6, etc.
    24 vertue] virtue *R*
99. 6 sithe] sith *C*
    8 finis] finis. *C*; FINIS. *P*
    21 lenght] length *P, C*
    24 life *P*] lyfe *R, C*
    28 litle *P*] little *R, C*
    32 thoughts *P*] thoughtes *R, C*
100. 5 lend] len d *R*

[138]

MISPRINTS AND VARIANT READINGS

100. 7 tungs] tungs. *C;* tungs, *P*
  10 storme,] storme. *R, C, P.* In *G* the comma is very small, perhaps from another font
  17 preuayld] preuayd *C*
  18 mee,] mee *P, R*
  20 Tempora si] *One word in G*
  21 FINIS] The *F* is either in wrong font or broken. Cf. 13. 4
101. 1–102.20 (= leaf N iii)] *Omitted by P*
101. 1 Inuentions] Iuuentions *R*
  9 we] wee *C*
  10 wit,] wit. *R*
  12 wee] we *C*
  15 Beauties *R, C*] Beauties' *possibly G*
  23 Euen] Even *R*
  27 Lo thus *C*] Lothus *G, R*
102. 5 greeue *R, C*] greeuc *G apparently*
  18 beeing] being *R*
103. 1 *R* supplies the headline *of gallant Inuentions*
  14 blisse] bliss *C*
  17–18 *P* has asterisks to mark an omission between these lines
  23 sustayne. *P*] sustayne, *R, C*
  24 elswhere *P*] elsewhere *R, C*
  26 Ioy] Joy *C*
  33 slake. *P*] slake, *R, C*
104. 3 nor] uor *G apparently*
  10 hide] hide, *P, R, C*
  11 louers] lovers *C*
  12 neither] The *n* may be upside down in *G*
  15 til] till *C*
  18 her] the *C*
  20 tels] els *G, R, C;* [t]els *P*
  28 ordayne,] ordayne *P, R, C.* In *G* the *n* may be upside down and the comma may be a period
  30 scalde] sealde *P* (see the note on this line).   all *P*] al *R, C*
  32 pyning] pyuing *G*
  36 face] fate *C.* (See the note on this line)
105. 3 Between *bequests* and *within* a printer's lead shows distinctly in *G*

[139]

MISPRINTS AND VARIANT READINGS

105. 14 succor *P*] succour *R, C*
   22 carefull] careful *C*
   29 knap] kn ap *G*
   35 sweet] sw eet *G*
106. 10 ruthe] ruth *C.*   on] ou *G*
   22 Not, I] Not I, *R, C*; Not I; *P*
   24 neuer] ueuer *G possibly.*   spring] spring, *P, R, C*
   34 between] between, *P, R, C*
   35 seene] seene. *P, R, C*
107. 11 bee found] be found *C*
   13 litle *P*] little *R, C*
   19 heer] hur *C*
   20 wrought,] wrought. *C*
   21 brought. *P*] brought *R, C.* The period in *G* is blurred
   25 Poore] Poor *R*
   30 woonted] wonted *C*
   33 A glimpse] *One word in G*
   35 knew] knew, *R, C*; knew: *P.* The *w* is so badly blurred in *G* as possibly to hide some point of punctuation
108. 5 receiued] receined *G*
   11 life] life, *C*
   18 gladsom *P*] gladsome *R, C*
   19 say] say, *R, C*; say: *P*
   20 backe] back *C.*   ỹ] ẙ *R*
   27 confound:] confound, *R, C*; consound, *P.* In *G* the *f* is probably an *s*
109. 12 arise] arise, *P, C*
   13 place,] place *R, C*; place; *P*
   28 caught.] caught, *R, C*; caught *P*
   31 last,] last. *P, R, C*
110. 6 ioy,] ioy *C*; ioy! *P*
   7 greater] greate *P*
   8 great] great[er] *P*
   27 so,] so *P, C*
   33 askes,] askes *P, C*
111. 30 neyther] neither *C*
   32 say] ay *G, P, R, C*

[140]

MISPRINTS AND VARIANT READINGS

111. 34 prouoke] pronoke *G apparently*
112. 6 Mountaine] Mountaiue *G perhaps*
    10 ẙ] the *C*
    12 Iaw] Jaw *C;* jaw *P*
    25 seas'd *R, C*] seas,d *G;* seasd *P*
    26 earst,] earst *C, P*
    27 hee] he *C*
    33 That] TЧat *G*
113. 7 wheron] whereon *C*
    31 litle *P*] little *R, C*
    32 (alas,] (alas) *R;* ,alas! *P*
114. 2 t'embrace *C*] t'mbrace *G, P, R*
    10 payne. *P, R, C*] *G may have a colon*
    16 therfore as] therforeas *R;* theefore as *C;* therfore, as *P*
    17 the] *R puts this word in black letter (corresponding to roman letter of the present text); C prints it in roman*
    19 of] *In G the o is torn off, as is also the top of the l (in liue) just beneath*
    20 the same] *One word in G*
    26 ẘͭ] with *C;* wᵗʰ *P*
    29 chere] chere, *P, R, C*
    35 tell,] tell *P, C*
115. 6 neuer] nerer *P, C. (See the note on this line)*
    7 shee] she *C*
    9 cōplayne] cōplayne, *R, C;* complayne. *P*
    14 me] mee *P, R, C.*   shine] shine, *P, R, C*
    18 it] to *C*
    19 wee] we *P, C*
    26 &] and *P, R, C*
    28 not] no t *G*
    29 lēgth] lēgth. *R, C;* length: *P*
    34 profound] profounde *C*
116. 9 lamentacion] Lamentacion *C*
    11 William] *For the W cf. 4. 4–6, etc.*
    13 nor *P*] not *R, C*
    24 *In G the block-initial looks more like V*
    27 cares,] cares? *R, C;* cares *P*

[141]

MISPRINTS AND VARIANT READINGS

116. 28 why? *P*] why: *R, C*
117. 8 William] For the *W* cf. 4. 4–6, etc.
   11 liew] lieu *P, R*.   finde] fiude *G possibly*
   18 the same] *One word in G*
   23 selues] selves *C*
   32 William] For the *W* cf. 4. 4–6, etc.
118. 2 Hee] He *C*
    7 dye.] dye, *C*; dye! *P*
    9 scroule:] scroule, *R, C*
   19 now] uow *G*.   euery] euere *R*; euerie *C*; every *P*
   32 Muse, *P*] muse *R, C*
119. 21 lyues] lynes *C*. (See the note on this line)
   26 hope,] hope *P, C*
   31 Narscissus *P*] Narcissus *R, C*
   33 Restor'd] Restord *C*
   37 haue] have *C*
120. 6 wel *P*] well *R, C*
    9 an] a n *G*.   therfore] therefore *C*
   16 for] fot *R*

NOTES

NOTES

References are to pages and lines. For a word or a phrase on which no note is given, see the Glossarial Index. The following works are cited in the Notes by abbreviated titles:

Arber, Edward, editor. *A Transcript of the Registers of the Company of Stationers of London; 1554–1640 A.D.*, 5 vols., London and Birmingham, 1875–1894.

Camden, William. *Proverbs* (1614), in his *Remaines concerning Britain* (1674 ed., *Library of Old Authors*, 1870).

Chappell, William. *Popular Music of the Olden Time*, 2 vols., London, n.d.

E. E. T. S. = Early English Text Society Publications.

Handful (A) of Pleasant Delights (1584) By Clement Robinson and Divers Others, edited by Hyder E. Rollins, Harvard University Press, 1924.

Hazlitt, W. C. *English Proverbs and Proverbial Phrases*, 2d edition, London, 1882.

Heywood, John. *Woorkes*, London, 1562 (*The Proverbs and Epigrams of John Heywood*, Spenser Society reprint, 1867).

Lilly, Joseph. *A Collection of Seventy-Nine Black-Letter Ballads and Broadsides, Printed in the Reign of Queen Elizabeth, between the Years 1559 and 1597*, London, 1867. (Lilly wrote the preface and printed the book.)

Lyly, John. *Complete Works*, edited by R. W. Bond, 3 vols., Oxford, 1902.

N. E. D. = *The New English Dictionary*.

Paradise (The) of Dainty Devices. The original editions are cited, the date being given in each reference.

Tottel's *Miscellany* = popular title of *Songes and Sonettes, written by the ryght honorable Lorde Henry Howard late Earle of Surrey, and other*, 1557; edited by Edward Arber, *English Reprints*, 1870.

3. 1 *A. M.*] Anthony Munday (see the *Dictionary of National Biography*). Proctor in turn contributed verses to Munday's *Mirrour of Mutabilitie* (1579); a few are reprinted in Thomas Corser's *Collectanea Anglo-Poetica*, pt. IX, pp. 32–33.

6 *deuisde*] Notice the use of words throughout this preliminary poem that suggest the title of the *Paradise*.

NOTES

3. 21 *Owen Roydon*] See the discussion of Roydon in the Introduction, pp. xx–xxi, above.

22 *Sycophantes*] George Turbervile likewise prefaced his *Epitaphes, Epigrams, Songs and Sonets* (1567) with a poem addressed "To the rayling Route of Sycophants," a term by which he, like Roydon, meant critics.

4. 20 *Appelles*] Cf. 24.14. Many ballads on Apelles had been printed before the *Gorgeous Gallery* was published. Cf. also Lyly's play of *Alexander and Campaspe* (1584).

28 *Talke thou of that, &c.*] Referring to the Latin proverb, "Ne supra crepidam sutor judicaret." The proverb and the Apelles-shoemaker episode occur in Pliny's *Natural History*, XXXV, 36. 84–85. The same anecdote is told also by Valerius Maximus (VIII, 12. 3), though the name of Apelles does not occur and the proverb takes the form of "supra plantam ascendere vetuit." Greek parallels to this proverb are given in A. Otto's *Sprichwörter*. Cf. Lyly's *Euphues*, 1579 (Dedication), "The Shomaker must not go aboue his latchet"; Thomas Lodge's *Reply to Gosson*, 1580? (*Works*, ed. Hunterian Club, vol. I), p. 29, "when we wade aboue our shoe latchet *Appelles* wyll reprehende vs for coblers," and his *William Longbeard*, 1593 (*Works*, vol. II), p. 16, "William . . . began to presume aboue the latchet (as the prouerbe is)"; Robert Greene's *Carde of Fancie*, ca. 1587 (*Works*, ed. Grosart, IV, 102), "if *Appelles* . . . suffer the greasie Souter to take a view of his curious worke. . . ." The proverb "Ne sutor vltra crepidam" appears also in Erasmus's *Adagia* (I, vi, 16) and in his *Apophthegmata* (VI, 37); in Humfrey Gifford's *Posie of Gilloflowers*, 1580, I^v (*Complete Poems*, 1875); in Thomas Nashe's *Anatomy of Absurdity*, 1589 (*Works*, ed. McKerrow, I, 21); in the preface to Thomas Lodge's *Rosalynde*, 1590, A4 (*Works*, Hunterian Club, vol. I); in *A Health to the Gentlemanly profession of Seruingmen*, 1598 (W. C. Hazlitt's *Inedited Tracts*, 1868, p. 104); in Henry Crosse's *Vertues Common-wealth*, 1603 (ed. Grosart, p. 61); in John Taylor the Water Poet's *Works*, 1630 (Spenser Society reprint, p. 499), and in his *Swarme of Sectaries*, 1641, B2.

5. 3 *All men be false*] Perhaps Roydon had in mind the poem called "The complaint of a gentlewoman, being with child, falsely forsaken," that is printed in George Whetstone's *Rocke of Regard*, 1576 (Collier's reprint, p. 127). One stanza of it ends,

> I justly say, which wordes I rue,
> All men be false, and none be true.

NOTES

But more probably Roydon (like Whetstone himself) was imitating "The complaint of a woman Louer," a poem in the *Handful* (pp. 50, 111), which contains the lines,

> But now, alas, too soon I preeue,
> Al men are false, there is no choice.

10 *his freend*] 'His lover (Helen).'

23 *Menelaus wrath*] *Menelaus* is a genitive without ending. Other examples occur at 10. 20, 12. 7, 12. 13, 14. 8, 14. 36, 15. 12, etc.

24 *ioyes*] The rhyme leads one to expect *ioy*.

6. 6 *spoke, and sped*] Proverbial. Cf. 16. 30 n.

24 *time shal try them*] Proverbial. Cf. 15. 34 n.

7. 2 *The lamentable louer abiding, &c.*] The compiler of the *Gorgeous Gallery* "built" this poem from two poems in Thomas Howell's *Arbor of Amitie*, 1568, E2–E2ᵛ, F5–F6ᵛ (*Poems*, ed. A. B. Grosart, 1879, pp. 69–70, 91–94), called "The languishing Louer to his Ladie" (*A*) and "The Louer almost in dispaire" (*B*). In the *Gallery* poem there are almost no verbal changes, but lines from *A* are sandwiched with lines from *B* in a fashion that, to say the least, is curious. Thus, it begins with twelve lines from *A*, which are followed by thirty-four from *B*, two from *A*, two from *B*, two from *A*, two from *B*, two from *A*, and two from *B*. The last two groups borrowed from *B* are inserted in the *Gallery* in reverse order. Since this barefaced plagiarism of Howell has not been observed before, and since his *Arbor of Amitie* is not easily accessible, his poems are reprinted below (from Grosart's edition), with variations from the *Gallery* in diction, but not in spelling or punctuation, indicated by italics. The titles, which are of course not in the *Gallery*, are italicized in the original:

> [*A.*] *The languishing Lover to*
>   *his Ladie.*
>
> Health I thée sende, if he may giue,
>   that which himselfe doth misse:
> For thy swéete brest doth harbour whole,
>   my bloudy bale or blisse.
> I néede no scribe to scrie my care,
>   in restlesse rigour spreade:
> They that beholde my chaunged chéere,
>   alreadie iudge me dead,

NOTES

My baned limmes haue yeelded vp,
    their wonted ioy, to die:
My helthlesse hande doth nought but wring,
    and drie my dropping eie.
The *deathly* day in dole I passe,
    a thousand times I craue:
The noysome night, againe I wishe,
    the dolefull day to haue.
Eche howre to me most hatefull is,
    eche place doth vrge my woe.
No foode me feedes: close vp mine *eie*,
    to gastly graue I goe.
No phisicks arte can giue the salue,
    to heale my painefull parte:
Saue onely thou, the salue and sore,
    of this my captiue harte.
Thou hast the *forme* that cut the wound,
    of my vnholpen paine:
Thou canst and art the onely helpe,
    to heale the same againe.
In thée my wealth, in thée my woe,
    in thee to saue or spill.
In thée *my* lyfe, in thée my death,
    doth rest to worke thy will:
O salue thou then my secret sore,
    sith helth in thée *doe* stay:
And graunt with speede my iust request,
    whose want workes my decay.

[B.] *The Louer almost in dispaire, showeth his*
    great greefe and craues redresse.

THou art the braunch that swéetely springs,
    whose hart *so* sounde and true
Can onely chéere me wofull wight,
    or force *by* want to rue.
Then giue to me the sap I thirst,
    which gift may giue me ioy:
I meane thy firme and faithfull loue,
    whose want breedes mine anoy.
Remember yet *the friendly wordes*,
    ypast betwéene vs twaine:
Forget him not, for loue of thée,
    that sighes in secret paine.

NOTES

I oft doe séeme in companie,
   a gladsome face to beare:
But God thou knowst my inward woes,
   and cares that rent me there.
And that I may gush out my griefe,
   in secret place alone:
I bid my friends farewell in hast,
   I say I must be gone.
Then hast I fast with heauie hart,
   in this my dolefull case:
Where walkes no wight but I alone,
   in drowsie desart place.
And there I empt my laden hart,
   that swelde in fretting mone:
My sighes and *plaint* and panges I tell,
   vnto my selfe alone.
What shall I say, doe aske me once,
   why all these sorrowes bée:
I aunswere true, O foe or friend,
   they all are made for thée.
Once knit the linck that loue may *hast*,
   then shall my dolors cease:
It lies in thée and wilt thou not,
   the yeelding wight release?
O would to God it lay in me,
   to cure such griefe of thine:
Thou shouldst not long be voide of helpe,
   if twere in powre of mine.
But I would run and raunge in stormes,
   a thousand miles in paine:
Not fearing foyle of friends to haue,
   my Countnance whole againe.
And wilt thou then all mercilesse,
   more longer torment mée
In drawing back, sith my good helpe,
   is onely whole in thee?
Then sende me close the hewing knife,
   my wyder wounde to stratch:
And thou shalt sée by wofull griefe,
   of life a cleane dispatch.
When thou shalt saye and proue it true,
   my harte entirely loude:
Which lost the lyfe for Countnance sweete
   from whome he neuer moude.

NOTES

Write then vpon my *mournefull* toombe,
    these verses grauen aboue:
Here lies the heart, his truth to trie,
    that lost his life in loue.
Loe, saue or spill thou mayst me nowe,
    thou sitst in iudgement hie:
Where I poore man at barre doe stande,
    and lowde for life do crie.
Thou wilt not be so mercilesse,
    to slea a louing hart:
Small praise, it is, to conquer him,
    that durst no where to start.
Then heale the hart that loues thée well,
    vntill the day he die:
And firmely fast thy *fayth* on him,
    that's true continually.
Then shall I blesse the pleasant *plot*,
    Where *first I sawe thy face:*
And *say* the Gods haue thee *indude*,
    With *giftes of goodly* grace.
Whose vertues mixt with pittie great,
    hir *Counsell sought to* saue:
Who *being voyde of hir goode helpe*,
    long since had line in graue.

7. 16 *salue and sore*] A commonplace in Elizabethan poetry. Cf. "And none aliue may salue the sore," Tottel's *Miscellany*, p. 134; "it is not *Ouids* arte, Which I prescribe as salue for such a sore," W. A.'s *Speciall Remedie*, 1579, B3^v.

8. 7 *my countenance whole agayn*] The lover is telling what he would do to cure his lady's troubles if she were as badly off as he: 'I would run a thousand miles — not regarding the danger of succumbing — to restore thy countenance (i. e., thy good estate or prosperity).' Perhaps the reading should be *the* instead of *my*. *Of freends* is a generalizing plural, meaning 'of you, my friend.'

17 *at Bar doo stand*] Perhaps reminiscent of George Gascoigne's celebrated poem, "The arraignment of a Louer," which begins, "At Beautyes barre as I dyd stande" (*Complete Poems*, ed. W. C. Hazlitt, I, 36; MS. Ashmole 48, ed. Thomas Wright, Roxburghe Club, 1860, No. 75; Arber's *Transcript*, II, 376).

25 *mee lyfe*] Read *my lyfe*.

NOTES

30 *I tooke thy gloue*] Perhaps the author regarded his love-affair as a sort of challenge, of which his taking up the glove was an acceptance. But the glove may have been only a love-token. Cf. Chaucer, *Troilus*, V, 1013, "Hir glove he took, of which he was ful fayn."

9. 15 *Who neuer durst assaile, &c.*] Cf. *Measure for Measure*, I, iv, 77-79:

> Our doubts are traitors
> And make us lose the good we oft might win
> By fearing to attempt.

30 *Sith beggars haue no choyce*] Cf. Heywood's *Works*, 1562, p. 24, "Folke saie alwaie, beggers should be no choosers"; Robert Wilson, *The Coblers Prophesie*, 1594, D3, "What thinke ye as the Prouerb goes that beggers haue no [choice]?"; Beaumont and Fletcher, *The Scornful Lady*, V, iii, "Beggars must be no choosers." For other examples see A. H. Bullen, *Old English Plays*, IV, 367; Gabriel Harvey, *Works*, ed. Grosart, I, 20; Camden's *Proverbs*, p. 319; Joseph Reed, *The Register Office* (Mrs. Inchbald's *Collection of Farces*, III [1815], 150).

30 *nor neede had euer law*] Cf. George Turbervile, *Tragical Tales*, ca. 1574 (1837 reprint of the 1587 edition, pp. 238, 292),"But (as the auncient Prouerbe goes) *Perforce obaies no law*," "Sith neede obeyes no lawe"; Anthony Munday, *A Pleasant Comedy of Two Italian Gentlemen*, 1584, B4^v, G3^v (Malone Society reprint, lines 266, 1664), "Need hathe no lawe"; George Whetstone, *The Rocke of Regard*, 1576 (Collier's reprint, p. 253), "Necessitie obeys not lawe"; *A Health to the Gentlemanly profession of Seruingmen*, 1598 (ed. Hazlitt, p. 164), "Necessitie hath no Law"; William Rowley, *A Search for Money*, 1609 (Percy Society ed., p. 30), "necessity (being but a pettifogger) has no law." For further examples see Tyndale, *Works*, ed. Russell, II, 18; Robert Greene, *Works*, ed. Grosart, XIV, 55; Gabriel Harvey, *Works*, ed. Grosart, II, 35; R. C., *The Times Whistle*, 1616 (E. E. T. S. ed., p. 46); S. S., *The Honest Lawyer*, 1616, D^v; Richard Simpson, *The School of Shakspere*, II, 137; Richard Brathwaite, *Essays upon the Five Senses*, 1620 (2d ed., reprinted by Brydges, *Archaica*, vol. II), p. 26; James Shirley, *Love Tricks*, 1625 (*Works*, ed. Gifford and Dyce, I, 73); Charles Shadwell, *Works*, I (1720), 185. The proverb has been traced back to Publilius Syrus (*ca.* 42 B.C.), "Necessitas dat legem, non ipsa accipit."

NOTES

9. 31 *The subiecte Oxe*] Cf. Ovid, *Tristia*, IV, vi, 1–2:

> Tempore ruricolae patiens fit taurus aratri,
> Praebet et incurvo colla premenda jugo.

This passage was often quoted. Cf. the *Paradise*, 1576, B4, "The Oxe dooth yeelde vnto the yoke"; Thomas Watson, *Hekatompathia*, 1582, "sonnet" xlvii, 1, "In time the Bull is brought to weare the yoake"; Thomas Kyd, *The Spanish Tragedy, ca.* 1585?, II, i, 4, "In time the savage bull sustains the yoke"; Shakespeare, *Much Ado about Nothing*, I, i, 262–3, "Well, as time shall try: 'In time the savage bull doth bear the yoke'"; Jonson, *A Tale of a Tub*, 1633, III, iv, "Tempus edax — In time the stately ox" (cf. 93.2 n.).

10. 13 *assay the bayt . . . bane I bight*] 'Compelled me to make trial of the bait (the beauty of my mistress), in which now I bite (find) my destruction.' A ballad by Leonard Gibson, *ca.* 1570 (Lilly's *Ballads*, p. 116), says:

> Thinke, when you see baight, theres hidden a hooke,
> Whiche sure wyll bane you, if that you do bight.

Cf. 18.5.

21 *Danae*] Her father's name, "Acrysious" (Acrisius), was the title of a ballad which Richard Jones registered in 1568–1569 (Arber's *Transcript*, I, 386). References to her love-affair with Jupiter are among the Elizabethan commonplaces.

24 *highest seates . . . subiect to most winde*] Proverbial. Cf. 70. 28 n.; *Ancren Riwle, ca.* 1255 (ed. J. Morton, Camden Society, 1853, pp. 178, 226), "Euer so the hul is more and herre, so the wind is more theron," "Euer so herre tur, so haueth more wind"; Tottel's *Miscellany*, p. 157, "The highest tree in all the woode is rifest rent with blustring windes"; Samuel Brandon's *Virtuous Octavia*, 1598, A7ᵛ, "The tempest soonest teares The highest towers"; and Horace (*Carmina*, II, x, 9–11),

> Saepius ventis agitatur ingens
> Pinus et celsae graviore casu
> Decidunt turres.

11. 12 *a sternles ship*] Cf. Chaucer's *Troilus*, I, 416 f., "Al sterelees with-inne a boot am I A-mid the see, by-twixen windes two."

26 *No more then water soft, can stir a stedfast rocke*] This is the opposite of the regular proverbial expression. Cf. Lucretius, *De Rerum Natura*, I,

NOTES

313, "Stilicidi casus lapidem cavat"; Job (Vulgate version), xiv. 19, "Lapides excauant aquae"; *Ancren Riwle, ca.* 1255 (ed. Morton, p. 220), "Lutle dropen thurleth thene ulint thet ofte ualleth theron"; Lyly, *Euphues*, 1579 (*Works*, I, 225), "The softe droppes of raine pearce the hard Marble"; *Locrine*, 1595, C2ᵛ, "At length the water with continuall drops, Doth penetrate the hardest marble stone." See also Tottel's *Miscellany*, p. 56; Spenser's *Amoretti*, sonnet 18; *Tell-Trothes New-yeares Gift*, 1593 (ed. F. J. Furnivall, p. 27); Shakespeare's *Rape of Lucrece*, line 959; *Troilus and Cressida*, III, ii, 193; *Othello*, IV, iii, 47.

 37 *after calme . . . the stormes do come*] Cf. 51. 3 n.

 12. 7 *Dedales line*] Or rather, a 'Vulcan's line'; that is, the thread (a gift of Vulcan) with which Ariadne furnished Theseus to enable him to find his way out of the labyrinth. A ballad on Daedalus and Icarus that is at least as early in date as 1568 is printed in my *Old English Ballads* (1920), p. 329. Its first line is used as a tune in Thomas Howell's *Newe Sonets, and pretie Pamphlets, ca.* 1568, F4 (*Poems*, ed. Grosart, 1879, p. 51), and is quoted by Luxurioso in *The Return from Parnassus (ca.* 1598), I, i. Cf. also 68. 15.

 22 *streames shall soner turne*] A favorite asseveration. Cf. Ovid, *Ex Ponto*, IV, v, 43, "Fluminaque in fontes cursu reditura supino"; Cressida's apostrophe to the river "Simoys" to "retorne bakwarde to thy welle" if she shall prove false (Chaucer's *Troilus*, IV, stanza 222); and Samuel Brandon's *Virtuous Octavia*, 1598, B8ᵛ, "And *Tyber* should his flowing streames recall: Before his loue should euer thinke on change." See 62. 3.

 25 *All plagues . . . may fall on me*] That is, as leprosy befell the faithless Cressida. See the note on line 29.

 29 *wofull ende that Cressed made*] In Robert Henryson's *Testament of Cresseid (ca.* 1500) the faithless heroine is punished with leprosy. The *Testament*, which was generally thought to be Chaucer's own work, completely ruined the reputation of his lovely Criseyde. Literally dozens of references to Cressida's leprosy appear in Elizabethan works. See the history of her degradation given in my article on "The Troilus-Cressida Story from Chaucer to Shakespeare," *Publications of the Modern Language Association of America*, XXXII (1917), 383-429.

 13. 30 *The pleasant passed sportes: that spent the day to ende*] 'The pleasing but bygone delights of love that filled the day completely.'

 34 *Pyramus . . . Thisby*] Cf. 103. 1 n. The conclusion of these *if* clauses is awkwardly postponed.

[153]

NOTES

14. 2–3 *Eneas . . . Didos lyfe*] A favorite topic for ballad-writers. Several ballads dealing with Dido and Aeneas were entered at Stationers' Hall in 1564–1565 (Arber's *Transcript*, I, 263, 270); another, by Thomas Pridioxe, of perhaps even earlier date, is preserved in Additional MS. 15,233 (*The Moral Play of Wit and Science*, ed. Halliwell-Phillipps, 1848, p. 88). For the very popular ballad of "The Wandering Prince of Troy," which was usually referred to by Elizabethans simply as "Queen Dido" or "Troy Town," see the *Roxburghe Ballads*, VI, 548, and my article in the *Publications of the Modern Language Association of America*, XXXVIII (1923), 134.

4 *and end*] Read an end.

4–5 *If these . . . dying deathes remaine*] 'If these (Dido, Thisbe, etc.) have won an end of their tormenting pains by dying, why do I remain in the great torment of seeming to be dying a death and yet live?'

8–9 *do please mee . . . As dying bodies ioy, &c.*] That is, 'they don't please me at all, but rather fill me with fear or doubt.'

34 *Alcumena . . . the treble night*] Cf. Chaucer's *Troilus*, III, 1427 f.; and Anthony Munday's *Pleasant Comedy of Two Italian Gentlemen*, 1584, E2ᵛ, "But prolong ẙ night, as when *Iupiter* thy father with *Alcmena* lay." In Thomas Heywood's *Silver Age*, 1613 (*Dramatic Works*, 1874, III, 98), Jupiter says:

> Three nights I haue put in one to take our fill
> Of daliance with this beauteous *Theban* dame.

William Browne, *Britannia's Pastorals*, bk. II, song 1 (*Whole Works*, ed. Hazlitt, I, 169), speaks of

> the dread *Olimpicke Ioue*
> That dark't three dayes to frolicke with his Loue.

But Hyginus in his twenty-ninth fable merely remarks of Jupiter, "Tam libens cum ea [Alcmene] concubuit, vt vnum diem vsurparet, duas noctes congeminaret."

36 *Troylus sister*] I. e., Polyxena, who at the demand of the ghost of Achilles was sacrificed by Pyrrhus on the tomb of the dead warrior. A poem on the wooing of Polyxena by Achilles, called *Loues Leprosie*, by Thomas Powell, was printed in 1598 (ed. Percy Society, VI, 63 ff.). Cf. 56. 8, 63. 19.

15. 4 *childe of mighty Ioue*] Pallas Athene (Minerva). Cf. 64. 15.

8 *fine . . . finde*] Notice the play on words. Cf. 19. 9 n., 110. 23 n.

13 *I should*] 'I ought (to have).'

[154]

NOTES

15 *lothest to forgo*] 'That (i. e., what) I am' is understood.

31 *Forbid vs meat . . . to send*] I. e., 'forbid us to meet and also to send speech or message.'

34 *time . . . doth try mee*] Cf. Henry Porter's *Two Angry Women of Abington*, 1599 (*Tudor Facsimile Texts*, 1911, H3ᵛ), "Time & truth tries all, & tis an olde prouerbe"; Shakespeare's *Much Ado about Nothing*, I, i, 262; Hazlitt's *Proverbs*, p. 419; *Handful*, p. 5; and 6. 24.

38 *I do*] Read I doo.

16. 6 *my mystresse shall thee see*] Cf. Chaucer's *Troilus*, II, 1090 ff.:

> He kiste tho the lettre that he shette,
> And seyde, "lettre, a blisful destenee
> Thee shapen is, my lady shal thee see."

27 *thy bewayling words*] Perhaps the lover means that his lady (like the supposed authoress of the last poem in this book) had on occasion bewailed her love-pangs in verse. Cf. also 57.8 n. But *bewayling* may be a misprint for *beguiling* (cf. 18. 6).

30 *To speake and . . . speede*] Cf. Gower, *Confessio Amantis* (I, 1293), "For specheles may noman spede"; Heywood, *Works*, 1562 (pp. 31, 157), "Nought venter nought haue. spare to speake spare to speede"; Richard Hill, *Commonplace-Book*, ca. 1536 (ed. R. Dyboski, E. E. T. S., p. 132), "He that spareth to speke, ofte spareth to spede. Qui parcit fari, parcit sibi dona parari"; Hazlitt's *Proverbs*, p. 355; and 6.6.

17. 2 *that wemen choose to change*] Repeated in line 29 below.

12 *by pearcing spur*] 'Because of the spur that pierces him.'

14f. *to leaue that I did loue, Or lothe*] Perhaps there is an influence here of Lord Vaux's very popular poem, "The aged louer renounceth loue" (Tottel's *Miscellany*, p. 173), which begins, "I Lothe that I did loue, In youth that I thought swete." Cf. 35. 21 n.

17 *striue . . . against the streame*] In the form "Strong hit is to rowe a-yeyn the séé that floweth," this occurs in the *Proverbs of Alfred*, ca. 1250 (Skeat's ed., 1907, p. 16). Cf. Heywood's *Works*, 1562, pp. 55, 160, "Foly it is . . . To stryue against the streme," "He striueth agaynst the streme, by custums scoole That striuer is either a fishe or a foole"; Camden's *Proverbs*, p. 326, "It is hard striving against a stream."

25 *am I not to learne*] I. e., 'I have not to be instructed,' 'I don't need to be instructed.' Lines 24–25 mean, 'Though I am not clever in gen-

NOTES

eral and cannot always discern what is best, yet I need no instruction in the attempts of craft to take rank as truth.'

17. 29 *that wemen, &c.*] Cf. 17. 2 n.

38 *My*] Read Mee.

18. 8–9 *all . . . those: that vse such craft I wish . . . to liue with Lasars dish*] This ungallant wish was expressed by many other Elizabethan lover-poets. So "To his cruel Mistresse" (*Tragical Tales, ca.* 1574, 1837 reprint of the 1587 edition, p. 369) George Turbervile wrote:

> And if I may not haue
>   the thing I would enioy:
> I pray the gods to plague thee
>   as they did the dame of Troy.
> I meane that Creside coy
>   that linkt her with a Greeke:
> And left the lusty Troyan Duke,
>   of all his loue to seeke.
> And so they wil, I trust,
>   a mirror make of thee:
> That beuties darlings may beware,
>   when they thy scourge shal see.

19. 9 *Queene*] The lines that follow indicate that the author is punning on *queen* and *quean*.

35 *trees that new dispoyled are*] Perhaps *new* should be *now*, indicating that the poet was writing of the autumn or the winter.

20. 31 *Who can beware by others harmes*] See 92. 25 n.

21. 2,20 *Fortune*] Cf. H. R. Patch, *The Tradition of the Goddess Fortuna*, Smith College Studies in Modern Languages, III (1922), 131–235.

31 *an horse doth run*] *An* is probably a misprint for *on*.

22. 11 *hugie heape*] George Peele (*Works*, ed. Bullen, II, 91, 164, 169) several times uses this phrase. Cf. also Tottel's *Miscellany*, p. 154, and the *Handful*, p. 10. The metre, if strictly followed, would demand the omission of *hugie*.

13 *still . . . my*] The metre would be improved by omitting one of these words.

23. 3 *boy his dart*] 'And does the blind boy strike (shoot in) his dart so sure?'

NOTES

21 *guiltlesse shee*] *Read* guiltlesse thee. On Cupid's arrows of lead and of gold see Boccaccio's *Amorosa Visione* (*Opere Volgari*, Florence, 1833, vol. XIV), xv; *Li Fablel dou Dieu d'Amours*, ed. Jubinal, p. 31; an anonymous poem of 1557 in Tottel's *Miscellany*, pp. 265–266; Spenser's *Colin Clout's Come Home Again*, 1595, line 807.

24. 14 *Apelles*] See 4. 20 n., 28 n.

18 *binde and lose*] Cf. Job, ix. 9, "bind the sweet influences of the Pleiades or loose the bands of Orion."

25. 39f. *men doo relent . . . that I should speed*] *Relent* means *repent* (though possibly the reading should be *resent*), as in the *Faerie Queene*, III, vi, 25, "Shee [Venus] inly sory was, and gan relent What shee had said."

26. 2 *To the tune of lusty Gallant*] This is a genuine broadside ballad. To this same tune one of the *Handful* ballads (p. 57) was to be sung. The music for *Lusty gallant* and various facts about the tune are given in Chappell's *Popular Music*, I, 91, II, 769.

11 *The frisking Fish*] Cf. *Shirburn Ballads, 1585–1616*, ed. Andrew Clark, p. 188, "The pretye frisking fish." *Frisking* means 'moving briskly or sportively.' So a ballad printed from Additional MS. 15,233 (*The Moral Play of Wit and Science*, ed. Halliwell-Phillipps, p. 76) says:

> The friskinge fleas resemble well
> The wringlinge worme to me.

27. 22 *a birde in hand*] Cf. *Churchyardes Charge*, 1580 (Collier's reprint, p. 31), "A birde is better sure in fiste, Than five in feeld"; Camden's *Proverbs*, pp. 319, 329, "Better one bird in the hand than ten in the wood," "One bird in hand is better than two in the bush"; R. C., *The Times Whistle*, 1616 (E.E.T.S. ed., p. 106), "one thrush I'th' hand is worth more then are two i' th' bush"; Martin Parker, "Good Counsel for Young Wooers," *Roxburghe Ballads*, I, 426, "And one bird in hand is worth two in the bush." In *Don Quixote*, pt. I, bk. iv, ch. iv (or, as often cited, pt. I, ch. xxxi), the proverb appears as "y que más vale pájaro en mano que buitre volando," — literally, "a sparrow in the fist is worth more than a flying bittor," — which Smollett translated as "a bird in hand is worth two in the bush." Likewise Plutarch's comment, in his essay "Of Garrulity" (*Moralia*), "νήπιος, ὅς τὰ ἕτοιμα λιπὼν, ἀνέτοιμα διώκει" (which, by the way, is quoted by the scholiast on Theocritus, XI, 75), means literally, "he is foolish who,

NOTES

neglecting things at hand, seeks things that are not at hand," but is often translated as "a bird in hand," etc.

28. 2 *The Lady beloued exclaymeth*] The metre of this poem is very irregular.

25 *speake in the same*] I. e., speak concerning, in regard to, the faithless conduct of her lover.

36 *lure mee to thy fist*] As a falcon is brought to the lure.

40–47 *The wretched hound, &c.*] These lines (cf. 29. 9 n.) are imitated from the *Handful*, lines 1810–1817,

> The hound that serues his Maisters will,
>   in raunging here and there,
> The moyling Horse, that labours still,
>   his burthen great to beare:
>   In lew of paine, receiues againe,
>   of him which did him owe:
>   As Natures heast, wiles most & least
>   them thankefull for to showe,

and line 1819,

> as Nature doth them binde.

46–47 *Who . . . Disdayne not them to know*] 'The hound and horse find relief from (at the hands of) their masters, who disdain not to acknowledge them in their old age,' — i. e., who don't cut them off as if they didn't know them.

29. 9 *My teares run, &c.*] Perhaps suggested by line 1460 of the *Handful*, "That stil mine eies run down like streams."

24 *beloued*] Read beloued's.

25 *Since needes ye will mee singe*] 'Since you of necessity wish me to sing.'

38 *my hart*] Probably (as the antithetic style indicates) the reading should be *my hurt*.

30. 11 "This poem is quaintly quibbling in substance, and defective both in rhyme and rhythm: yet the burden of it is not altogether unpleasing" (Park). The rhyme and rhythm, however, are not unusually defective.

17 *wel like*] Read wel linke.

24 *I heare*] *I heard* might be expected.

31. 9 *when Cupid scaled first the Fort*] The tune is named from the first line of Lord Vaux's poem, "Thassault of Cupide vpon the fort where the

NOTES

louers hart lay wounded," in Tottel's *Miscellany*, pp. 172–173. Several lines are borrowed outright from Vaux's poem, though the present song, as Park observed, "alludes to naval, and his Lordship's to military tactics." A very interesting moralization of the Tottel poem, a ballad called "The Cruel Assault of Gods Fort" (*ca.* 1560), is reprinted in J. P. Collier's *Old Ballads*, p. 29 (Percy Society, vol. I, 1840).

34 *A*] The key-word should be *Yet*.

32. 5–6 *With Powder . . . Barke*] These lines are borrowed from Lord Vaux's poem:

> With powder and with pellets prest,
> To bring the fort to spoile and sacke.

8 *And now the shot the ayre doth darke*] So Lord Vaux: "And dims the ayre with misty smokes."

10–13 *Then Ignorance . . . thy Boate*] With this stanza compare Lord Vaux's lines:

> Good will the master of the shot,
> Stode in the rampyre braue and proud:
> For spence of powder he spared not,
> Assault assault to crye aloude.

33. 3 *the deafe can mone no noyse*] *Read* the deafe can moue no noyse, — i. e., no noise can move (affect, influence) the deaf.

7 *time with daughter his*] "Truth is allegorically said to be the daughter of Time" (Park). Cf. Gascoigne, *The Grief of Joy*, 1576 (*Complete Poems*, ed. Hazlitt, II, 280), "Treweth (Tymes daughter)."

34. 4 *rule the roste*] Proverbial for 'to be master.' Examples are too numerous to need citation.

35. 10 *pleasurest*] A queer word, in place of which one would, from Luke, xiii. 7, expect *cumberest*.

13–16 *when that death did heare, &c.*] Compare this grimly humorous passage in Samuel Rowlands's *Terrible Battell* (*ca.* 1606), C2:

> This Poet thus a sonneting we found,
> Riming himselfe euen almost out of breath,
> *Cupid* (quoth he) thy cruell Dart doth wound,
> Oh graunt me loue, or else come gentle *Death:*
> I heard him say, come gentle death in Iest:
> And in good earnest graunted his request.

NOTES

35. 21 *Tune of I lothe that I did loue*] The tune, which is named from the first line of Lord Vaux's "The aged louer renounceth loue," Tottel's *Miscellany*, pp. 173–175 (cf. 17. 14 n.), will be found in Chappell's *Popular Music*, I, 216, and in Additional MS. 38,599, fol. 134ᵛ. Vaux's poem was registered for publication in broadside-ballad form in 1563–1564 (cf. Rollins, *Analytical Index*, 1924, No. 48). It is quoted in the grave-digging scene in *Hamlet*.

31–33 *O Atropos ... mee die*] Professor Kittredge suggests a comparison with Pistol's rant in *2 Henry IV*, II, iv, 211–213:

> Then death rock me asleep, abridge my doleful days!
> Why, then, let grievous, ghastly, gaping wounds
> Untwine the Sisters Three! Come, Atropos, I say!

Cf. 60. 19.

36. 14 *For when bewitch shee had*] This poem borrows most liberally from three separate poems in the *Handful*. Compare 36.14–17 with the *Handful*, lines 463–466:

> Her beautie thee bewitcht,
> thy minde that erst was free:
> Her corps so comely framd, thou saiest,
> did force thee to agree.

Compare 36.18–45 with the *Handful*, lines 1327–1330, 1335–1338, 1365–1380, 1391–1394:

> ¶And as the Gods do know,
> and world can witnesse beare:
> I neuer serued other Saint,
> nor Idoll other where.

> ¶No toile, nor labour great,
> could wearie me herein:
> For stil I had a *Iasons* heart,
> the golden fleece to win.

> ¶And for my part I sweare,
> by all the Gods aboue,
> I neuer thought of other friend,
> nor sought for other loue.
> ¶The same consent in her,
> I saw ful oft appeare,
> If eies could see, or head could iudge,
> or eare had power to heare.

NOTES

¶Yet loe words are but winde,
    an other new come guest,
Hath won her fauour (as I feare)
    as fancies rise in brest.
Her friend that wel deserues,
    is out of countenaunce quite,
She makes the game to see me shoot,
    while others hit the white.

¶In these vnconstant daies,
    such troth these women haue:
As wauering as the aspen leaf
    they are, so God me saue.

Compare 36.50–53 with the *Handful*, lines 1447–1450:

What paps (alas) did giue him food,
That thus vnkindly workes my wo?
What beast is of so cruell moode,
to hate the hart that loues him so?

And compare them also with Thomas Howell's *Newe Sonets, and pretie Pamphlets*, ca. 1568 (*Poems*, ed. Grosart, 1879, p. 133):

What Paps did giue hir foode, that nought regardes my wo?
    What Tiger fearce alas coulde hate, the harte that loude hir so.

    34 *woordes bee . . . winde*] Cf. Spenser, *The Shepherds' Calendar*, 1579 ("October," line 36), "Sike words bene wynd, and wasten soone in vayne"; *The Phoenix Nest*, 1593 (Collier's reprint, p. 31), "Your word is but winde, and no sooner spoken than gone"; *Shirburn Ballads* (ed. Andrew Clark, p. 284), "But words are winde that fleets away"; *Ballads . . . from the Collections of Sir James Balfour*, 1639 (ed. James Maidment, 1834, p. 1), "There is an old saying, that words are but winde"; Hazlitt's *Proverbs*, p. 499, "Words are but wind, but blows unkind"; and 86.2.

    37. 20 *cruelly*] Read Cruelty.

    21 *Whose edge of Enuy hard, &c.*] 'Whose edge hath been wrought by cruel Malice in Venus's forge.'

    31 *A greater greefe be not begonne*] Optative use: 'May a greater grief be not begun.' The passage reminds one of Hamlet's "To be or not to be" soliloquy.

    44 *thy*] Read my.

NOTES

38. 3f. *Tune of Attend thee go play thee*] The tune takes its name from the first line of "The scoffe of a Ladie, as pretie as may be," a ballad preserved in the *Handful*, pp. 12–14. In the *Marriage of Wit and Wisdom*, 1579 (Shakespeare Society ed., p. 20), Wantonness sings a song "to the tune of 'Attend the goe playe the,'" probably in imitation, not of the *Handful* ballad, which was old, but of the *Gallery* ballad, which was new.

5 *light of loue*] "A very proper Dittie: To the tune of Lightie Loue" (*ca.* 1570) is reprinted in Lilly's *Ballads*, p. 113. The tune of this name (which is twice mentioned by Shakespeare), together with much information about it, is given in Chappell's *Popular Music*, I, 221–225. Cf. 84.14; and *Handful*, p. 84.

32 *Camma*] Cf. *A poore Knight his Pallace of priuate pleasures*, 1579, B3, "And *Camma* lyeth behinde [i. e., in her tomb] as faythfull as the best." The story of Camma, Synorix, and Sinnatus — which is the subject of Tennyson's *Cup*, a play that on its original production ran in London for a hundred and thirty nights — was told in two lost ballads that were registered in 1569–1570 (Arber's *Transcript*, I, 414, 416) under the titles, "Sinorex Cania et Sinatus" and "the Revenge yat a Woman of Grece toke of hym that slewe hyr husbounde." The latter was obviously summarized from the chapter in Sir Thomas North's *Diall of Princes*, 1557 (fols. 85^v–87), called "Of the reuengement that a vvoman of Gretia toke of him, that had killed her husband, in hope to haue her in mariage." On fol. 86^v North printed a ballad, beginning "To the Dian, whose endles reigne doth stretche," which Camma is said to have sung. The story is told also by Plutarch (*De Mulierum Virtute*); by Count Baldassare Castiglione (*The Courtier*, translated by Sir Thomas Hoby, 1588 ed., bk. III, Aa3); by George Pettie (*A petite Pallace of Pettie his pleasure*, 1576, ed. Gollancz, I, 11–48); and by Humfrey Gifford (*A Posie of Gilloflowers*, 1580, P4^v–Q2, *Complete Poems*, 1875, pp. 128–131). See further the discussion in W. E. H. Lecky's *History of European Morals*, II (1869), 361 f.

39. 2 *Phedra*] Phaedra is the subject of tragedies by Euripides, Seneca, and Racine. See the note next below.

6 *Hippolite*] The following summary of the story of Phaedra and Hippolytus is given in Thomas Heywood's annotations in his *Pleasant Dialogues and Dramma's*, 1637 (ed. W. Bang, p. 292):

Hippolitus, the sonne of *Theseus* and *Hyppolita* the Amazon, who when his father was abroad, his step-mother *Phædra* sollicited him to incestuous love, which he re-

NOTES

fusing, she accused him to his father that he would have forced her, but when hee perceived him to give credid to her false information, he tooke his Chariot and horses to flie his fury, but by the way his steeds being frighted with Sea-calves, ran with him to the mountaines, and dashed the Coach in pieces, and him also, he lived in the yeare of the world, 2743.

21 *The Louer wounded, &c.*] The title is borrowed from the *Handful*, p. 55, "The Louer being wounded with his Ladis beutie, requireth mercy. To the tune of Apelles." Most of the lines are taken either from that poem or from "The complaint of a woman Louer, To the tune of, Raging loue" (*Handful*, pp. 50–51). Compare 39. 28–40. 9 with the *Handful*, lines 1607–1618:

> And since I can no way deuise,
> To stay the rage of my desire,
>   with sighs and trembling tears I craue
>   my deare on me some pitie haue.
> ¶In vewing thee, I tooke such ioy,
> As one that sought his quiet rest:
> Vntill I felt the fethered boy,
> Ay flickring in my captiue brest:
>   Since that time loe, in deepe dispaire,
>   all voide of ioy, my time I weare.

Compare 40.16–41.7 with the *Handful*, lines 1451–1468:

> ¶Like as the simple Turtle true,
> In mourning groanes I spend the day:
> My daily cares night dooth renew,
> To thinke how he did me betray:
>   And when my weary limmes wold rest,
>   My sleepe vnsound hath dreadfull dreams,
> Thus greeuous greefes my hart doth wrest
> That stil mine eies run down like streams:
> ¶And yet, full oft it dooth me good,
> To haunt the place where he hath bcene,
> To kisse the ground whereon he stoode,
> When he (alas) my loue did win.
>   To kisse the Bed wheron we laye?
>   Now may I thinke vnto my paine,
>   O blisfull place full oft I say:
>   Render to me my loue againe.

NOTES

Compare 41.8–42.11 with the *Handful*, lines 1619–1630:

> ¶The wofull prisoner *Palemon*,
> And *Troylus* eke kinge *Pyramus* sonne,
> Constrained by loue did neuer mone:
> As I my deer for thee haue done.
>   Let pitie then requite my paines,
> My life and death in thee remaines.
> ¶If constant loue may reape his hire,
> And faith vnfained may purchace:
> Great hope I haue to my desire.
> Your gentle hart wil grant me grace,
>   Til then (my deer) in few words plaine,
> In pensiue thoughts I shall remaine.

For the tune of *Where is the life that late I led* (which is derived from a lost ballad referred to in *The Taming of the Shrew*, IV, i, 143, and in *2 Henry IV*, V, iii, 147) see my discussion in the *Handful*, pp. 88 f.

40. 33 *clot of clay*] The ground of the place where the lovers first met.

41. 8 *Monsier dom Dieg*] Cf. Alexander Craig, *The Pilgrime and Heremite*, 1631 (Hunterian Club ed., p. 8):

> For *Don-Diëgo* had died in Desart,
> Wert not *Rodorico* did him there convert.
>   Thus, it may fall so,
>   That I thy *Rodorico*,
>   May finde ease to thy woe,
> And heale thy hurt Heart.

The story of Dom Diego was familiar because of its appearance in William Painter's *Palace of Pleasure*, 1567 (vol. II, novel 29). The argument, as given in Joseph Haslewood's edition (1813, II, 490), runs as follows:

Dom Diego a gentleman of Spayne fell in loue with fayre Gineura, and she with him: their loue by meanes of one that enuied Dom Diego his happy choyse, was by default of light credit on hir part interrupted. He constant of mynde, fell into despayre, and abandoninge all his frends and liuing, repayred to the Pyrene Mountaynes, where he led a sauage lyfe for certayne monethes, and afterwardes knowne by one of hys freendes, was (by marueylous circumstaunce) reconciled to hys froward mistresse, and maryed.

This story is told also by Bandello (*Novelle*, pt. I, novel 27), by Belleforest (I, 382), by Sir Geoffrey Fenton (*Certaine Tragicall Discourses*, 1567, fols.

NOTES

265ff.), and by George Whetstone (*The Rocke of Regard*, 1576, pt. II, Collier's reprint, pp. 93–104). Fenton calls the heroine "Genivera," Whetstone "Genevora" and once "Genevra." Cf. also Richard Linche's *Diella. Certain Sonnets, adjoined to the amorous Poem of Dom Diego and Gyneura*, 1596 (Arber's *English Garner*, VII, 185–240).

 9 *Priams noble sonne*] Troilus.

 12 *Romeus*] The poet's knowledge of this story no doubt came from Arthur Brooke's *Tragicall Historye of Romeus and Iuliet* (1562) and from Painter's *Palace of Pleasure*. The first ballad on this subject seems to have been "A newe ballad of Romeo and Juliett," which was licensed on August 5, 1596 (Arber's *Transcript*, III, 68), after Shakespeare's tragedy had been performed. Romeo and Juliet are mentioned in the *Handful*, p. 45, and in *A poore Knight his Pallace*, 1579, B3ᵛ, E2ᵛ.

 44. 3 *eache thing, &c.*] This 'stanza' appears to lack four lines; but actually the poem is written in iambic septenary couplets, and the division into stanzas was made arbitrarily by the printer.

 19 *threatned mee to die*] 'Threatened me with dying, or with death.'

 45. 2 *The desperate Louer*] Eight of the ten stanzas of this poem, under the title "The louer refused of his loue imbraceth death," are printed among the works of "Uncertain Authors" in Tottel's *Miscellany*, pp. 168–169. Tottel's (*T*) omits lines 24–27 and 40–43 of the present version, and has as its fourth stanza (that is, between lines 15 and 16 of this version) the lines that make up the seventh stanza (lines 28–31) here. All other variations, except those of mere orthography, are pointed out below. Perhaps Proctor followed a manuscript or a broadside copy rather than any edition of Tottel's *Miscellany*:

  4 *ioyful dayes bee*] youthfull yeres are *T*
  5 *pleasant yeres be*] ioyfull dayes are *T*
  8 *all is*] ioyes are *T*
  10 *Desireth*] Desirous *T*
  13 *in middest of*] amids the *T*
  15 *most I doo*] is my most *T*
  16 *that*] how *T*
  19 *seeketh*] sekes *T*
  29 *death*] life *T*
  31 *I see*] That is *T*. *cruell*] deadly *T*
  32 *would you*] will ye *T*

NOTES

45. 33 *would*] will *T*
    34 *shee*] you *T*
    36 *by*] with *T*
    38 *would*] will *T*

46. 14 *whom shame did force, &c.*] The phrase is pleonastic. The lines mean, 'If thy heart is angry towards him to flee from whose faith (or constancy) shame once compelled thee.'

20-21 *But hindre him in loue ... thy due disdain*] A very difficult passage, which apparently means something like this: 'But do you (imperative) hinder (thwart, deny) in love him who hinders (doth refrayne) all others, him whose treachery once procured for me thy disdain.' Obviously the lover is asking his lady not to favor some rival who has told her a false tale which caused her to repulse her lover when, in reality, he was faithful.

26 *tickle stay*] 'Inconstant state.' Cf. Heywood's *Works*, 1562, p. 157:

> Time is tickell.
> Chaunce is fickell.
> Man is brickell.

47. 27 *Of a happy wished time*] Under the title of "Time trieth truth" this poem is printed among the works of "Uncertain Authors" in Tottel's *Miscellany*, p. 168. The variations between the two texts are so numerous that I reprint the whole of Tottel's text:

> Eche thing I se hath time which time must trye my truth,
> Which truth deserues a special trust, on trust gret frendship groweth
> And frendship may not faile where faithfulnesse is founde,
> And faithfulnesse is ful of frute, and fruteful thinges be sounde.
> And sound is good at proufe, and proufe is prince of praise,
> And precious praise is such a pearle as seldome ner decayes.
> All these thinges time tries forth, which time I must abide,
> How shold I boldly credite craue till time my truth haue tryed.
> For as I found a time to fall in fansies frame,
> So I do wishe a lucky time for to declare the same.
> If hap may answere hope and hope may haue his hire,
> Then shall my hart possesse in peace the time that I desire.

28 *Eche thing must haue a time*] Cf. Ecclesiastes, iii. 1–8; John Skelton, "On Tyme" (*Poetical Works*, ed. Dyce, 1856, I, 160–161),

> Ye may here now, in this ryme,
> How euery thing must haue a tyme.

NOTES

32 *The sound*] Park suggests — with good reason, as Tottel's text shows — the reading *And sound*.

48. 21–22 *To aske and to obtayne, that Fortune were so swifte . . . gyfte*] Perhaps *so* should be *too*. Then the lines would mean, 'To ask and at once to obtain, that fortune were too swift, for unto each noble gift the ready way is to labor.'

25 *with sad aduice*] I. e., with serious consideration or thought. The lover means that he is seriously determined to hope.

28 *constre*] Construe. Cf. Lyly, *Euphues and his England*, 1580 (*Works*, II, 129), "The Gentlewomen clustred about them both . . . to hear how cunningly *Philautus* could conster"; George Peele, *The Arraignment of Paris*, 1584, II, i (*Works*, ed. Bullen, I, 27), "We must not conster hereof as you mean, But take the sense as it is plainly meant."

30 *The*] Read ¶The.

49. 12 *eefe*] I. e., eath (easy). This is the only example of the word given in the *N. E. D.*

50. 20 *A due*] I. e., adieu.

51. 3 *stormes faire calmes haue brought*] Cf. Thomas Usk, *The Testament of Love*, ca. 1387, I, v, 88 (Skeat's Chaucer, VII, 23), "After grete stormes the weder is often mery and smothe"; Sir Thomas Wyatt, *Poems* (ed. A. K. Foxwell, I, 157), "After great stormes the cawme retornis, And plesanter it is thereby"; John Redford, *The Moral Play of Wit and Science* (ed. Halliwell, Shakespeare Society, 1848, p. 45), "After stormy clowdes cumth wether clere"; Lyly, *Euphues and his England*, 1580 (*Works*, II, 130), "Fayre weather commeth after a foule storme"; Camden's *Proverbs*, p. 318, "After a storm comes a calm"; *Othello*, II, i, 187 f., "If after every tempest come such calms, May the winds blow till they have waken'd death!"; Matthew Henry's commentary on Acts, ix. 31, "After a storm comes a calm." See also *Piers Ploughman*, C, passus XXI, 456 f.; H. L. Collmann, *Ballads and Broadsides*, Roxburghe Club, 1912, p. 74; *Roxburghe Ballads*, I, 127; *Mirror for Magistrates*, ed. Haslewood, I, 299; and 11.37.

4 *After sharp showres, the sunne shyneth*] Cf. Charles Kingsley, *Dolcino to Margaret*:

>The world goes up and the world goes down,
> And the sunshine follows the rain.

[167]

NOTES

George Whetstone (*The Rocke of Regard*, 1576, Collier's reprint, p. 105) says that "after stormes wee may some sunne shine see."

51. 19 *Ryuers scarce will quenche*] Cf. *3 Henry VI*, IV, viii, 7–8:

> A little fire is quickly trodden out;
> Which, being suffer'd, rivers cannot quench.

27 *may deuorce, and lay*] 'May be divorced (removed) and laid.'

52. 2 *The Louer wisheth, &c.*] This poem is borrowed from the *Paradise*, 1576, F3ᵛ, where it is signed "M. B.," that is, Master Bewe (whoever *he* may have been). The *Paradise* version has only ten lines, which differ in many particulars from the present text. It runs thus:

> I Would to God I were *Acteon*, that *Diana* did disguise,
> To walke the Forest vp and doune, whereas my ladie lies:
> An Harte of heere and hewe, I wishe that I were so,
> So that my Ladie knewe me, onely, and no mo.
> The shalyng Nutts and Maste, that falleth from the tree,
> Should well suffice for my repast, might I my ladie see:
> It should not greeue me, there in frost, to lye vpon the grounde,
> Delite should easly quite the coste, what euill so that I founde.
> Sometyme that I might saie, when I sawe her alone,
> Beholde, see yonder slaue aldaie, that walketh the woodds alone.
>   Finis.   M. B.

Proctor may have inserted the poem in the *Gorgeous Gallery* from memory, or perhaps he followed a manuscript copy.

12 *shaling nuts*] This is the only example of an adjective *shaling* given in the *N. E. D.*, where the meaning suggested is "falling from the husk as ripe." The word had, however, as appears from the preceding note, occurred in the 1576 edition of the *Paradise;* and occasionally "shale" is found as an intransitive verb, — cf. William Corkine, *Ayres*, 1610, No. vii (E. H. Fellowes, *English Madrigal Verse*, 1920, p. 391), "Shall beauty shale upon the ground?" The transitive "shale" (to remove husks or shells) is not uncommon.

17–18 *Arthur Fletchar*] I have been unable to trace this person.

20 *Mids Ditis dennes*] 'Amidst the dens, or caves, of Dis (Pluto).' Cf. W. A.'s *Speciall Remedie*, 1579, B3ᵛ, "most famous men . . . Whose deedes remaine in depth of *Ditis* Den"; and Thomas Lodge's *Scillaes Metamorphosis*, 1589, C4 (*Works*, ed. Hunterian Club, vol. I), "*Furie* and *Rage*, *Wan-hope*, *Dispaire*, and *Woe* From *Ditis* den by *Ate* sent, drewe nie."

NOTES

20 *Erebus Dames*] The Gorgons. Cf. *Aeneid*, VI, 289, "Gorgones Harpyaeque et forma tricorporis umbrae."

21 *thy monstrous mates*] I. e., the other Gorgons.

53. 5 *hath pearst in earth,*] The comma should be after *pearst* (i. e., struck through) instead of after *earth*.

9 *The craggy Rocks . . . once is rend*] 'Even the craggy rocks and the sturdiest oaks are (shall be inevitably) one day stark (i. e., utterly) rotten and rent asunder.' For the phrase "craggy rocks" cf. *Handful*, pp. 55, 74.

10 *payd*] *Payd all* would improve the metre.

13 *A Lady writeth, &c.*] Note that this poem is in *ottava rima*, a form introduced into English from the Italian by Wyatt and Surrey.

19–22 *What cruelty? . . . ballance lay*] The meaning seems to be: 'Whatever cruelty, whatever trustless treason was ever heard in any tragical complaint, — all was less than this (of yours), if I may weigh my deserts against yours.' This paraphrase, however, ignores *iust* (line 19). Professor Kittredge suggests the reading *trustles treasons lust* (not *iust*), meaning 'delight in trustless treason,' — a suggestion that seems to me to offer the only solution of this difficult passage.

23–26 *Wherfore . . . genorositie*] The meaning is: 'Wherefore, unkind one, — since there is no wight alive worthier in prowess or beauty, or any that in comely port and nobility of lineage approaches thee by much (i. e., even afar off), — why dost thou,' etc.

28 *serbillitie*] This word is not given in the *N. E. D.* I presume it is a misprint for *stability*, which fits the sense. Park altered it to *servillitie*.

31 *F iii*] Read G iij.

54. 2 *write ye*] Read wit ye.

16 *The heauens iustles, &c.*] 'I will say that the heavens are without justice in case that on me (for my faithful love) they show a so-called just revenge.'

18–19 *that monstrous vice Ingratitude*] A good, quotable phrase, like Byron's "low vice, curiosity," and Shakespeare's "formal vice, iniquity."

20 *Angell of great price*] Lucifer. Cf. 1 Timothy, iii. 6.

23–25 *bend . . . send . . . mend*] This rhyme violates the scheme of the *ottava rima*.

28 *I meane it not*] A line is missing here, as the rhyming scheme proves. It was no doubt dropped by the compositor. The omission is noticed by Park also, but not by Collier or the Roxburghe Club.

NOTES

54. 30 *must*] Read muse (i. e., wonder), *to rhyme with* accuse (line 27) and with the word in the line omitted after line 28.

55. 2–5 *I will . . . dayes*] As the rhyme shows, *will* (line 2) should be omitted. The passage means: 'But I will not willingly (forsake) thee, no matter what trials I have to submit to; yet, in order to escape this hard hap and trouble, I can and will end these doleful days of mine.'

6 *In onely way*] The reading probably should be *I onely way* (i. e., weigh, consider); that is, 'all that daunts me is the thought of dying while in your disfavor.'

11 *The Louer vnto his Lady beloued*] This poem is written in four iambic pentameter quatrains plus a concluding couplet, thus bearing some resemblance to the eighteen-line "sonnets" that make up Thomas Watson's *Hekatompathia* (1582).

16 *Wisdoms watch*] Read Wisdoms match (i. e., 'because you are her match in wisdom').

20 *so much worth*] The sense requires *so much are worth* or *are so much worth*, either of which would fit the metre.

21 *thy proofe I know, the trusty waight*] '(Unlike the gods) I know thy proof (know thee by experience), I know thy trusty weight (the value to be put on you).'

22 *Of Tygars milke, thou fostred wert*] Cf. 60. 2 n.

23 *Cipres Well*] "Cypris' [i. e., Venus's] well," with its "infected poyson colde," is, I suppose, the fountain of bitter water in Venus's garden of which Apuleius tells in his story of Cupid and Psyche. Some readers may like to be reminded of "Vilikins and his Dinah" (*Christy's Plantation Melodies*, No. 5 [1856], pp. 11–12):

> As Villikens was a-walking the garding all round,
> He spied his dear Dinah laying dead on the ground;
> A bottle of *cold poison* lay down by her side,
> And a billet-dux, which said— 'twas by poison she died.
>   Singing, Tu-ra-li, &c.

For *chaung of fraight* perhaps we should read *chaunges fraight* (i. e., fraught).

26 *Narcissus*] A book on the Narcissus story was printed in English in 1560. Part of a ballad on the same subject is preserved in the *Handful*, pp. 29–31.

28 *Of thine owne, from others flame to swell*] "Some word must be missing here"(Park). Perhaps the line should be, *Of thine owne flame*, etc. Instead of *swell* the rhyme leads one to expect *swelt.*

56. 2 *The Louer, &c.*] An interesting example of a sonnet of the so-called English, or Shakespearean, type, — a type introduced by Henry Howard, Earl of Surrey. Its presence here seems to have escaped notice. See also 69. 2 n.

6 *shee*] Diana.

7 *Hart . . . did shunne*] 'A hart that her coy beauty did shun.'

8 *shee whose blud*] Polyxena. Cf. 14. 36 n.

9 *Whose face*] *Read* Nor shee whose face. I do not know to whom this amended line refers, — possibly to Ariadne.

10 *shee that wan, &c.*] 'She that won by means of the judgment of Paris,' namely Venus.

12 *shee whose eyes*] Cressida. Cf. 12. 29 n.

13 *that knew in loue no law*] According to Chaucer (but not Boccaccio), Troilus had never been in love until he saw Cressida (*Troilus*, I, st. 29).

21 *Behold you Dames* $\overset{t}{y}$ *raigne in fames*] Similarly, Stephen Peele's "Proper New Balade Expressyng the Fames" (J. P. Collier's *Old Ballads*, p. 53, Percy Society, vol. I, and H. L. Collmann's *Ballads and Broadsides*, No. 71, Roxburghe Club, 1912) begins:

> You London dames whose passing fames
> Through all the worlde is spread.

27 *In forhed, &c.*] The line should be punctuated thus: *In forhed feature beareth brunt; in face, &c.* The meaning is, 'In her forehead shapeliness is preëminent.'

28 *in shape is shame*] I suppose that *shame* means *modesty:* 'she has a modest figure,' — to say nothing of her lively looks and high-colored cheeks!

57. 8 *her saying late set forth*] Her "saying" was a motto, or device, or posy, "I burn and cannot flee"; and it was "set forth" (put into circulation), not by her, but by one of her admirers in a poem which was meant to be laudatory but which the author of the present ditty thinks did her injustice.

10 *Shee is none such . . . would disdayne*] 'She is no such person as, even if she wished, could disdain anybody.'

NOTES

57. 12 *lothe of any lyfe*] 'Loath that any life.'

14 *M, her brest*] M.'s breast. There is a poem called "A praise of m[istress]. M." in Tottel's *Miscellany*, p. 266, that may have suggested this production.

17 *The Louer deceyued, &c.*] As Mr. Charles Crawford points out in his edition of *Englands Parnassus* (1913, pp. xviii–xix), this poem — or, more accurately, the first two stanzas of it — appears also in *A light Bondell of liuly discourses called Churchyardes Charge*, 1580 (Collier's reprint, pp. 51–52). Churchyard's poem, "A Farewell to a Fondlyng," runs thus:

> The heate is past that did me fret,
> The fire is out that nature wrought;
> The plants of love, which youth did set,
> Are drie and dedde within my thought:
> The frost hath kilde the kindly sappe
> Whiche kept the harte in livly state;
> The sodaine stormes and thonder clappe
> Hath tourned love to mortall hate.
>
> The miste is gone that bleard myne eyes,
> The lowryng clouds I see appere:
> Although the blinde eats many flies,
> I would she knewe my sight is clere.
> Her sweete, disceivyng, flattryng face
> Did make me thinke the crowe was white:
> I muse how she had sutche a grace
> To seeme a hauke, and be a kite.

There seems to be no reason for denying Churchyard's authorship of the poem as it stands in the *Gorgeous Gallery*.

29 *the blinde eate many flyes*] Proverbial. "Bewar therfore; the blinde et many a fly," is the refrain of "A Balade: warning Men to Beware of Deceitful Women," by John Lydgate (Skeat's Chaucer, VII, 295). Cf. *The Image of Ypocresye*, 1533 (*Ballads from Manuscripts*, ed. F. J. Furnivall, I, 182, 224), "with Twenty thousand lyes, Do make the blind Eate flyes," "The blind men Eat vpp flees"; J. G. Nichols, *Narratives of the Reformation* (Camden Society), p. 202, "The blynd dothe eate manye a flye"; *Bannatyne MS.*, 1568 (Hunterian Club ed., IV, 751), "God wait the blind eitis mony a fle"; Lyly, *Euphues*, 1579 (*Works*, I, 214, cf. II, 63), "the blinde man doth eate many a Fly"; Gabriel Harvey, *Pierces Supererogation*, 1593 (*Works*, ed. Grosart, II, 138), "blind men swallow-downe many

NOTES

flyes"; *Englishmen for My Money*, 1597 (Dodsley-Hazlitt, *Old Plays*, X, 503), "Sometimes the blind may catch a hare. — Ay, sir, but he will first eat many a fly." "The Blynd eates many a fly" is the title of a ballad that was registered for publication on April 12, 1627 (Arber's *Transcript*, IV, 176; *Roxburghe Ballads*, VIII, 683); a play of the same title is mentioned in Philip Henslowe's *Diary* (ed. W. W. Greg, II, 233) during the year 1602–1603. See further John Skelton's *Works*, ed. Alexander Dyce, I, 239; Heywood's *Works*, 1562, pp. 60, 153, 166; Robert Greene's *Works*, ed. Grosart, VIII, 81, XI, 150, 159; and Camden's *Proverbs*, p. 332.

32 *that you were white*] 'That you were gracious, or favorable.' Cf. Chaucer's *Troilus*, III, stanza 224, "ye caused al this fare . . . for alle your wordes whyte." Most probably, however, *that you* is a misprint for *the crow* (the reading given in the stanza quoted above from *Churchyardes Charge*), as the two following lines show clearly that the author had birds in mind. To make one think a crow white was a proverbial expression. See 97. 5 n.

58. 3 *seeme a Hauke, and bee a kyte*] I. e., to seem of a noble disposition, like a falcon, and in reality to be as base as a vulture.

4–11 *Where precious ware, &c.*] A highly sententious stanza, the style of which is strongly suggestive of Thomas Churchyard (cf. 57. 17 n.). Several of the lines ought to have become proverbial sayings.

21 *A true description of Loue*] This poem was presumably intended to be a sonnet, though it has a curious rhyme-scheme of three quatrains plus a couplet, all with interlinking rhymes (*abbaabbaabbabb*).

22 *Aske what loue is? . . . passion*] *Passion* is trisyllabic; *occasion* in line 29 is tetrasyllabic. For a discussion of Elizabethan definitions of love see C. R. Baskervill, "Bassanio as an Ideal Lover," *The Manly Anniversary Studies in Language and Literature*, 1923, pp. 95 ff.

31 ff. *Where wee therby . . . cheefly on denaye*] Mr. Kittredge notes that *leaue* (line 32) is a misprint for *leane*, and solves the riddle of these puzzling lines in this illuminating paraphrase: 'We thereby are subject to the law (control) of those (i. e., women) whose frailty is such that they ought to lean upon our support; (as would be the condition of things) in case we had not acquired the custom of praying for hope and health to such creatures as have their chief glory in denying men's prayers!'

59. 11 *No minde of malice I protest*] 'I protest that (in thus accusing you) I have no malicious intent.' The author means that he is forced against his will to tell the truth.

NOTES

59. 16 *Vlisses wife*] Cf. 15. 2, 64. 16 n; *Handful*, p. 63 n. In his conversations with William Drummond, Ben Jonson told this anecdote: "A Gentleman reading a poem [Sir John Davies's *Orchestra*, 1596] that began with

> Wher is that man that never yet did hear
> Of fair Penelope, Ulisses Queene?

calling his Cook, asked If he had ever hard of her? Who ansuering, No, demonstrate to him,

> Lo, ther the man that never yet did hear
> Of fair Penelope, Ulisses Queene!"

See *Conversations*, ed. R. F. Patterson, 1923, p. 44. By *mate the sore* the *Gallery* poet means 'sorely subdue thee,' i. e., make you bitterly ashamed of your faithlessness.

16 *wishly*] Possibly this is a form of *wistly* (i.e., mute, silent); but I believe, with Park, that it is a misprint for *wifely*. In John Phillip's *Patient Grissell* (1566) the phrase *wifly troth* occurs five or six times.

23 *borne is bond by kinde*] I. e., is born to a natural condition of bondage or slavery.

24 *Doth not, &c.*] This line should for uniformity be a septenary instead of an Alexandrine.

60. 2 *Tygars whelpe*] A very common figure. Cf. 55.22, 74.10; and Tottel's *Miscellany*, p. 56 (also pp. 80, 140, 259),

> For though hard rockes among
> She semes to haue bene bred:
> And of the Tigre long
> Bene nourished, and fed.

The ultimate source of the figure (cf. the *Handful*, p. 55) is the *Aeneid*, IV, 365–367, where Dido reproaches Aeneas:

> Nec tibi diva parens, generis nec Dardanus auctor,
> Perfide, sed duris genuit te cautibus horrens
> Caucasus, Hyrcanaeque admorunt ubera tigres.

19 *ye Sisters*] The Fates. Cf. 35. 31–33 n.

25 *And that eche*] *And that eche one* would make the rhythm more regular, but it is not necessary.

NOTES

26 *hath*] I. e., may have.

61. 2 *did I write*] *Read* did write.

5 *bring the newes*] 'Bring thee news.'

7 *hee*] The spirit of the dead lover.

11 *flying fame*] A ballad-tune of this name is often met with. See Chappell's *Popular Music*, I, 198; and 120. 16.

14 *this Letter red*] 'This letter having been read'; though *red* could also be an imperative.

15 *thou wilt the same*] I. e., thou wilt wish to burn the letter.

16 *they*] People in general, visitors to the tomb. But probably *they* should be *thou*.

18 *graunt mee this*] *This* is the prayer, given in line 19, which the lover wants his lady to pray in behalf of his soul.

23 *so will*] These words should be omitted to restore the pentameter movement of the *ottava rima*.

29–30 *rocke . . . ply . . . one inche*] This reminds one of Scott's *Lady of the Lake*, canto V, stanza 10:

> Come one, come all! this rock shall fly
> From its firm base as soon as I.

31 *A file, &c.*] A new stanza should begin here.

62. 3 *When Ryuers take their course, &c.*] Cf. 12. 22 n.

4 *for better or for worse*] A more or less proverbial phrase influenced by its occurrence in the Book of Common Prayer. Cf. also Thomas Deloney, *Thomas of Reading*, ca. 1598 (*Works*, ed. F. O. Mann, p. 244), "Be it better, or be it worse, Please you the man that beares the purse." This same proverb is repeated also in John Taylor the Water Poet's *Epigrammes*, 1651, A5ᵛ, and — with slight variations — in Camden's *Proverbs*, p. 319.

10 *than that, which*] The rhythm would profit by the omission of two of these words. *That which* could be omitted without affecting the meaning.

17 *prise*] A line is missing after *prise*, so that lines 17–20 (as numbered in my text) are unintelligible. The omission is noticed by Park, but not by Collier or the Roxburghe Club.

18 *septier*] This word (for *sceptre*) is here trisyllabic.

25–28 *My hart like Waxe . . . your Image to pourtray*] To make sense of this passage, *of* in line 27 must be emended to *or* and *best* in line 28 to *rest*: 'being like wax, my heart did not easily submit to more than one

NOTES

stroke before Cupid succeeded in taking away (from it) one splinter or scale, the rest being left with your image portrayed on it.' The poet means that with one stroke Cupid chiselled his lady's image on his soft heart; that the stroke took away a little piece of his heart, but the part that remains is stamped with her image.

62. 29 *desendeth*] Read defendeth (with Park, Collier, and the Roxburghe Club).

63. 3 *Those peeces somewhat, you resemble shall*] This conceit is practically duplicated by Michael Drayton, John Donne, and Abraham Cowley. In "The Heart," 1619 (*Minor Poems*, ed. Cyril Brett, 1907, p. 63), Drayton writes:

> Madame, two Hearts we brake,
> And from them both did take
> The best, one Heart to make. . . .
>
> Were it cymented, or sowne,
> By Shreds or Pieces knowne,
> We each might find our owne.

In "The Broken Heart," lines 23–32, Donne (*Poems*, ed. H. J. C. Grierson, I, 48) declares:

> Love, alas,
> At one first blow did shiver it as glasse.
>
> Yet nothing can to nothing fall,
>   Nor any place be empty quite,
> Therefore I thinke my breast hath all
>   Those peeces still, though they be not unite;
> And now as broken glasses show
> A hundred lesser faces, so
>   My ragges of heart can like, wish, and adore,
>   But after one such love, can love no more.

So, in "The Heart-breaking," Cowley (*Poems*, ed. A. R. Waller, p. 127) says:

> And now (alas) each little broken part
>   Feels the whole pain of all my *Heart:*
>   And every smallest corner still
> *Lives* with that torment which the *Whole* did *kill.*

8 *raste*] Read rafte (i. e., took away, plundered).

NOTES

9 *Surrey*] Henry Howard, Earl of Surrey, whose poems were familiar through their inclusion in Tottel's *Miscellany*.

12 *a staming stock*] A fine or excellent stem (as of a plant or tree). So the word *stamming* is defined in the *N. E. D.*, which cites no other instance of its use earlier than 1800. The definition seems to me very doubtful, but I have nothing better to suggest.

15 *flowing dew so sweete*] A figurative expression for his speech, which was sweet like honey-dew. Compare the description of Nestor's talk given in the *Iliad*, I, 249.

19 *Hectors sister*] On Polyxena cf. 14. 36 n.

26 *That D, should . . . the Aple haue*] Gascoigne, in the "seconde songe" of his *Grief of Joy* (1576, st. 4), applies this idea to Queen Elizabeth; and George Peele also, in his play *The Arraignment of Paris* (1584), makes Venus, Pallas, and Juno mutually agree to give the golden apple to the one mortal who far surpasses them in beauty, Elizabeth. Likewise in a ballad by Nicholas Udall (*Ballads from Manuscripts*, ed. Furnivall, I, 397 f.) which was sung before Anne Boleyn on her coronation-day in May, 1533, Paris is represented as giving the apple for beauty direct to that Queen.

29 *seemely spaste*] 'Suitably (or beautifully) spacious (high).'

30 *beame*] The reading *beames* might be expected.

64. 2 *I feare . . . further wade*] This line is rhythmically defective. The required hexameter movement would be restored by the reading, *I feare Promethius fall, I dare no further wade*.

3 *Whom loue embraced with the shape, &c.*] 'Whom (i. e., Prometheus) love for the shape (i. e., man) that he had so finely made embraced, or captivated.' The poet means that, just as Prometheus felt for the beautiful creature, man, whom he had created, so great a love that in trying to help him he was driven from heaven, so he (the poet) in creating in his verse a similarly beautiful image may experience a like punishment.

7 *other Dames*] Some such reading as *other Dames who do* is necessary to fit the metrical scheme.

8 *slights that flame*] Collier and the Roxburghe Club read *flights that flame*, a reading to which the alliteration lends countenance. But *slights* (i. e., sleights, tricks) makes good sense.

9 *of Natures case*] Probably *case* is a misprint for *care:* the "other Dames" complain that Nature took care to make Mistress D. beautiful but had small regard for them.

NOTES

64. 15 *gendred was of Ioue his braines*] 'Was engendered of Jove's brains.' Cf. 15. 4 n.

16 *Vlisses wyfe*] Cf. 59. 16 n. An early sixteenth-century ballad on Penelope, and the music for it, are preserved in MS. Egerton 2009, fol. 39^v.

17 *in ventring of the same*] 'If Penelope wished to venture a contest on the subject of chastity, she should be equalled, yea indeed surpassed, by D.' In *Have With You to Saffron-Walden*, 1596 (*Works*, ed. McKerrow, III, 112, cf. IV, 358), Nashe refers to Lycophron, "who, notwithstanding *Homers* praises of her [i. e., Penelope], saith shee lay with all her wooers"; and the same year Thomas Willoby ("The victorie of English Chastitie," *Willobie his Avisa*, ed. Grosart, 1880, Hughes, 1904, p. 156), says that

> Some greatly doubt your *Grecian* dame
> Where [= whether] all be true that Poets faine. . . .
> Where old Penelops doubtfull fame,
> *Selfe Chastity* may put to shame.

18 *Lucresse*] Ballads called "the grevious complaynt of Lucrece" and "the Death of Lucryssia," registered in 1568–1569 and 1569–1570 (Arber's *Transcript*, I, 379, 416), had made the story of the rape of Lucrece familiar before the date of the *Gorgeous Gallery*.

28 *Thesiphon*] To Tisiphone, one of the Furies, the poet apparently assigns the duty (of cutting the thread of life) that Atropos (cf. line 26), one of the Fates, performed.

32 *Lesse hatred cannot want, &c.*] Mr. Kittredge explains the passage thus: 'Less hatred cannot be lacking (i. e., no less hatred must exist in the minds of those ladies whom I have judged inferior to D.) than the hatred that inspired Juno, though they have less power to revenge than Juno had.' In line 33 *she* would fit the sense better than *they* does.

34 *if it were like*] I. e., like the might of Juno against Troy.

35 *Ouid . . . whose greefe by Muses grew*] The poet adopts the view that Ovid's poems were the actual, as they were the alleged, reason for his exile. According to Henry Crosse (*Vertues Common-wealth*, 1603, Q3, ed. Grosart, p. 121), "*Ouid* for his wanton *Ars amandi*, was exiled by *Augustus*." But Nashe in 1592 (*Works*, ed. McKerrow, I, 286) wrote: "*Ouid* once saw *Augustus* in a place where he would not haue beene seene; he was exilde presently." The real cause of the exile is unknown.

NOTES

65. 3 *I Spake . . . to gayne*] 'I spoke (asked a lady's favor) to prosper in my suit, although I meant it not (i. e., wasn't sincere).'

5 *would writh w̃ the wind*] This probably means, 'I found (that one lady) of whom I had no such fear would change as the wind changes'; i. e., I found mutability in a woman of whom I expected constancy.

7–8 *Nothing in which . . . beauty but rustie*] Unintelligible. Line 7 is defective.

16 *In vsing for pleasure, &c.*] I can make no meaning out of this line. Another word seems to be required by the metre, unless *pleasure* is pronounced in three syllables or *beates* in two.

17 *in byrding, to beat well the bush*] Cf. John Heywood, *Works*, 1562, p. 7, "And while I at length debate and beate the bushe, There shall steppe in other men, and catche the burdes"; Spenser, *The Shepherds' Calendar*, 1579 ("October," line 17), "I beate the bush, the byrds to them doe flye"; Thomas Watson, *Hekatompathia*, 1582, "sonnet" xlviii, 2, "When *Birders* beate the bush"; "The Lover's Complaint," *ca.* 1620 (*Roxburghe Ballads*, II, 309 f.), "Hard hap had I to beate the bush, And another to catch the bird," "He still doth beate the bush, Although the bird be lost"; John Taylor the Water Poet, *Bull, Beare, and Horse*, 1638, A6 (*Works*, ed. Spenser Society, vol. III), "Yet *some may Catch the Bush, some beat the Birds.*" See also the *Handful*, p. 109.

19 *try ere I trust*] A very common proverb. Cf. 69.10, 100.3; *Handful*, p. 105; Ecclesiasticus, vi. 7, xxxvii. 4.

20 *I finde iust*] I. e., people who are just.

21 *I iet not*] 'I do not revel or go proudly.' Cf. Nicholas Breton, *A Floorish upon Fancie*, 1582 (ed. Park, pp. 5, 75), "To jet in brave attire, to please their mistris eye," "Take delight to jet in brave attire"; *Shirburn Ballads* (ed. Andrew Clark, p. 51), "in Jigges and Jagges we iet it out."

21 *Geminie, Tawre*] Gemini and Taurus, the zodiacal signs, are introduced without meaning, solely because of the alliteration.

22 *In bluttring who bleares mee? I leaue them with Lawre*] "This line must be left to some arch expounder of metrical enigmas" (Park). Here again, for the sake of apt alliteration's artful aid, the poet becomes unintelligible. The first half-line may mean, 'In blurting out words who can blear (dim, surpass) me?' Possibly the second half means, 'I leave to them the laurel' (i. e., they win the victory from me).

NOTES

65. 23 *in burning to bight*] An involved statement of a simple proverb. Cf. "Brend child fur dredeth," *Proverbs of Hending*, line 184; "Brent child of fier hath mych drede," *The Romaunt of the Rose*, line 1820 (Chaucer Society, 1891); "The ybernde uer dret," *Ayenbite of Inwyt* (ed. Richard Morris, E.E.T.S., 1866, p. 116); "Brente honde fire dredith," Richard Hill, *Commonplace-Book*, ca. 1536 (ed. Dyboski, E.E.T.S., 1907, p. 129); "For brint barne the fyre ay dreids," Robert Sempill, 1572 (*Satirical Poems*, ed. James Cranstoun, Scottish Text Society, 1891, I, 217); "the burnt childe dreadith fier," Gabriel Harvey (*Works*, ed. Grosart, I, 134), in a letter to Spenser, ca. 1575; "As children brent doe after dread the flame," George Whetstone, *The Rocke of Regard*, 1576 (Collier's reprint, p. 31); "The childe that hath burnte his fingers, dreades the candle," *The Passionate Morrice*, 1593 (ed. Furnivall, New Shakspere Society, 1876, p. 74); "Brunt bairn with fyre the danger dreidis," Alexander Montgomerie, *The Cherrie and the Slae*, 1597 (*Poems*, ed. Cranstoun, Scottish Text Society, 1887, p. 17); "The burnt child dreads the fire," Ben Jonson, *The Devil is an Ass*, 1616, I, ii. See, further, Lilly's *Ballads*, p. 114; Lyly's *Euphues and his England*, 1580 (*Works*, II, 92); *Alcilia*, 1595, G4ᵛ (ed. Grosart, 1879, p. 56); Camden's *Proverbs*, pp. 320, 332; R. C.'s *Times Whistle*, 1616 (E.E.T.S., 1871, p. 102).

25 *Forseeing the weede, &c.*] Perhaps he means, 'I foresee (and avoid) the weed (harm in general) and the loss that comes from going on another's bond, and I foresee the futility of plowing the sea, of sowing in sand.' Line 26 is proverbial. Cf. Juvenal, *Satires*, VII, 48-49, "Nos tamen hoc agimus tenuique in pulvere sulcos Ducimus et litus sterili versamus aratro"; Ovid, *Heroides*, V, 115-116, "Quid facis, Oenone? quid arenae semina mandas? Non profecturis litora bubus aras"; Sannazaro, *Arcadia* (1504), eclogue 8,

> Nell' onde solca, e nell' arene semina,
> E 'l vago vento spera in rete accogliere,
> Chi sue speranze fonda in cor di femmina;

Anthony Munday, *A Pleasant Comedy of Two Italian Gentlemen*, 1584, D2 (Malone Society reprint),

> He plowghes the seas, and fishes in the lande,
> And loseth all the labour of them both,
> He fondly reares his fortresse on the sande.
> That buildes his trust vpon a womans troth;

NOTES

Alcilia, 1595, H (ed. Grosart, p. 57),

> He ploughs on sand, and sows vpon the wind,
> That hopes for constant loue in wemenkinde;

Robert Southwell (1560–1595), "Love's Servile Lot" (*Poetical Works*, 1856, p. 65), "Plough not the seas, sow not the sands"; Phineas Fletcher, *Sicelides*, 1614, II, ii, 1 (*Works*, ed. Grosart, 1869, III, 31, cf. pp. 230, 234), "Who sowes the seas, or plowes the easy shore?"

66. 2 *Of patience*] This quatrain is much older than 1578. It is scribbled on the margin of the Durham MS. of Thomas Hoccleve's poems (as Mr. Charles Crawford pointed out in his introduction to *Englands Parnassus*, pp. xvi–xvii), whence it is reprinted in the E.E.T.S. edition of the *Minor Poems* of Hoccleve, p. 224, note. Furnivall, editor of the *Minor Poems*, dated the scribbling "c. 1500?" In the MS. the quatrain runs thus:

> A sufficyent salve for eache disease,
> The cheff revenge for cruell yre,
> Ys patyence, the present ease
> For to delaye eche flamy fyre.

Mr. Crawford remarks that "the date of the scribbling [is] about 1540," as the lines show the influence of Sir Thomas Elyot's *Boke named The Gouernour*. I can trace no such influence, but I presume he refers to this passage (1531 ed., ed. H. H. S. Croft, 1880, II, 277), "Pacience is a noble vertue ... and is the vainquisshour of iniuries, the suer defence agayne all affectes and passions of the soule."

12 *Of will, and reason*] These lines also occur in the Durham MS. mentioned in the foregoing note:

> I count his conquest greate,
> That canne, by reasons scylle,
> Subdue affections heate,
> And conquer wanton wyll.

Sir Thomas Elyot (*op. cit.*, ed. Croft, II, 10) expresses a similar idea,

> If luste or anger do thy mynde assaile,
> Subdue occasion, and thou shalte sone preuaile;

and this couplet appears also in *Englands Parnassus*, 1600 (ed. Crawford, No. 1251).

NOTES

66. 13 *this*] Park's suggestion of *his* is supported by the MS. version quoted above.

26 *Of beauty, and chastity*] There is a poem on this theme in the *Paradise*, 1576, G2. It contains the lines:

> Twixt comelinesse and chastitie,
> A deadly strife is thought to be.

Cf. MS. Sloane 1210, *ca.* 1450 (*Reliquiae Antiquae*, II, 40), "The fayrere woman tho more gyglott"; John Taylor the Water Poet, *Works*, 1630 (Spenser Society reprint, p. 46), "For 'tis a maxime, Those haue euer bin, That are most faire without, most foule within."

67. 20 *And woorthy got to bee retayned*] 'And, once got, it is worthy to be retained.'

34 *A proper Posie*] In *Every Man in his Humour*, II, ii, Ben Jonson satirizes such posies or mottoes as this, in the inscriptions he gives for two rings:

> Though Fancy sleep,
> My love is deep.

> The deeper the sweeter,
> I'll be judg'd by Saint Peter.

68. 2 *The Louer, &c.*] The six-line iambic pentameter stanza (rhyming *ababcc*) in which this poem is written was used by Spenser for the eclogue on January in *The Shepherds' Calendar* (1579) and by Shakespeare in *Venus and Adonis*. Cf. also 72. 9 n., 73. 2 n., 82. 5 n., 94. 2 n., 116. 24 n.

15 *Dedalus, Minotaure*] Cf. 12.7 n.

21 *findes*] A better reading would be *find;* but to grammar the *Gorgeous Gallery* pays slight attention.

69. 2 *How to choose, &c.*] Another example of a "Shakespearean" sonnet. Cf. 56.2 n.

5 *soone repenting proofe*] 'By experience that soon makes one repent.'

10 *Trust not to much, &c.*] Proverbial. Cf. 65.19 n.

18 *The Louer beeing, &c.*] Under the title "Of sufferance cometh ease" (cf. Heywood's *Works*, 1562, pp. 18, 134; Camden's *Proverbs*, 1614, p. 329; Thomas Howell's *H. His Deuises*, 1581, E3^v; Shakespeare's *2 Henry IV*, V, iv, 28), this poem appears in the *Paradise*, 1576, D3^v, over the

NOTES

initials "E. S." (which are usually, but without much warrant, explained as the initials of Dr. Edwin Sandys, Archbishop of York). In all later editions of the *Paradise* (1578–1606) the signature is changed to that of Lord Vaux. The texts, except for two totally different lines, agree fairly well. All the variations between the 1576 edition of the *Paradise* and the present text, save those of spelling and punctuation, are listed in the notes that immediately follow:

22 *when*] where *P*

23 *moodes*] moode *P*.   *when*] where *P*

25 *case*] cause *P*

28 *leuid*] I. e., *levèd*, meaning 'believed in,' 'trusted,' a later use of the word than any given in the *N. E. D.*   *P. has* loued.

29 *that*] the *P*

30 *I wrought but for my freend*] I wrote but for my selfe *P*

31 *As if the troth were truely tryde, by prooft*] As, who would proue extremitie, by proofe *P*. *Prooft* is evidently a misprint, perhaps for *prooff*.

33 *to*] of *P*.   *things proue not as they seeme*] This "olde troth" occurs in Phaedrus's *Fables*, IV, ii, 16, "Non semper ea sunt quae videntur." Cf. Longfellow's *Psalm of Life*, "And things are not what they seem."

70. 2–3 *Wherby ... needeth not to kicke*] 'Whereby it may befall them (the persons just mentioned, who think they can interpret my verses) to be so hasty in judgment as to cause certain persons to be suspected who have no cause to kick.' The author means that persons of whom he isn't thinking at all may object to his verses.

3 *them be suspecte*] them selues suspect *P*

5 *accuse ... may*] amisse ... might *P*

17 *On tops of trees*] W. S. Gilbert has a song ("The First Lord's Song") in which this expression occurs:

> Now, landsmen all, whoever you may be,
> If you want to rise to the top of the tree.

17 *that groundles path*] *Groundles* may be an adverb, and *path* may be a verb, as in *Julius Caesar*, II, i, 83, "For if thou path, thy native semblance on."

28 *On mountaynes high it hath most power*] Proverbial. Cf. 10. 24 n.; Thomas Churchyard, *Shore's Wife*, 1593 (Collier's reprint, — *Illustrations of Old English Literature*, 1866, vol. II, — p. 16), "The winde is great upon

[183]

NOTES

the highest hilles"; George Whetstone, *The Rocke of Regard*, 1576 (Collier's reprint, p. 41), "But highest trees in fine have hardest fall"; Gascoigne, *The Grief of Joy*, 1577 ("fourthe songe," stanza 14), "As highest clymes are most afearde to fall"; Robert Greene, *Philomela*, 1592 (*Works*, ed. Grosart, XI, 192), "The highest trees abide the sharpest stormes."

71. 9 *To helpe the poore, the sicke, the blinde*] Cf. Luke, xiv. 13.

35 *wit*] Read with.

72. 9 *The paynfull plight, &c.*] Another example of the *Venus and Adonis* stanza (cf. 68. 2 n.). Under the title of "Beyng troubled in mynde, he writeth as followeth," and signed with the initials of Jasper Heywood, this poem appears in the *Paradise*, 1576, L3 (Heywood's name is signed in all the other editions from 1578 to 1606). Every variation between the two texts, except those of spelling and punctuation, is given in the notes below:

11 *sweete*] sweate P

12 *which*] that P.   *which doth the same*] I. e., 'which the same doth.'

17 *which*] that P

18 *alwayes*] alwaie P

19 *matched*] mated P. *Mated* (i. e., checkmated, rebuffed) makes better sense than *matched*. This poem is echoed by a piece of Thomas Howell's which begins, "The bitter smarte that straines my mated minde" (*H. His Deuises*, 1581, F4–G, ed. Raleigh, 1906, p. 51).

21 *betwixt*] betwene P

24 *their*] the P

26 *panges*] paines P

27 *hap*] hope P.   *none*] no P

73. 2 *The Louer, &c.*] Written in the *Venus and Adonis* stanza. Cf. 68. 2 n.

6 *vnwillingly*] *Unwilling* would fit the metre better.

9 *lickering*] The *N.E.D.* defines this word as "?lickerish = lustful," but gives no other example of its use.

17 *I tread vpon the snake*] Cf. 79. 32 n.

74. 10 *if thou no tigre bee*] Cf. 60. 2 n.

17 *ensue Eneas race*] 'Imitate the course (action) of Aeneas (in betraying Dido).' *Eneas* is a genitive, and so is *Carthage* in line 21.

21 *from Carthage Queene*] On Dido, cf. 14. 3 n. See note on line 17.

24 *surpassed dayes*] This use of *surpassed* in the meaning of 'bygone' is earlier than the one example given in the *N. E. D.*

[184]

NOTES

75. 10 *Aesons sonne*] Jason.

13 *I should distroy thy seede*] As Medea, when Jason wished to put her aside for Creusa, killed her own children and fled to Athens. Cf. 83. 25 n.

30 *disgest*] Digest, 'stomach.' Cf. *How a Man May Chuse a Good Wife from a Bad*, 1602, A4ᵛ, Dᵛ: "my heart is not so light, It can disgest the least conceit of ioy"; "a husband gaue her words Of great reproofe . . . Which she poore soule disgested patiently."

32 *Baccus beldame Nonne*] "By a learned and reverend friend it has been suggested, that the word *nonne*, alias *nun*, may be here used as a general name for a votary or priestess: one of the titles of the female attendants on the rites of Bacchus being *Mænades*, in the singular *Mænas*, an epithet betokening their frantic or bedlam behaviour, arising from their religious enthusiasm or mania. He therefore supposes 'beldame' to be either a misprint for 'bedlam,' or to be used in an improper sense; as an old hag is frequently called a 'beldam,' in opposition to its original meaning, 'a fine lady'" (Park). Cf. George Turbervile, *Epitaphes*, 1567 (Collier's reprint, 1867, p. 58), "A colde and crooked beldam shalt in lothsome cabbin lie"; and see the description of the Mænads in the *Aeneid*, IV, 300–304.

76. 15 *it is not Italy, as sometimes it hath bin*] 'Italy is not, as formerly it was (e. g., in the days of Aeneas), a place in which to do great deeds.' The wife means that a desire for fame or action is not what has taken her husband to Italy.

77. 11 *They win more fame . . . then those that run away*] An interesting contrast to the familiar proverb, "He who fights and runs away May live to fight another day."

26 *Leanders cunning art*] There were dozens of references to Hero and Leander before the Marlowe-Chapman version of the story appeared (1598). A ballad of "Leanders loue to loyall Hero" (1614) is reprinted in my *Pepysian Garland* (1922), p. 49, where various facts about other ballads on the story are given.

29 *loth to depart*] Because of its frequent use in love-poems, this phrase assumed almost proverbial significance. Cf. *Zepheria*, 1594, canzon 22:

> Well sayd I herein that I did but seeme it,
> (Loth to depart) he still retayn'd to me.

Ballads were often sung to the tune of *Loath to departe* (cf. Clark's *Shirburn Ballads*, p. 354). Music of this name was composed by the celebrated Eliza-

[185]

NOTES

bethan musician John Dowland (cf. Halliwell-Phillipps, *Manuscript Rarities of Cambridge*, p. 8).

77. 33 *Although not so*] 'Although if you don't agree so.'

35 *L iii*] Read K iii.   *Another*] Read An other.

78. 4 *I greet thee well of hartinesse . . . Caruer bee*] 'I greet you well; you may take as much as you like (of my heart and heartiness).'

79. 1 *Pretie pamphlets*] This title may have been suggested by that of Thomas Howell's *New Sonets, and pretie Pamphlets* (ca. 1568), especially since two of the poems in his *Arbor of Amitie* (1568) were appropriated by the compiler of the *Gallery* (see 7. 2 n.). Cf. 36. 14 n.

11 *Learne of the Ant*] Referring to the well-known fable of the grasshopper and the ant. Cf. Proverbs, vi. 6 ff., "Go to the ant," etc.; Tottel's *Miscellany*, p. 138,

> I saw, how that the litle ant in somer still dothe runne
> To seke her foode, wherby to liue in winter for to come.

14 *where worthy honors wun*] That is, *wone* (dwell).

22 *for erring lewd astray*] 'For going astray lewdly (foolishly, ignorantly).'

30 *thought*] Read though.

32 *In greenest Grasse, the lurking Adder lyes*] Cf. 73. 17; Tottel's *Miscellany*, pp. 6, 200, "I know vnder the grene the serpent how he lurkes," "Lurker of kinde like serpent layd to bite"; Lyly, *Euphues*, 1579 (*Works*, I, 202), "Doe we not commonly see . . . that in the greenest grasse is the greatest Serpent?"; *Shirburn Ballads* (ed. Clark, p. 283), "In greenest grasse the Serpent lyes"; *Macbeth*, I, v, 66–67, "Look like the innocent flower, But be the serpent under 't"; Alexander Craig, *Amorose Songes*, 1606 (*Works*, ed. Hunterian Club, H4), "In greenest Grasse the deadly Adder lowrs," "In greenest Grasse lies hid the stinging Adder." The figure occurs also in the *Handful*, p. 10, and at least four times in the *Paradise*, 1576 (B3, C2ᵛ, H2, H3). Its ultimate source is perhaps Virgil's "latet anguis in herba" (*Eclogues*, III, 93). Cf. Thomas Lodge, *Reply to Gosson*, 1580? (*Works*, ed. Hunterian Club, vol. I), p. 32, "*latet anguis in herba*, vnder your fare show of conscience take heede you cloake not your abuse"; and Hodg Turbervil (i. e., Edmund Gayton), *Walk Knaves Walk*, 1659, p. 4, "*Latit Anguis in herba*: that is that Serpent the Devill lurks in their holes."

[186]

NOTES

80. 2 *Inuidus alterius, &c.*] "Invidus alterius macrescit rebus opimis," Horace, *Epistles*, I, ii, 57.

8 *To serue his vse, &c.*] The rhyme shows (as Park noted) that this line should run, *Although hee hath enough to serue his vse.*

11 *Hee thinkes . . . claw*] 'He thinks much of that which he fails to secure.'

12 *And findes . . . hap*] 'And for it (his failure to obtain what he covets) he finds the fault, or blame, in luckless chance.'

25 *our Queene his*] I. e., our Queen's. This old form of the genitive is rendered more unusual by the connection of *his* with a feminine noun, and by the presence of *her* in the same line. Ballads often ended like this poem, with a prayer for the ruling sovereign.

81. 2 *Helen*] This poem is not unusual in theme, but merely follows the Elizabethan convention of treating Helen with scant respect. Similar to it are Proctor's "Helens Complaint" in his *Triumph of Truth, ca.* 1584 (Collier's reprint, — *Illustrations of Old English Literature*, 1866, vol. II, — pp. 23 f.), and Richard Barnfield's *Hellens Rape. Or A light Lanthorne for light Ladies*, 1594 (*Poems*, ed. Arber, pp. 38–40). Cf. also Shakespeare (*The Rape of Lucrece*, lines 1471 f.),

> Show me the strumpet that began this stir,
> That with my nails her beauty I may tear;

and John Taylor the Water Poet (*Works*, 1630, Spenser Society reprint, p. 271), "When youthfull *Paris* stole the lustfull Punke, Faire *Hellen*." Few Elizabethans thought of Helen either as a "good woman" in Chaucer's sense, or as "a daughter of the gods, divinely tall, and most divinely fair"; they hated her as a harlot that had brought destruction on the Trojans, who were, so the story had it, the ancestors of the Britons. The poem is written in heroic couplets, although there are a few Alexandrines (e. g., lines 7, 8, 12, 28).

82. 5 *A Louers lyfe*] Another example of the *Venus and Adonis* stanza (cf. 68. 2 n.), though lines 34–35 are very irregular.

19 *Not seene, they thinke themselues vnminded bee*] Cf. the proverb, "Out of sight, out of mind."

30 *Rosamond*] The reference is to Rosamunda (Rosemond, Rosimund), who after her father's death was forced to marry Alboin (A.D. 567), king of the Lombards. Alboin made a drinking-cup out of her father's

NOTES

skull, and as a jest (cf. line 31) he compelled Rosamunda to drink from it. In revenge she murdered him (A.D. 573) to marry her lover Helmichis. Later Rosamunda plotted to murder Helmichis; but, when he had drunk from the poisoned cup which she had prepared, he discovered her treachery and forced her to drink too. The author of the *Gorgeous Gallery* poem perhaps got his information about this story from George Turbervile's *Tragical Tales* (see the 1837 reprint of the 1587 edition, pp. 142–158), where the Rosamunda episode forms the fifth tale. (That Turbervile's *Tragical Tales* first appeared *ca.* 1574 I have shown in *Modern Philology*, XV [1918], 137–139.) But the story occurs in many other places: e. g., Paulus Diaconus, *De Gestis Longobardorum*, I, 27, II, 28; Godfrey of Viterbo, *Pantheon*, no. xvii; Gregory of Tours, *Historia Francorum* (Société de l'Histoire de France), IV, 41; Gower, *Confessio Amantis*, I, 2459–2646; Belleforest (following Bandello, pt. III, novel 18), *Histoires Tragiques*, IV, 550. Rosamunda is the heroine of Rucellai's *Rosmunda* (1515), of Sir William Davenant's *Albovine* (1629), of Alfieri's *Rosmunda* (1780), and of Swinburne's *Rosamund Queen of the Lombards* (1899). See further the discussion by Paris, *Journal des Savants*, 1889, pp. 616 ff.; by Olrik, *Danske Ridderviser*, I, 165 ff.; and by Genzmer, *Herrig's Archiv für das Studium der neueren Sprachen und Literaturen*, CXLII (1921), 1–8. See also Lydgate's *Fall of Princes*, bk. VIII, 3256–3381.

82. 32 *Itrascus*] I cannot explain this allusion; but see Tottel's *Miscellany*, p. 190:

> Thinke on Etrascus worthy loue that lasted thirty yeres,
> Which could not long atcheue his hartes desired choyse,
> Yet at the ende he founde rewarde that made him to reioyce.

35 *they plunge in payne*] The much-ridiculed ballad on George Mannington in the *Handful*, p. 65, begins with the oft-quoted line, "I waile in wo, I plunge in pain."

83. 2 *Axeres*] Anaxarete, whose disdain caused Iphis to hang himself to her gate-post, and who for her cruelty was turned to stone by the gods (Ovid, *Metamorphoses*, XIV, 748 ff.). A ballad called "the vnfortunate ende of Iphis sonne vnto Teucer kynge of Troye" was registered in 1569–1570 (Arber's *Transcript*, I, 403). "The storie of Axeres and the worthie Iphijs" is referred to by Thomas Nashe (*Works*, ed. McKerrow, III, 67).

NOTES

See also the *Handful*, p. 45; and cf. Leonard Gibson, "A very proper Dittie," *ca.* 1570 (Lilly's *Ballads*, p. 116),

> Anexes so daintie example may bee,
> Whose lightie loue caused yong Iphis his woe
> His true loue was tryed by death, as you see,
> Her lightie loue forced the knight therunto.

6 *disdayne*] Read disdayned.

11 *Willow willow willow*] Willow was the emblem of ill luck in love, and many "willow songs" were written during the sixteenth century. One of the earliest — with the refrain of "For all a grene wyllow is my garland" — was the work of John Heywood; it is reprinted, among many other places, in Halliwell-Phillipps's edition of *The Moral Play of Wit and Science*, 1848, p. 86. A very good "willow song" occurs also in Thomas Deloney's *Gentle Craft*, part II, *ca.* 1598 (*Works*, ed. Mann, p. 165); another is in Robert Jones's *Muses Gardin for Delights*, 1610 (cf. Thomas Evans, *Old Ballads*, 1810, I, 63). More famous than any other, however, is the ballad from which Desdemona sings in the fourth act of *Othello* and which is reprinted in Percy's *Reliques*, 1765 (ed. H. B. Wheatley, I, 199), and in the *Roxburghe Ballads*, I, 171. See also the discussion and the music given in Chappell's *Popular Music*, I, 206 ff. Of an altogether different type from any of these is the "willow song" that concludes the comedy of *Sir Giles Goosecap* (1606). Cf. Thomas Howell's poem entitled

> ¶All of greene Willow, Willow, Willow, Willow,
> Sithe all of greene Willow shall be my Garland

(*H. His Deuises*, 1581, C2, ed. Raleigh, 1906, p. 23).

25 *periurde as Iason*] Referring to Jason's unfaithfulness to Medea, whom he put aside to marry Creusa (or Glauce). Cf. 75. 13 n. A poem called "The pitious complaint of Medea, forsaken of Jason," is in Whetstone's *Rocke of Regard*, 1576 (Collier's reprint, p. 108). "*The story of Jason how he gotte the golden flece and how he Ded begyle Media* oute of laten into englesshe by Nycholas Whyte" was registered for publication in 1565–1566 (Arber's *Transcript*, I, 299).

29 *with showes gallant gay*] 'With fine and beautiful ornaments (or garments).'

84. 2 *phrases fine philed*] Cf. the *Handful*, line 1480.

NOTES

84. 14 *Light of loue*] Cf. 38. 5 n.

25 *willow will*] Read willow willow.

86. 2 *thy wordes are but winde*] Cf. 36. 34 n.

8 *soone hot, and soone colde*] Cf. Heywood's *Works*, 1562, pp. 5, 72, "Than perceiue they well, hotte loue soone colde," "Sone whot, sone colde"; Hazlitt's *Proverbs*, p. 354; *Handful*, p. 87.

15 *A gloze of fawning freendship*] The metre of this poem varies uncertainly between septenary couplets and poulter's measure.

27 *I haue not I*] The repetition of the pronoun is a favorite Elizabethan mannerism. Cf. Tottel's *Miscellany*, p. 90, "I can not, I no, no, it will not be"; Nicholas Breton, *A Floorish upon Fancie*, 1582 (ed. Park, p. 104), "That what to doo, I know not I"; *Two Gentlemen of Verona*, V, iv, 132, "I care not for her, I"; and 109. 33.

87. 3 *goes to gaze of*] 'Goes to gaze at.' Cf. line 19.

10 *Our gaze vngaynd*] 'The object of our gaze not yet gained.' Cf. *Troilus and Cressida*, I, ii, 315, "Men prize the thing ungain'd more than it is."

22 *Shuns*] The context requires *shuts*, i. e., shuts up, encloses. The *N. E. D.* gives *shun* in the sense of hide or screen, but its earliest example is dated 1627.

88. 8, 10 *In minde, and loyall hart, Till breathing lyfe depart*] These trimeter (instead of tetrameter) lines violate the metrical scheme.

17–18 *Whom . . . mee, to play my parte*] Either *whom* or *mee* is redundant.

22 *loytryng loue, reapes troubled toyle*] A commonplace that is almost proverbial. A ballad on this theme, beginning "In lingeringe Love mislikinge growes," was registered in 1564–1565 and is reprinted in Lyly's *Works*, III, 463 (cf. the *Handful*, p. 103). Cf. also *The Passionate Morrice*, 1593 (ed. F. J. Furnivall, New Shakspere Society, 1876, pp. 87, 97), "Lingring loue breedes mislike," "Liking wil not be long a dooing." The same idea is expressed in the proverb, "Happy's the wooing that's not long a-doing." Cf. the *Handful*, p. 87.

89. 26 *it greeues vs to forgo*] Apparently repeated from line 24 by the compositor's mistake.

27 *Wee nothing brought, &c.*] Cf. 1 Timothy, vi. 7; Job, i. 21; Chaucer, *The Clerk's Tale*, lines 871–872, "'Naked out of my fadres hous,' quod she, 'I cam, and naked moot I turne agayn'"; George Peele, *Edward I*, 1593,

NOTES

scene vii, "Naked came we into the worlde naked are wee turned out of the good townes into the wildernesse"; "Young Andrew" (*Bishop Percy's Folio Manuscript*, ed. Hales and Furnivall, II, 331), "then naked thou came into this world, and naked thou shalt returne againe"; and 98. 6.

 31 *Liue then, to leaue thy life, &c.*] 'Live, then, such a life as will make thee ready to leave (thy life) at any time.'

 33 *sweet is sower*] Cf. Hazlitt's *Proverbs*, p. 362, "Sweet sauce begins to wax sour," "Sweet meat will have sour sauce"; *Jack Jugler* (F. J. Child, *Four Old Plays*, p. 16), "It hath byn a saying, of tyme long That swete mete woll haue soure sauce among"; *Colyn Blowbols Testament*, line 121 (Hazlitt's *Remains of the Early Popular Poetry*, I, 98), "Sharpe sawce was ordeigned for swete mete"; *Mirror for Magistrates*, ed. Joseph Haslewood, I, 76, "The prouerbe sayth, sweete meate will haue of sauces sower."

90. 5 *Wee gloze in that, &c.*] 'We delight in that which we see to be uncertain.'

 18 *Diues*] Ballads called "of the Ryche man and poore Lazarus" and "Dyves and Lazerus" had been registered in 1557–1558 and 1570–1571 (Arber's *Transcript*, I, 76, 436). A traditional song on this subject is preserved in F. J. Child's *English and Scottish Popular Ballads*, No. 56. Mention is made of "The merry ballad Of Diverus and Lazarus" in John Fletcher's *Monsieur Thomas*, III, iii. Proctor himself was the author of a poem on "Dives's lamentation" that is printed in his *Triumph of Truth*, ca. 1584 (Collier's reprint, 1866, pp. 24 ff.). A comma after *golde* would make the meaning of this line clearer. *Mirror*, as also in line 26, page 92, seems to refer to such works as the *Mirror for Magistrates*.

 19 *Nemrods*] Like Dives, the mighty hunter Nimrod (Genesis, x. 8–9) was a favorite example with the ballad-writers. They were particularly fond of citing him as an illustration of the power of death. Cf. "The triumphe of death," ca. 1575 (Rollins, *Old English Ballads*, p. 263):

> Not *Nemrod*, with his sturdy lookes,
> could me repulse; but forcibly
> (As standes in first of *Moyses* bookes),
> amiddes his pryde and tyranny,
> Doune, doune, he fell confusedly,
> and (nilling-wise) thus catching, fall;
> By wofull force became my thrall.

NOTES

90. 20 *preter*] I. e., past. Except as used in tense-connections, this is the only example of *preter* given in the *N.E.D. Learn* of course means *teach* (cf. 92. 26).

91. 5 *benumbde*] *Benumbed*, pronounced in three syllables, would fit the metre better.

10 *My idle youth . . . what therof ensueth*] 'That my idle youth found out (by experience) the evils which result from lewdness.'

20 *iudgd them speake, of rigor*] 'I thought they spoke from harshness of judgment, not from good will.'

21 *Who toulde . . . for hire did hault*] 'Those who spoke of gain (reward) seemed to me to be trying to deceive me for their own benefit.'

22 *what now I wish by skill*] 'What now as a result of reason or judgment I wish (I had).'

25 *Such idle steps . . . such releefe*] I cannot explain this line. The stanza, however, evidently means, 'Experience makes me lament — the more my grief! — because in my youth I didn't shun such idle steps lest, once that youth had passed, I might find myself destitute (as actually I am now finding myself).'

27 *what preuayles to wish I would I had*] 'What avails to wish, "I would I had (done so)"?'

28 *time delayd, may not bee calde agayne*] Cf. 102. 8 n.

30 (*it*) Read it.

92. 4 *attacht with death his page*] 'Arrested by Death's messenger,' i. e., by Old Age. On the traditional Messengers of Death (*Boten des Todes*) see Bolte and Polívka, *Anmerkungen zu den Kinder- u. Hausmärchen*, III, 293 ff.; Lydgate, *Minor Poems*, ed. J. O. Halliwell [-Phillipps], Percy Society, II, 241 ff. Cf. also 95. 11; Tottel's *Miscellany*, p. 174; and Robert Greene, *Neuer Too Late*, 1590 (*Works*, ed. Grosart, VIII, 150), "Doth the sommons of death appeare in your gray head, and yet fleshly desires raigne in your hart?"

15 *mestiue*] Mournful. This and a similar use of *mestive* in stanza 7 of John Davies's *Holy Rood*, 1609 (*Works*, ed. Grosart, vol. I), are the only examples of the word given in the *N.E.D.* In John Phillip's *Patient Grissell*, 1566, B3, the phrase *mestfull harts* occurs; and in Thomas Lodge's *Famous History of Robert, Second Duke of Normandy*, 1591, I, *mestfull families*.

NOTES

16 *cankered knobs*] Ulcerous or cancerous knobs, — plague-sores, — used here figuratively of the effects of sin.

25 *Fœlix quem, &c.*] This proverb occurs in the *Speculum Stultorum* of the twelfth century (Thomas Wright, *Anglo-Latin Satirical Poets*, I, 145). It is printed at the end of D. Sterrie's "sonet declaring the Lamentation of Beckles, a Market Towne in Suffolke," 1586 (H. L. Collmann, *Ballads and Broadsides*, No. 87, Roxburghe Club, 1912). Cf. also Chaucer, *Troilus*, III, 329, "For wyse ben by foles harm chastysed"; the Durham MS. of Hoccleve's *Minor Poems* (ed. Furnivall, E.E.T.S., p. 224), "Felix quem faciunt aliena pericula cautum: Fortunate is he who hathe the happe to bewarre by an-other mannes clappe"; Hugh Latimer, *Seven Sermons*, 1549 (Arber, *English Reprints*, 1869), p. 61, "Here is of bywalkers. Thys hystorye would be remembred, the Prouerbe is. *Felix quem faciunt aliena pericula cautum.* Happy is he that can beware by an other mans ieoperdy"; *The Passionate Morrice*, 1593 (ed. Furnivall, New Shakspere Society, 1876, p. 75), "To take heede by another mans harme, is a louing warning"; Henry Porter, *The Two Angry Women of Abington*, 1599 (*Tudor Facsimile Texts*, G^v), "For happy is he whom other mens harmes do make to beware"; George Chapman, *An Humourous Day's Mirth*, 1599, scene 12, "Felix quem faciunt aliena pericula cautum"; Samuel Clarke, "Epistle to the Reader," in *A Mirrour or Looking-Glasse*, 1671, vol. II, "The very Heathen could say: *Fœlix quem faciunt aliena pericula cautum:* Happy is he that by other mens harms, learns to beware"; "Fayre Warning" (*Roxburghe Ballads*, I, 370), the refrain of which runs,

> O happy is he whom other men's harmes
> Can make to beware, and to shun Satan's charmes;

Plautus, *Mercator*, IV, vii, 40, "Feliciter is sapit qui periculo alieno sapit"; and 20. 31. See, further, Erasmus's *Adagia* (trans. Richard Taverner, 1552, fol. 3); Edmond Elviden's *Neweyeres gift*, 1570 (Huth's *Fugitive Tracts*, First Series); Lyly's *Midas*, 1592 (*Works*, III, 153; cf. I, 189); Samuel Rowlands's *Greenes Ghost*, 1602, F2; and Fielding's *Tom Jones*, bk. XII, ch. vii.

28 *with tryall tript*] I. e., 'tried and tripped by sad experience.'

93. 2 *A proper Sonet, how time consumeth all*] The metrical flow of these quatrains is very irregular. The theme suggests Ovid's familiar phrase, "tempus edax rerum" (*Metamorphoses*, XV, 234), which is quoted by Philip Stubbes (*The Anatomie of Abuses*, 1583, ed. Furnivall, pt. II, pp.

NOTES

1–2); by Matthew Grove, 1587 (*Poems*, ed. Grosart, 1878, pp. 97–100); by Thomas Nashe (preface to Greene's *Menaphon*, 1589, Greene's *Works*, ed. Grosart, VI, 15); and by Ben Jonson (*A Tale of a Tub*, 1633, III, iv). Cf. *Love's Labour's Lost*, I, i, 4, "cormorant devouring Time"; and 9. 31 n.

93. 7 *as Grasse doth fade away*] Cf. Isaiah, xl. 6 ff.; Psalms, ciii. 15 f.; *Shirburn Ballads*, ed. Clark, p. 149,

> Thy youth is as the growinge grasse;
> thine age resembleth withered hay.

An early ballad reprinted in H. L. Collmann's *Ballads and Broadsides*, No. 48 (Roxburghe Club, 1912), has the line, "All flesh is grasse, the *Scripture saith, and vadeth like a flowre," with this marginal note: "*Esaie. 40.6. Eccl. 14. 17. 18. 1 Pet. 1. 24. Iames. 1. 10. and in many places more." Cf. 99. 33.

11 *stay*] A poor rhyme for *ioy* (line 9).

94. 2 *A Mirror of Mortallity*] Written in the *Venus and Adonis* stanza (cf. 68. 2 n.). The poem is reprinted in Edward Farr's *Select Poetry* (Parker Society, 1845), II, 400 f.

5 *of yong delights*] This phrase spoils the rhythm and the rhyme. It should be omitted. Cf. line 28.

12 *Must each*] *And must each* would improve the rhythm. Probably, however, some noun like *man* has dropped out after *each*.

22 *Like as the flower, bedect, &c.*] Cf. 90. 8.

26 *certayn wee shall dye*] Cf. Chaucer's *Clerk's Tale*, lines 64–70; and the *Chronicon Adæ de Usk* (1377–1404), ed. E. M. Thompson, p. 55, "Hic me jubet quiescere Plato, cum nil sit cercius morte, nil incercius hora mortis."

31 *vse thy talent*] Cf. Matthew, xxv. 14–30; and 97. 27.

95. 2 *A briefe dialogue*] On dialogue-poems in general see J. E. Wells, *A Manual of the Writings in Middle English*, 1916, pp. 411 ff., 829 ff.

11 *of death*] These words are metrically superfluous. On Death's Messengers see 92. 4 n.

12 *Permit a while*] 'Give me permission (to live) a while longer.'

20 *shrine*] I. e., 'enshrine (bury) myself.'

96. 2 *Aeger Diues habet, &c.*] The stanza of five octosyllabic couplets is

NOTES

in the same form as that of Wordsworth's "She was a Phantom of Delight." The title is from Cato's *Disticha*, IV, 5:

> Quum fueris locuples, corpus curare memento.
> Aeger dives habet nummos, se non habet ipsum.

12 *Diues*] Cf. 90. 18 n.

12 *pealfe*] For employing this word Puttenham (*The Arte of English Poesie*, 1589, ed. Arber, pp. 266, 281) vigorously assailed Timothy Kendall: "Another of our bad rymers that very indecently said. *A misers mynde thou hast, thou hast a Princes pelfe*. A lewd terme to be giuen to a Princes treasure (*pelfe*). . . . These and such other base wordes do greatly disgrace the thing and the speaker or writer"; "Another of our vulgar makers, spake as illfaringly in this verse written to the dispraise of a rich man and couetous. Thou hast a misers minde (thou hast a princes pelfe) a lewde terme to be spoken of a princes treasure, which in no respect nor for any cause is to be called pelfe, though it were neuer so meane." See the discussion of these passages in my "New Facts about George Turbervile," *Modern Philology*, XV (1918), 513–514.

27 *hee remembreth not to dye*] 'He doesn't think of dying.' The phrase is an adaptation of *memento mori*; hence the infinitive construction.

97. 5 *the Crow is white*] Cf. 57. 32 n., and these passages in John Heywood's *Works*, 1562, p. 155:

> I wyll say the crowe is whyte. art thou so lyght,
> What is thy credence, when the crowe cumth in syght.
>
> Ye must say the crowe is whyte, in any case,
> Not nowe, but we were made sey so a longe space.
>
> I will say the crowe is whyte. wylt thou so?
> When euery man seeth hir blacke: go foole go.

Just so Philautus tells Camilla (Lyly, *Euphues and his England*, 1580, *Works*, II, 133), "I would sweare the Crow were white, if thou shouldest but say it." Humfrey Gifford in his *Posie of Gilloflowers* (1580, "A Delectable Dreame") has, "I cannot say the crow is white."

27 *tallent*] Cf. 94. 31 n.

98. 6 *Wee nothing had*] Cf. 89. 27 n.

31 *Hee leapes the lake, &c.*] 'He leaps over obstacles while others stop to look at them'; i. e., he is a man of action. It is just possible that this is

NOTES

a reference to Boiardo's hero (*Orlando Innamorato*, II, viii), who 'leaps the lake' because giants destroy the bridge whenever he tries to cross.

99. 2–3 *As Solomon . . . tombed lye*] A septenary couplet here interrupts the regular heroic verse.

9 *Respice finem*] Cf. Richard Hill's *Commonplace-Book*, ca. 1536 (ed. R. Dyboski, E.E.T.S., 1907, p. 131), "Quicquid agas, prudenter agas, et respice finem, Whan thow doste any thynge, think on the ende"; *A Comedy of Errors*, IV, iv, 45, "Mistress, 'respice finem,' respect your end"; Hazlitt's *Proverbs*, p. 413 (from a fifteenth-century MS.), "Think on the end ere you begin, and you will never be thrall to sin." See also Alexander Neville's translation (1563) of Seneca's *Oedipus*, act IV.

20 *Ruddocks*] Gold coins. Cf. Thomas Deloney, *The Gentle Craft*, part II, ca. 1598 (*Works*, ed. Mann, p. 151), "He looks for a golden girle . . . that might bring him the red ruddocks chinking in a bag"; Lyly, *Midas*, 1589 (*Works*, III, 125), "So he haue golden ruddocks in his bagges."

27 *the valiaunts*] This is merely a form of *valiaunst*, a word used twice before. The meaning is superlative, 'most valiant.' Cf. line 31.

33 *but a withered grasse*] Cf. 93. 7 n.

34 *Mors omnibus communis*] Cf. *Hamlet*, I, ii, 72 ff.:

"Thou know'st 'tis common; all that lives must die,
Passing through nature to eternity."

"Ay, madam, it is common."

George Eliot writes of Maggie Tulliver: "The most fragmentary examples [of Latin] were her favourites. *Mors omnibus est communis* would have been jejune, only she liked to know the Latin."

100. 3 *Try, ere thou trust*] Cf. 65. 19 n.

8 *paynt their prates*] 'Make their prating seem sincere.'

9 *clungs*] This ungrammatical form (for *clung*) was used to secure a rhyme with *tungs*. Cf. 116. 2 n.

12 *no fie*] *Oh fie*, as Park suggested, would be the more usual expression here.

14 *sance*] 'Sans' (Fr., *without*). "From this old orthography Mr. Douce thinks that the word had not obtained a French pronunciation. Illustr. of Shaksp. i. 301" (Park). Spelled *saunce*, the word occurs frequently in George Whetstone's *Rocke of Regard*, 1576 (Collier's reprint, 1867, pp.

NOTES

116, 124, 135, 262, etc.). Cf. *As You Like It*, II, vii, 166, "Sans teeth, sans eyes, sans taste, sans every thing."

19 *Donec eris fœlix, &c.*] From Ovid's *Tristia*, I, ix, 5–6. In Sir Thomas Elyot's *Boke named the Gouernour*, 1531 (ed. Croft, II, 164), the verses are translated thus:

> Whiles fortune the fauoureth frendes thou hast plentie,
> The tyme beinge troublous thou arte all alone.

Cf. Chaucer's *Boethius*, bk. III, prose 5 (but see also Proverbs, xix. 4, and Ecclesiasticus, vi. 8–12, xxxvii. 4), "Certes, swiche folk as weleful fortune maketh freendes, contrarious fortune maketh hem enemys"; and Milton's *Samson Agonistes*, lines 191–193,

> In prosperous days
> They [friends] swarm, but in adverse withdraw their head,
> Not to be found, though sought.

In Richard Hill's *Commonplace-Book, ca.* 1536 (ed. R. Dyboski, E.E.T.S., p. 133), similar Latin verses are given,

> Tempore felici, multi numerantur amici;
> Cum fortuna perit, nullus amicus erit;

and on p. 129 the same idea is epitomized as "Powerte partith felishipe." The author of the *Gallery* poem may have borrowed his Latin from the *Paradise*, 1576, E4^v (where it forms the title of a poem), rather than directly from Ovid.

101. 32 ¶*The*] Read T. P.

102. 8 *time past, may not be calde agayne*] A variation of the proverbs which declare that "the tide tarrieth no man," "time lost cannot be won again," and "time stays not the fool's leisure." Cf. Chaucer, *House of Fame*, III, 1257 f., "For tyme y-lost, this knowen ye, By no way may recovered be"; *The Clerk's Tale*, line 63, "Ay fleeth the tyme, it nil no man abyde"; Gower, *Confessio Amantis*, III, 577 f., IV, 1486 f., "For noman mai his time lore Recovere," "Bot so wys man yit nevere stod, Which mai recovere time lore"; Froissart, *Rondelés*, xiv, "Le temps perdu ne poet on recouvrer"; Heywood, *Works*, 1562, p. 6, "Take time whan time comth, lest time steale away"; and 91.28. In Collier's *Illustrations of Early English Popular Litera-*

[197]

NOTES

ture, vol. II (1864), there is a play by George Wapull entitled "The Tide Taryeth No Man," 1576.

102. 20 At the bottom of the page an old hand has written, "FS. by IH." For F. S. see 102.3; for I. H. see 117.34 and note.

103. 1 *The History of Pyramus and Thisbie*] In his monograph on *Die Pyramus- & Thisbe-Sage*, 1891, pt. II, Georg Hart lists most of the English versions of this story. Among the more important are those given in Chaucer's *Legend of Good Women* and Gower's *Confessio Amantis* (bk. III); a "Boke of Perymus and Thesbye" that may have appeared in 1553 and in 1562 (cf. 115. 30–31 n.); a "Romance" written toward the end of the sixteenth century and preserved in a Balliol College manuscript; and a "Poem" by Dunstan Gale that was dedicated in 1596 but seems to have appeared first as an appendix to Robert Greene's *History of Arbasto*, 1617. Golding's translation of Ovid's *Metamorphoses* (1567) had also helped to make the story familiar. The author of the *Gallery* poem professes to be 'truly translating.' Presumably Hart had pondered over that remark, but he merely observes (p. 17), "Ob diese tragische Liebesgeschichte eine Uebersetzung, oder eine freie Bearbeitung ist, vermag ich nicht anzugeben." Since most of the versions of the story are not accessible to me, I too am unable to say what author the poem translates from (but cf. 104. 20 n., 105. 19 n., and 115. 30 n.). It may be added that "The tayl of Pirramus and tesbe" is mentioned in *The Complaint of Scotland* (1549), and that an exceedingly interesting ballad on Pyramus and Thisbe (whose names, however, are not mentioned) is reprinted in the *Roxburghe Ballads*, I, 175 ff. A puppet-show on the lovers ("King *Ninus* motion") was referred to in 1615 by John Taylor the Water Poet (*Works*, 1630, Spenser Society reprint, p. 321). Dr. Douglas Bush, who has made a much more careful study of the matter than I have, kindly informs me that the closest parallel he has found to the poem is the Pyramus-Thisbe story, told in prose, in *Les xv liures de la Metamorphose D'ouide (Poëte treselegāt) contenans L'olympe des Histoires poëtiques traduictz de Latin en Francoys* (1539), fols. 54b–58a. He has also discovered another version of the story, identical in substance but written in verse, in *Les Histoires des Poetes* (1595). Cf. *Piramus et Tisbé, poème du XII*ᵉ *Siècle*, ed. C. de Boer, Paris, 1921, which is also printed, but from another source, in Barbazan and Méon's *Fabliaux et Contes*, IV (1808), 326–354.

17 *in pearced harts ẙ dwel*] A line was omitted here by the printer, with the result that line 18 is unintelligible.

[198]

NOTES

18 *babe & mother*] From what follows, these would appear to be Cupid and Venus.

19 *withstand*] Another frank disregard of grammar in the interest of rhyme. Cf. 100. 9 n.

20 *they*] Referring back to line 18.

22 *poore fooles*] This means practically 'poor souls.' *Fool* was a common term of endearment. Cf. 112. 13; and *King Lear*, V, iii, 305, "And my poor fool [i. e., Cordelia] is hang'd!"

24 *twayn*] This may be meant for *tween* (between); but the line may mean, 'except the two by themselves alone.'

31 *no ioy may glad, ẙ heuens ẙ passeth vnder*] 'No joy that happens under the heavens may make them glad.'

104. 7 *weary*] I. e., wary.

10–11 *hide . . . finde*] Assonance instead of rhyme; but *finde* is probably a misprint for *bide*.

20 *mine Auctor*] The author is undoubtedly Ovid, who says that the fathers forbade meetings but who gives no cause for their action.

22 *(alas) the while*] 'Alas the while!'

23 *loueday*] A day set for a meeting at which to settle amicably a dispute. Cf. John Heywood, *Works*, 1562, p. 56, "Yet should ye that waie rather breake a loue daie."

23 *their mallice to begyle*] 'To assuage their (the parents') malice, or quarrel.'

29 *bounde*] I. e., doth bound (lay down limits).

30 *scalde*] Read sealde.

32 *many*] Grammar would be better satisfied with *many a*.

33 *dayly sithe*] *Sithe* is a fairly common form for *sigh*. The *Oxford Spelling Book* of 1726 says that *sigh* is pronounced *sithe*, "according to the common way of speaking." The *N. E. D.* cites Robert Armin's *Two Maids of More-clacke*, 1609, E4, "Be smilefull, and expresse no griefe in sithes." In the *Gallery*, however, *sithe* is, I think, a misprint for *sight*. Cf. lines 2, 3, 30.

34 *what depth . . . indrowned bee*] The *in* of the verb goes in meaning with *what depth*: i. e., 'in what depth may they be drowned!'

35 *now*] Perhaps a misprint for *not*.

36 *face*] Read fate.

105. 9 *thou happy hand, these*] 'Thou happy hand that these.'

[199]

NOTES

105. 15 *Venus Temple*] Cf. 5. 23 n.

16 *I korue*] I. e., 'ikorve,' 'ykorve,' the past participle of *carve*.

16 *mindes*] Rhyme is responsible for *mindes* instead of the proper form *mind*. Cf. 103. 19 n.

19 *Vertue . . . the flame*] "This and the following lines appear to be derived from Ovid. Metamorph. i. 521 [–524]" (Park).

30 *The feeble thread, yet stayes*] 'The feeble thread (of life, spun for me by the Fates) that still supports.'

31 *Goddes brest?*] 'Goddess's breast.' The question-mark should be omitted.

33 *causeles not*] I. e., not without cause.

34 *Vulcane*] A reference to the story of how Mars and Venus in amorous dalliance were ensnared by Vulcan, familiar through Ovid's *De Arte Amandi*. A scene based upon this episode occurs in Thomas Heywood's play of *The Brazen Age* (1613).

34 *your common shame*] 'To the shame of both Mars and you (Venus).'

106. 16–17 *so please . . . body ease*] Notice that Pyramus ends his lament (as if he were concluding a scene or an act of an Elizabethan play) with a couplet. Cf. 109. 8–9 n.

17 *when you lust*] I. e., whenever it pleases you.

20 *wit, denayeth the some to thinke*] '(My) wisdom is too little even to conceive the sum (of Thisbe's woes).'

24 *spring*] Read *springs*.

25 *Dame Rhetorique*] Elegant speech or language. Cf. Marlowe, *Hero and Leander*, I, 338, "Who taught thee Rhetoricke to deceiue a maid?" Mr. Kittredge suggests that the author had in mind *The Franklin's Prologue*, lines 47–49 (*Canterbury Tales*, F, 719–721),

> I lerned never rethoryk certeyn;
> Thing that I speke, it moot be bare and pleyn.
> I sleep never on the mount of Pernaso;

or else the Prologue (lines 1–3) to the *Satires* of Persius,

> Nec fonte labra prolui caballino,
> nec in bicipiti somniasse Parnaso
> memini, ut repente sic poeta prodirem.

[200]

NOTES

Cf. also *Emaricdulfe. Sonnets written By E. C.*, 1595, sonnet 4:

> My forlorne muse that neuer trode the path
> That leades to top of hie Pierion mount,
> Nor neuer washt within the liuesome bath
> Of learnings spring, bright Aganippe fount. ...

    30 *lightes*] I. e., light's.
    37 *assured finde, shall bring*] 'Assuredly find that which shall bring.'
107. 14 *Which ... the issue had*] 'A rift, the course of which had, as it appeared, its issue through (on the other side of) the wall.'
    27 *wo begun*] Woe-begone.
    29 *her ... her*] 'Fortune's ... Thisbe's.'
    34 *Let in his face*] 'A glimpse of light the pendant emitted just in front of his visage, (which glimpse was) let in his face,' i. e., was cast into or shone into his face. Perhaps *let* should be *lept*: 'a glimpse of light which the pendant emitted leapt into his face.'
108. 2–15 *Though many tokens, &c.*] Pyramus utters his joy in a sonnet of the Shakespearean type. Cf. 111. 2–15.
    3 *redust*] Reduced. The word is used in the Latin sense of *leading back*. Cf. a ballad of 1566–1567 preserved in Lilly's *Ballads*, p. 169:

> O Lorde, I say, in mynd!
> Reduce and bryng to thee in truth all wicked Jewes vnkynd.

    13 *abandon*] Park suggests the reading *abandon'd*. In that case the meaning might be: 'Who but Thisbe could have eased a captive (who had) abandoned (hope)?' But probably the correct reading is *a bounden*.
    35 *In their respect, that*] 'In comparison with those that.'
109. 2 *such*] Notice that this word 'rhymes' with *speeche*.
    8–9 *see ... bee*] Thisbe's speech ends in a couplet. Cf. 106. 16–17 n., and see 109. 30–31, 110. 4–5, 111. 14–15.
    14 *dollours*] Read dolorous (for the sake of the rhyme).
    17 *so*] The omission of this word would improve the metre.
    18 *the tenth, that*] 'The tenth of the sorrows that.'
    30–31 *taste ... last*] Cf. 109. 8–9 n.
    33 *I doubt not I*] Cf. 86. 27 n.
110. 4–5 *brest ... rest*] Cf. 109. 8–9 n.
    7 *so*] The omission of this word would improve the metre. Or per-

NOTES

haps the reading should be *so great* here and *greater* in line 8, which needs another syllable.

110. 23 *cursed scyte . . . perfect sight*] Notice the pun on *scyte* (site) and *sight* (seeing).

32 *This standes full yll: to purpose, &c.*] 'This is not fitting to be done.' *Made* translates the Latin *facio*.

35 *yee this*] 'Yea this' (i. e., battering down the wall).

111. 2–15 This lament of Pyramus (cf. 108. 2–15) is an irregular sonnet, rhyming *aaaabcbcdedeff*.

3 *I doo you know*] 'I cause (make) you to know.'

4 *Minus*] Or rather, Ninus. In the comedy of Pyramus and Thisbe in *A Midsummer Night's Dream* the rustics call the king "Ninny."

9 *seas'de*] Seized.

14–15 *report . . . resort*] Cf. 109. 8–9 n.

21 *the feare*] Read they feare.

24 *that erst*] Read than erst.

25 *this*] Read thus.

26 *haue shapen so*] 'Hath so shaped (managed) it.'

34 *More hardyer, &c.*] 'More boldly than before she now urged her foot to hasten.'

112. 2 *What wil ye more*] 'What further do you wish me to tell?'

11 *brest*] Read best (i. e., beast).

13 *poore foole*] Cf. 103. 22 n.

15 *whose ruthful mone . . . denye*] 'For succor she fled to a hollow tree, which did not deny succor to her ruthful moan.'

16 *Liones*] The pronouns *he* and *his* in lines 19 ff. do not indicate the sex of the "liones"; they are neuter, not masculine, gender.

22 *smoaking*] Steaming with the warm blood of its victims.

24 *as fier*] 'As if fire.' So also in line 25, 'as if his corps.'

25 *in his tayle*] 'On (against) his tail.'

35 *the words*] Read these words.

35 *out abrade*] 'Shouted out.' This is the latest example of *abraid* in this sense given in the *N. E. D.*

36 *¶The*] Read The.

113. 2 *The lamentacion of Piramus*, which extends through 114. 24, is in rhyme royal, although the printers ignored the division into seven-line stanzas.

NOTES

18 *here only shew*] Read *her only slew*.

21 *mee (too) heere*] Read *me to her*.

23 *thy corps*] Probably the reading should be either *the corps* or (preferably) *her corps*.

26 *then woonted fine*] 'Than customary end (than the usual, natural death).'

28–31 *And that, &c.*] 'And what increases my grief is that nothing is left of her body.'

32 *If the dead corps, &c.*] Expressing a wish: 'Oh, if only the dead corps were yet to be seen and buried!'

114. 4 *thou hast the meane outchast*] 'Thou hast chased away (deprived me of) the means of (obtaining) this poor joy' (i. e., the joy of embracing and kissing her dead body).

27 *glush*] Not in the *N.E.D.* It evidently means *gush*, for which it may actually be a misprint.

33 *who ... had kept the hollow tree*] 'Who had stayed in the hollow tree.' Cf. the phrase "to keep (i. e., remain in) one's bed."

34 *Least hap, &c.*] 'Lest her lover's long wait may seem to him as if he were mocked.'

36 *her fel*] 'Befell to her.'

115. 4 *sights*] I. e., sighs. Cf. the *Paradise*, 1576, K^v, "Then should my sights, to quiet breast retire."

5 *him a kerchefe saw, &c.*] *Hit* (it) is pleonastic. The line means, 'she saw him, how he kissed and strained a handkerchief.'

6 *Shee neuer drew*] *Neuer* must be a misprint for *neerer*.

15 *canst be free, to shed*] 'Canst be free from shedding.'

17 *his, & mine*] 'His life and mine.'

24 *lastest throwes*] 'Latest (final) throes (of death).'

30–31 *Alas my loue, &c.*] The *N. E. D.*, as an illustration of *define* meaning *come to an end*, quotes lines 30–31, "(Alas my loue) and liue ye yet, did not your life define By Lyones rage?", but refers only to "1562, *Pyramus & Th.*" I can find no trace of the existence of any such work (but cf. 103. 1 n.). A "boke intituled Perymus and Thesbye" was entered in the Stationers' Register for 1562–1563 to William Griffith (Arber, *Transcript*, I, 215); and a quarto in black-letter, licensed in 1562 to T. Hacket, is mentioned in Thomas Warton's *History of English Poetry*, IV (1824), 243, but not, so far as I see, in the Register. If the editor of the *N. E. D.* actually had

NOTES

seen a 1562 edition and has quoted from it, not from the *Gorgeous Gallery*, the relations of the two poems obviously need investigating.

115. 34–35 *a profound sighe . . . did depart*] 'A profound sigh, cast out from the bottom of his heart, did divide (separate) his body and soul.'

116. 2 *strake*] Strake (i. e., struck) is used to rhyme with *sake*. Cf. 105. 16 n.

11 *William Gruffith*] This poem was registered for publication by Richard Jones on December 20, 1577 (Arber's *Transcript*, II, 322), six months after he had secured his license for the *Gorgeous Gallery* itself. In the Stationers' entry it was called "the lamentacon of a gentlewoman vpon the Death of hir late Deceased frende William Gryffith gent." It was probably published (in broadside form) before the *Gorgeous Gallery*, to which it was added as a filler. The epitaph is a very curious production, ostensibly the work of a woman who objected to the earlier epitaph that one of Gruffith's male friends had written. About Gruffith himself I have been able to find no information. There is no reason for attempting to identify him with the well-known printer William Griffith. Possibly he was the W. G. who contributed to *The Copy of a letter, lately written in meeter, by a yonge Gentilwoman*, — a pamphlet printed by Richard Jones in 1566 and reprinted in J. P. Collier's *Illustrations of Early English Popular Literature*, vol. II, — "A Love-letter, or an earnest perswasion of a Lover." In this poetical epistle W. G. remarks that "sixe yeares long . . . I bod for thee," addressing himself apparently to "Is. W.," the "yonge Gentilwoman" mentioned on the title-page.

The humility with which the gentlewoman of the *Gorgeous Gallery* makes trial of the art of poetry is anticipated by a passage in *Phyllyp Sparowe* (*ca.* 1515, lines 770–773, 820–822), where Skelton writes as a woman:

> I am but a yong mayd,
> And cannot in effect
> My style as yet direct
> With Englysh wordes elect. . . .
> Yet as a woman may,
> My wyt I shall assay
> An epytaphe to wryght.

12–23 *A doutfull . . . ruthe to ringe*] This introduction is evidently the work, not of the poetess, but of the "builder" of the *Gorgeous Gallery*, Thomas Proctor.

NOTES

13 *nor forcing life*] 'Not caring anything about life.' Cf. the *Paradise*, 1580, K, "I [Death] force nor friend nor faith."

24 *With Poets pen, &c.*] The poem proper is written in the *Venus and Adonis* stanza. Cf. 68. 2 n.

25 *Mineruæs mate*] 'Minerva's companion,' i. e., a wise woman.

27 *Can cure my cursed cares*] The context here, as well as the plain statement at 120. 6–7, shows that the line is incorrect. *Can't cure*, not *can cure*, is what the poetess means.

28 *For why?*] This means *because*, and the question-mark should be omitted.

117. 6 *Wit wants to will*] 'Knowledge (the ability to write) is lacking to will (my intention of writing).'

17 *pay my pate, &c.*] 'To wear black would reveal my secret love and, as a result (in reward), bring hatred on my head.'

31 *Damon . . . Pithias*] Several ballads on this subject were in circulation before 1578, to say nothing of the play of *Damon and Pythias* which Richard Edwards, compiler of the *Paradise*, had written.

34 *I. and H.*] Possibly the *I. H.* who wrote of Gruffith's death to small effect was Jasper Heywood. His initials are signed thus to poems in the 1576 edition of the *Paradise* and elsewhere. Cf. 102.20 n.

35 *Rime Ruffe*] I. e., doggerel rhymes. So Chaucer's Parson "can nat geste — rum, ram, ruf — by lettre." In his notes on *The Parson's Tale* (Chaucer's *Works*, V [1894], 446) Skeat gives a parallel phrase from George Peele's *Old Wives' Tale* ("It may be, this rim-ram-ruf is too rude an encounter"), and calls attention to an instance of "rym and raf" in Wright's edition of Walter Map, p. 340. Cf. also George Gascoigne (*Complete Poems*, ed. Hazlitt, I, 412), "To rumble rime in raffe and ruffe"; *Emaricdulfe*, 1595, sonnet 4,

> Smile on these rough-hewd lines, these ragged words
> That neuer stil'd from the Castalian spring;

Thomas Nashe, *Summers Last Will*, 1600 (*Works*, ed. McKerrow, III, 252), "The Poet is bribde . . . to hold him halfe the night with riffe raffe of the rumming of Elanor"; and 119. 20, "ragged rymes."

36 *It hangs at Pawles*] I suppose she means that the epitaph written by I. H. hangs (i. e., is pasted up) at St. Paul's Cathedral; for elegies and ballads smeared the doors, windows, and advertising posts in and near the building.

NOTES

118. 4 *neuer will refuse*] Unintelligible to me.

20 *Some Zoylus sot*] 'Some fool like Zoilus,' the Greek grammarian (†320 B.C.), whose vicious attacks on the Homeric poems gave him the title of "the Scourge of Homer."

22 *Momus match*] 'An equal of Momus.' Cf. 4. 3.

119. 2, 3, 8 *her . . . shee . . . her*] "This appears as though Death wore a female form to females" (Park).

5 *Hap death, holde life*] 'Whether death come or life remain.'

15 *Caliope*] No doubt Euterpe or Erato would have been a more appropriate muse to speak of, if the poetess had had more of "Pallas learned skill."

19 *Doo wayle, to want*] 'Do bewail to lack' (i. e., because I lack).

21 *lyues*] Read lines.

37 *a sticking place*] Cf. *Macbeth*, I, vii, 60–61, "But screw your courage to the sticking-place, And we'll not fail."

120. 4 *bluntish*] 'Rather, or somewhat, blunt.' This is the earliest example of *bluntish* (meaning unfeeling or callous) given in the *N. E. D.*

10 *drinke vp all, my sorrow*] Cf. the *Handful*, p. 31, "And make them drinke their owne disease"; Chaucer, *The Franklin's Tale*, line 214, "With-outen coppe he drank al his penaunce"; Chaucer, *Troilus*, III, 1035, "But goodly drinketh up al his distresse."

16 *dare I not*] 'I dare not' (give my name).

16 *flying fame*] Cf. 61. 11 n.

17 *byting bugs will barke*] 'Biting bugbears (bogies) will bark.' A curious expression, showing how the necessity for alliteration led the unskilled poetess into arrant nonsense. Cf. Thomas Churchyard, *The Worthines of Wales*, 1587, C2ᵛ (Spenser Society reprint),

> A kynd of sound, that makes a hurling noyse,
> To feare young babes, with brute of bugges and toyes;

and John Wilbye, *English Madrigals* (1598, No. 11), "No, no, these are but bugs to breed amazing."

INDEXES

INDEX OF FIRST LINES, TITLES, AND TUNES

First lines and titles are printed in roman type, and titles are enclosed in quotation-marks. Tunes are printed in italics.

	PAGE
"A. M. unto All Young Gentlemen in Commendation of this Gallery"	3
"Aeger Dives Habet Nummos"	96
"Aged Lover's Note at Length to Learn to Die, The"	44
All wealth I must forsake and pleasures eke forego	35
"Another Complaint on Fortune"	21
"Another Loving Letter"	78
Ask what love is it is a passion	58
Attend thee go play thee	38
Ay me ay me I sigh to see	93
Be steadfast to thine own	27
"Beauty and Chastity, Of"	66
"Beauty is a Pleasant Path to Destruction"	101
Because my heart is not mine own	78
Behold me here whose youth to withered years	91
Behold these high and mighty men	70
Behold you dames that reign in fames	56
Bitter sweet that strains my yielded heart, The	72
"Brief Caveat to Shun Fawning Friends, A"	100
"Brief Dialogue between Sickness and Worldly Desire, A"	95
Busy bees whose pains do never miss, The	3
But I suppose the same good will	67
"Caveat to Young Men to Shun the Snares of Cupid's Crafty Sleights, A"	42
Chastity a virtue rare	66
Conscience pure withouten spot, A	67
Dear heart as erst I was so will I still remain	61
Dear lady decked with comeliness	88
Deem as ye list upon good cause	30
Desire hath driven from me my will	24
"Desperate Lover Exclaimeth his Lady's Cruelty and Threateneth to Kill Himself, The"	45
Doubtful dying doleful dame, A	116
Each thing must have a time	47
"Epitaph upon the Death of Arthur Fletcher of Bangor, An"	52
Even he that whilom was thy faithful friend	16
Everlasting bondage doth he choose, An	66
"Excellent Sonnet Wherein the Lover Exclaimeth against Detraction, An"	31
Faithful cannot fly nor wander to nor fro, The	51

[209]

INDEX OF FIRST LINES, ETC.

"Fall of Folly Exampled by Needy Age, The" 91
Fancy is fierce desire is bold 67
Farewell my friend whom fortune forced to fly 102
"Fine and Friendly Letter of the Lover to his Beloved, A" 34
Finest tongue can tell the smoothest tale, The 67
"Flatterers and Faithful Friends, Of" 67
For beauty's sake though love doth dread thy might 55
"Friendship Found by Chance, Of" 67
Friendship found by chance is such, The 67
From limbo lake where dismal fiends do lie 81
Glittering shows of Flora's dames, The 26
"Gloze of Fawning Friendship, A" 86
God wot my friend our life full soon decays 67
"Good Will Got by Due Desert, Of" 67
Greedy man whose heart with hate doth swell, The 80
"Happy Wished Time, Of a" 47
Health I thee send if he may give 7
Heat is past that did me fret, The 57
"History of Pyramus and Thisbe Truly Translated, The" 103
How can the cripple get in running race the game 21
"How to Choose a Faithful Friend" 69
Hugy heap of cares that in this world I find, The 22
I count this conquest great 66
I loathe that I did love 35
I spake when I meant not 65
I would I were Actaeon whom Diana did disguise 52
If Chaucer yet did live whose English tongue 63
If ever wight had cause to moan 42
If only sight suffice my heart to loose or bind 48
If pity once may move thy heart 39
Imagine when these blurred lines thus scribbled 74
In Babylon a stately seat 103
In doubtful dreading thoughts as I gan call to mind 21
"In the Commendation of Faithful Love" 51
"In the Praise of a Beautiful and Virtuous Virgin Whose Name Begins with M" 56
"In the Praise of the Rare Beauty and Manifold Virtues of Mistress D." . . . 63
"Invidus Alterius Rebus Macrescit Opimis" 80
"Lady Beloved Assureth her Lover to be his Own and not to Change, The" . 61
"Lady Beloved Exclaimeth of the Great Untruth of her Lover, The" 28
"Lady Writeth unto her Lover Wherein she Most Earnestly Chargeth him with Ingratitude, A" 53
"Lamentable Lover Abiding in the Bitter Bale of Direful Doubts towards his Lady's Loyalty, The" 7

INDEX OF FIRST LINES, ETC.

"Lamentation of a Gentlewoman upon the Death of her Friend William Gruffith, The" 116
"Lamentation of Pyramus for the Loss of his Love Thisbe, The" 113
"Lawless Lust, Of" 66
Leave vading plumes no more vaunt gallant youth 79
"Letter Sent from beyond the Seas to his Lover, A" 77
"Letter Written by a Young Gentlewoman and Sent to her Husband Unawares into Italy, A" 74
Like as the hawk is led by lure to draw from tree to tree 34
Lo here the state of every mortal wight 99
"Lover Approving his Lady Unkind is Forced Unwilling to Utter his Mind, A" 83
"Lover Being Accused of Suspicion of Flattery Pleadeth Not Guilty, The" . 69
"Lover Being Blinded with the Faithless Love of his Lady is Contented to Remit her Fault, The" 45
"Lover Being Newly Caught in Cupid's Snares Complaineth on the Gods of Love, The" 22
"Lover Being Overmuch Wearied with Servile Life, The" 68
"Lover Complaineth of his Lady's Unconstancy, The" 35
"Lover Deceived by his Lady's Unconstancy Writeth unto her, The" . . . 57
"Lover Declareth his Painful Plight, The" 29
"Lover Describeth his Painful Plight and Requireth Speedy Redress, The" . 59
"Lover Describeth the Dangerous State of Ambition, The" 70
"Lover Exhorteth his Lady to be Constant, The" 38
"Lover Extolleth as well the Rare Virtues of his Lady Beloved as also her Incomparable Beauty, The" 24
"Lover Forsaken Writeth to his Lady a Desperate Farewell, The" 16
"Lover Grievously Complaineth against the Unjust Dealing of his Lady Beloved, The" 49
"Lover Having his Beloved in Suspicion Declareth his Doubtful Mind, The" 30
"Lover Having Sustained Overmuch Wrong Wisheth Speedy Death, The" . 37
"Lover in Bondage Looketh for Releasement, The" 33
"Lover in Distress Exclaimeth against Fortune, The" 21
"Lover in Great Distress Comforteth Himself with Hope, The" 50
"Lover in the Praise of his Beloved and Comparison of her Beauty, The" . 56
"Lover Persuadeth Himself to Patience against Envy, The" 48
"Lover Persuadeth his Beloved to Beware the Deceits of Strange Suitors, The" 27
"Lover Recounteth his Faithful Diligence toward his Beloved, The" . . . 73
"Lover to his Beloved by the Name of Fair and False, The" 59
"Lover unto his Lady Beloved of her Disdainfulness toward him, The" . . 55
"Lover Wisheth Himself an Hart in the Forest as Actaeon Was, The" . . 52
"Lover Wounded with his Lady's Beauty Craveth Mercy, The" 39
"Lover's Farewell at his Departure Persuadeth his Beloved to Constancy, The" 25
"Lover's Fatal Farewell at his Death, The" 35
"Lover's Life, A" 82

INDEX OF FIRST LINES, ETC.

"Loving Epistle Written by Ruphilus to his Lady Elriza, A" 9
Lusty gallant 26
"Maze of Maidens, A" 87
"Mirror of Mortality, A" 94
My fancy feeds upon the sugared gall 73
My joyful days be past 45
My love what misliking in me do you find 83
"Narsetus a Woeful Youth in his Exile Writeth to Rosana" 13
Not light of love lady 38
Not she for whom proud Troy did fall and burn 56
Now cease to sing your siren songs 86
O cruel heart with falsehood infect 59
O heavy heart whose harms be hid 50
O wretched wight whom henceforth may I trust 53
"Owen Roydon to the Curious Company of Sycophants" 3
"Painful Plight of a Lover Remaining in Doubtful Hope of his Lady's Favor, The" 72
Pass forth in doleful dumps my verse 31
"Patience, Of" 66
"Pretty Pamphlets" 79
"Pretty Parables and Proverbs of Love" 65
"Proctor's Precepts" 79
"Proper Ditty to the tune of Lusty gallant, A" 26
"Proper Posy for a Handkerchief, A" 67
"Proper Sonnet How Time Consumeth All Earthly Things, A" 93
"Pure Conscience, Of a" 67
"Respice Finem" 99
"Reward of Whoredom by the Fall of Helen, The" 81
See gallants see this gallery of delights 3
Shall clammy clay shroud such a gallant gloze 94
"Short Epistle Written in the Behalf of N.B. to M.H., A" 88
Since needs ye will me sing give ear unto the voice 29
Since that thou didst me love 45
Since thou unjust hast caught a lust 49
Slave of servile sort that born is bond by kind, The 59
Some women feign that Paris was 5
Sovereign salve there is for each disease, A 66
"T. P. his Farewell unto his Faithful Friend F. S." 102
Tedious toil the cares which lovers taste, The 82
This is the day wherein my irksome life 113
Though fortune cannot favor according to my will 25
Though that my years full far do stand aloof 69
"Three Things to be Shunned, Of" 66
Three things who seeks for praise must fly 66

INDEX OF FIRST LINES, ETC.

Through beauty's sugared baits	101
"To a Gentlewoman that Said All Men be False"	5
To darksome cave where crawling worms remain	95
To seem for to revenge each wrong in hasty wise	69
To stay thy musing mind he did this pistle frame	13
To thee I write whose life and death thy faith may save	77
Too feeble is the thread that holdeth me in life	37
"True Description of Love, A"	58
Try ere thou trust unto a fawning friend	100
Twice hath my quaking hand withdrawn this pen away	9
"View of Vainglory, A"	89
"Virtuous Life Age and Death, Of a"	67
Wealthy chuff for all his wealth, The	96
What motion more may move a man to mind	89
When Cupid scaled first the fort	31
When shall relief release my woe	33
When that I weigh with wit and eke consider now	46
Where is the life that late I led	39
Who goes to gaze of every gallant girl	87
Who seeketh the renown to have	66
Who sees the ill and seeks to shun the same	98
Why askest thou the cause wherefore I am so sad	44
"Will and Reason, Of"	66
Willow willow willow	83
"Win Fame and Keep it"	98
"Wisdom, Of"	66
With poet's pen I do not press to write	116
With speedy wings my feathered woes pursues	68
"Worthy Comparison of Virtue against All Worldly Pomp, A"	46
Would God I had never seen the tears	28
Ye grisly ghosts which walk below in black	52
You graves of grisly ghosts	35

GLOSSARIAL INDEX

References are to pages. Numbers in parentheses refer to lines of the text, an *n.* to the note on a line. The glossary contains lexicographical material, much of it, of course, familiar to any educated person.

A., W., *A Special Remedy*, xv, 150, 168
abandon, *expel, banish*, 40 (22)
abasid (abased), *cast down*, 105 (10)
abrade, 112 (35) n.
accounted, *equated, compared*, 89 (5)
Achilles, 14 (36) n., 63 (19) n.
acquench, *quench*, 29 (36)
Acrisius, 152
Actaeon, 52 (3), 56 (6)
adaunt, *quell, subdue*, 32 (7)
addrest, *furnished with*, 32 (3)
adew, a due (adieu), 25 (45), 50 (20), 76 (17), 77 (29), 120 (3)
Admetus, 119 (29)
advance, *help on, aid*, 21 (12), 60 (27), 68 (25)
advice, *opinion*, 10 (17); *consideration, thought*, 48 (25)
Aeneas, 14 (2) n., 74 (17, 20)
aeole, *Aeolus*, 36 (45)
Aeson, 75 (10) n. *See* Jason
Aetna, Mount, 68 (6)
affection, *passion*, 66 (15)
afore, *before*, 62 (32)
Agamemnon, 12 (27)
Alboin, King, 187 f.
Alcestis, 119 (33)
Alcilia, 180 f.
Alcmene, 14 (34) n.
Alfieri, Vittorio, 188
Alfred, The Proverbs of, 155
allow, *recognize, admit*, 15 (11)
alow, *low down*, 52 (8)
alowe. *See* allow
amain, *with main force, violently*, 81 (17)
among, *all the while, continually*, 50 (9); *all over, throughout*, 108 (21)
Anaxarete, 83 (2) n.
Anchises, 74 (20)
Ancren Riwle, 152 f.
and (an), *if*, 16 (16)

[214]

GLOSSARIAL INDEX

annoy, *annoyance*, 7 (20), 60 (31), 96 (29), 99 (13)
ant, the, and the grasshopper, 79 (11) n.
Apelles, *a Greek painter of the time of Alexander the Great*, 4 (20 n., 26, 28 n.), 24 (14)
Apollo, 60 (13)
appease, *grow calm*, 23 (27)
approve, *prove, test*, 83 (9), 84 (24), 102 (3)
Apuleius, Lucius, 170
Arber, Edward, xiii n., xiv n., xix n., 150, 152, 154, 162, 165, 173, 178, 187 ff., 195, 203 f.; editor of Tottel's *Miscellany, q. v.*
Ariadne, 12 (7) n., 56 (9) n.
armid (armed), *furnished with claws*, 112 (23)
Armin, Robert, 199
arrive, *approach*, 53 (25)
as, *as if*, 112 (24, 25); *that* (result), 9 (19), 10 (2, 18), 69 (12)
assay, *make trial of*, 19 (15), 35 (35), 69 (13), 90 (15), 107 (17)
assay, *attempt*, 55 (3); at all assays, *on every occasion*, 52 (30)
assemble, *unite*, 115 (16)
assemblies, *social entertainments*, 105 (11)
Atropos, 35 (31), 64 (26), 64 (28) n.   *See* Fates
attached, *arrested*, 92 (4)
attempt, *try with afflictions*, 86 (17)
awrong, 74 (26)
awry, *wrongly*, 69 (26); *out of the right course*, 118 (6)
Axeres.   *See* Anaxarete
Ayenbite of Inwyt, 180
ayer (heir), 10 (20)

B., M., 168
Babylon, Pyramus and Thisbe at, 103 (3)
Bacchus, 75 (32) n.
back friends, *false friends*, 11 (7)
bait, assay the, 10 (13) n.
Balfour, Sir James, *Ballads*, 161
balk, *ignore, overlook*, 93 (21)
ballads, examples of, in the *Gorgeous Gallery*, xxii; referred to, 146, 152, 153, 157, 162, 185, 187; registrations of, 152, 154, 160, 162, 165, 173, 178, 188, 190 f., 204. *See* Balfour, Clark, Collmann, Lilly, Percy, *Roxburghe Ballads*
ban, *curse*, 12 (3), 19 (5)
band, *bond, promise*, 27 (24), 65 (25) n.; *bond, chain*, 31 (21), 32 (22); *bounds*, 107 (16)
Bandello, Matteo, 164, 188
bane, *destruction*, 10 (13) n., 18 (5)
baned, *doomed*, 7 (9)
Bang, Willy, 162
Bangor, Wales, 52 (18)

[215]

GLOSSARIAL INDEX

Barbazan and Méon, *Fabliaux*, 198
Barnfield, Richard, 187
Baskervill, C. R., 173
bate (bait), 87 (20)
beams, *glances*, 56 (25)
bear away the bell, *surpass*, 36 (40)
Beaumont and Fletcher, 151.   *See* Fletcher, John
Beckles, lamentation of, 193
beclogged, *encumbered*, 74 (13)
beguile, *assuage*, 104 (23)
behest, *vow, promise*, 18 (16)
beldame nun, 75 (32) n.
Belleforest, François de, 164, 188
bent, *wrinkled (of the brows)*, 48 (17); *determined*, 75 (36)
beraft (bereft), 23 (22)
besprent, *sprinkled*, 13 (23), 112 (30)
Bewe, Master, xxi, 168
bewray, *reveal, disclose*, 9 (5), 105 (35), 106 (15), 110 (18), 117 (16); *betray*, 12 (13) 109 (7)
bewreathed, *entwined*, 68 (11)
Bible, Holy, cited, 159, 166, 169, 179, 184, 190, 197; quoted, 153, 157, 186, 194
bide, *suffer, endure*, 6 (2), 30 (6); *remain*, 18 (17)
bight (bite), 10 (13) n., 65 (23) n.
bill, *letter*, 74 (8), 75 (9), 76 (25)
bind, *force, obligate*, 24 (18), 28 (43), 36 (5), etc.
bird, *woman*, 26 (29, 32, 34)
birding, *hunting for birds*, 65 (17)
blase (blaze), *splendor, brilliancy*, 24 (9), 87 (13)
blast, *reputation*, 63 (13)
blear, *dim (the eyes), hoodwink*, 24 (9), 57 (27), 65 (22) n., 96 (26)
blink, *glimpse*, 107 (8)
blist, *blessed*, 107 (15)
blubbering, blubbered, *tearful*, 43 (2, 30)
bluntish, 120 (4) n.
bluttring, *blurting out (words)*, 65 (22) n.
board, *dining-table*, 50 (9)
Boccaccio, Giovanni, 157, 171
Boer, C. de, 198
Boiardo, Matteo M., 196
boiling breast, 81 (15), 82 (13, 33), 83 (3)
Boleyn, Anne, 177
Bolte, Johannes, 192
Bond, R. W., editor of John Lyly, *q. v.*
bond, *in the condition of servitude*, 59 (23) n.
Book of Common Prayer, 175

GLOSSARIAL INDEX

boord. *See* board
boot, *advantage*, 49 (29)
bound, *restrict*, 104 (29)
bourdes, *jests, raillery*, 49 (20)
braggest, *most boastful*, 87 (13)
Brandon, Samuel, 152 f.
brast, *burst*, 44 (29), 50 (29)
Brathwaite, Richard, 151
brave, *handsome, fair*, 3 (5), 81 (28), 86 (16), 87 (13, 21), etc.
breed, *cause*, 7 (20)
bren, *burn*, 51 (18)
Breton, Nicholas, xxii f., 179, 190
Brett, Cyril, 176
brickle, *fragile, brittle*, 46 (26) n., 49 (8), 98 (11)
bright, *beautiful*, 13 (27), 14 (35), 19 (2), etc.
Britannia, 74 (22)
brittle, *fickle*, 9 (23)
broil, *burn (with love)*, 44 (4)
Brooke, Arthur, 165
brued (brewed), 64 (16)
brunt, bear the, *stand the test, surpass*, 56 (27) n.
brute (bruit), *reputation*, 69 (22), 102 (15); *the message of Death*, 95 (23)
Brydges, Sir Egerton, 151
bugs, 120 (17) n.
Bullen, A. H., 151, 156, 167
Bush, Douglas, 198
but, *only*, 57 (11); *unless, except*, 48 (14), 106 (29)
but if, *unless*, 22 (27)
by, *because of*, 17 (12); *with, in respect to*, 58 (8)
Byron, George Gordon, Lord, 169

C., E. *See Emaricdulfe*
C., R., 151, 157, 180
Calliope, 119 (15) n.
Camden, William, *Proverbs*, 151, 155, 157, 167, 173, 175, 180, 182
Camden Society, 152
Camma, 38 (32) n.
can, *have*, 4 (28); *be able*, 59 (17); *gan, began to*, 112 (7)
carking, *fretting*, 92 (15, 29), 101 (25)
carpingly, *disdainfully*, 4 (10)
Carthage, 74 (21) n.
carver, 78 (4) n.
case, *condition, state*, 64 (9)
Castiglione, Baldassare, 162
Cato, Dionysius, 195

[217]

GLOSSARIAL INDEX

caveat, 42 (13)
Cervantes, 157
champion, *one who stoutly maintains any cause*, 4 (25)
Chapman, George, xxi, 185, 193
Chappell, William, 157, 160, 162, 175, 189
chaps, (*contemptuously for*) *human jaws*, 119 (22)
Charon, 60 (20)
chastity conflicts with beauty, 66 (26)
Chaucer, 63 (7), 151–155, 171, 173, 187, 190, 193 f., 197 f., 200, 205 f.
Chaucer Society, 180
cheer, *countenance, mien*, 15 (18)
chiding chaps, *censuring lips*, 119 (22)
Child, F. J., 191
Christy's Plantation Melodies, 170
Chronicon Adae de Usk, 194
chuffe, *churl, boor*, 96 (4), 97 (14)
Churchyard, Thomas, xxi f., 157, 172 f., 183, 206
Cipres well, 55 (23) n.
claps, *sudden mishaps*, 117 (23)
Clark, Andrew, *Shirburn Ballads*, 157, 161, 179, 185 f., 194
Clarke, Samuel, 193
claw, pass by one's, *escape one's grasp*, 80 (11)
clear, *sound, without taint*, 27 (17)
clomb, *climbed*, 106 (24)
clungs, 100 (9) n.
Cocistus (Cocytus), *the river of wailing in Hades*, 52 (19)
cog, *deceive*, 85 (20)
colde (could), 104 (12)
Collier, J. P., xv–xix, 146, 151, 157, 159, 161, 165, 168 f., 171 f., 175 ff., 180, 183 ff., 187, 189, 191, 196 f., 204
Collmann, H. L., *Ballads*, 167, 171, 193 f.
colored, *insincere*, 100 (6)
Colyn Blowbols Testament, 191
common, *mutual*, 105 (34), 108 (30), 114 (13); *ordinary, natural*, 113 (27)
compact, *leagued*, 10 (15)
compast, *artfully contrived*, 63 (33)
Complaint of Scotland, The, 198
conceit, out of, *dissatisfied, displeased*, 36 (39)
confess, *acknowledge, disclose*, 62 (8)
constre, *construe*, 48 (28) n.
cool, *subdue*, 32 (15)
cope, *contest, fight*, 35 (36)
Copy of a Letter by a Young Gentlewoman, The, 204
Corkine, William, 168
cornerwise, *diagonally*, 107 (7)

[218]

GLOSSARIAL INDEX

corps(e), *a living human body*, 9 (10), 12 (17), 20 (19), 43 (10), etc.; *a dead body*, 79 (17), 83 (7)
correct, *corrected (by imprisonment)*, 47 (22)
corse, *a living body*, 23 (12); *a dead body*, 80 (15)
Corser, Thomas, 145
corsive, *corrosive*, 113 (12)
costs (coasts), *boundaries*, 35 (24)
coucht, *stuffed*, 92 (16)
count, *reckoning, esteem*, 72 (12)
countenance, 8 (7) n.; *demeanor, conduct*, 44 (24)
counterpaise, *counterpoise*, 34 (33)
countervail, *be equivalent in value to*, 88 (4); *compensate for*, 96 (21), 102 (10)
courtuous (courteous), 57 (15)
Cowley, Abraham, 176
coy, *disdainful*, 18 (28); *coyly*, 56 (7)
Craig, Alexander, 164, 186
Cranstoun, James, 180
crasde, crased, crasid (crazed), *bruised*, 18 (11), 39 (33), 59 (25)
Crawford, Charles, 172, 181
Cressida, 12 (22, 29) n., 36 (3), 38 (24), 46 (11), 56 (12) n., 59 (15), 78 (20). *See* Troilus
Cres(s)us (Croesus), 13 (16), 96 (8)
Creusa, 75 (13) n., 83 (25) n.
Croft, H. H. S., 181, 197
crop, *bite off*, 50 (3)
Crosse, Henry, 146, 178
cunning, *skill (as opposed to nature)*, 24 (11), 106 (23), etc.
Cupid, 9 (22), 23 (21) n., 31 (9) n., 60 (7), 62 (26), 64 (5), 78 (7, 23), 103 (18) n., 119 (10), 170
curious, *fastidious, dainty*, 3 (21), 96 (20)
Cypris's well, 170

D., Mrs., poem in praise of, 63 f.
Daedalus, 12 (7) n., 68 (15)
dainful, *disdainful*, 55 (23)
dame, *mother*, 55 (14)
Damon, 117 (31) n.
dampish, 99 (16, 21)
Danae, 10 (21) n., 14 (26)
dankish, *humid*, 89 (17), 94 (4)
Davenant, Sir William, 188
David, King, of Israel, 99 (3)
Davies, Sir John, 174, 192
deadly, *deathlike*, 115 (9); *deathlike in gloom*, 7 (11)
Death, messengers of, 92 (4) n.; personified as a woman, 206

[219]

GLOSSARIAL INDEX

debate, *quarreling*, 48 (12)
decaite (deceit), 101 (26)
decay, *destruction*, 113 (17)
decked ('decte'), *adorned*, 24 (20), 88 (3)
decline, *fall*, 51 (29)
declined, *deflected* (*from love*), 16 (32)
decreed, *determined, decided*, 6 (21)
Dedales line, 12 (7) n. *See* Daedalus
deem, *judge*, 69 (32), 70 (7), 71 (12), 91 (17), 109 (28); ?*repent*, 82 (16)
deface, *destroy*, 12 (34)
defend ('desend'), *resist the attack* (*of graving tools*), 62 (29) n.; *forbid*, 75 (13)
define, *come to an end*, 115 (30) n.
Dekker, Thomas, xxiii
Delicate Dainties to Sweeten Lovers' Lips Withal, xiv
Deloney, Thomas, 175, 189, 196
demand, *ask for, deserve*, 10 (11)
denay, *deny*, 17 (33), 106 (20), 110 (23)
denaye, *denial*, 59 (4)
depaint, *delineate, beautify*, 64 (11)
depart, *divide*, 25 (44), 115 (35)
descant, *dwell on, explain*, 76 (18)
desend. *See* defend
deserne (discern), 17 (24)
despight (despite), at thy, *in contempt of thee*, 4 (37)
deuise, *purpose, intention*, 6 (26)
deuorce (divorce), 51 (27) n.
dew, *speech*, 63 (15) n.
Diaconus, Paulus, 188
dialogue-poems, 194
Diana, goddess, 56 (6) n., 59 (18). *See* Actaeon, Phoebe
Dido, 14 (3) n., 74 (21) n.
Dis, *Pluto*, 168
disalowde, *censured*, 98 (3)
disease, *lack of ease*, 72 (22)
disgest, *digest*, 75 (30) n.
disgrace, *disfavor*, 11 (6), 55 (6)
disguise, *transform, change the shape of*, 52 (4)
dislyked, *disapproved of*, 4 (27)
dispatch, *end* (*of life*), 8 (11)
dispitous (despiteous), *insulting*, 60 (22)
disturn, *turn aside*, 62 (5)
Ditis dennes, 52 (20) n.
Dives, 90 (18) n., 96 (12)
do, *make, cause to*, 55 (29), 111 (3), 116 (29)
Dodsley, Robert, *Old Plays*, 173

[220]

GLOSSARIAL INDEX

doings, *'making,' poetry*, 3 (18)
dole, *grief, misery*, 82 (8, 35)
Dom Diego, 41 (8) n.
Donne, John, 176
doom ('dome'), *judgment*, 42 (27), 63 (22), 108 (29)
double, *tinged with duplicity*, 49 (10), 65 (8)
double, *double up, fold*, 34 (21)
doubleness, *duplicity*, 50 (2)
doubtful, *fearful, full of doubts*, 9 (35), 68 (26), 72 (13); *dubious*, 48 (19)
Douce, Francis, 196
Dowland, John, 186
draw strides, *walk*, 13 (22)
Drayton, Michael, 176
dreadly, *dreadful*, 105 (32)
dreads, *fears*, 79 (21)
driery (dreary), 59 (29)
drifts, *schemes, plots*, 58 (11)
drink one's sorrow, 120 (10) n.
drive, *pass (the time)*, 15 (25), 72 (22); *pass away, elapse*, 59 (29); *accomplish*, 110 (36)
driven, *impelled*, 9 (31)
dropping, *tearful*, 7 (10)
dross, 86 (20), 89 (33)
Drummond, William, 174
dryfts. *See* drifts
dumps, *mournful melodies*, 31 (10); *melancholy*, 82 (20)
Dyboski, R., 155, 180, 196 f.
Dyce, Alexander, 151, 166, 173
dynte (dint), *stroke, blow*, 61 (33)

Early English Text Society, 151, 155, 157, 180 f., 193, 196 f.
earnest, *something paid down to seal a bargain*, 77 (19)
earst (erst), *sooner*, 112 (26)
earwhile (erewhile), *formerly*, 75 (20)
Edwards, Richard, xiii, 205; probable compiler of *The Paradise of Dainty Devices q. v.*
eefe, 49 (12) n.
eft, *again, a second time*, 103 (32), 109 (9), 115 (36, 37)
eftsoons, *presently*, 80 (6), 82 (16)
eke, 21 (22, 32), 26 (17), 35 (3), etc.
Eliot, George, 196
Elizabeth, Queen, 80 (25) n., 177
Ellis, George, xv
Ellis, Sir Henry, xv f.
Elriza, epistle to, from Ruphilus, 9 ff.

[221]

GLOSSARIAL INDEX

els (else), 4 (11), 9 (13), etc.
Elviden, Edmond, 193
Elyot, Sir Thomas, 181, 197
Emaricdulfe, by E. C., 201, 205
embrace, *accept (as a friend)*, 24 (19)
embrew. *See* imbrew
empt, *empty*, 7 (29)
Eneas. *See* Aeneas
England's Parnassus, 172, 181
Englishmen for My Money, 173
ensue, *imitate*, 74 (17) n.
entice, *provoke, instigate*, 54 (22)
envy, *malice, enmity*, 37 (21)
equal, *impartial*, 23 (8)
Erasmus, Desiderius, 146, 193
erbe (herb), 105 (19) n.
Erebus, *Hades*, 52 (20) n.
estates, *persons of high degree*, 103 (5)
Ethna. *See* Aetna
Etrascus, 82 (32) n.
Europe, 119 (11)
Evans, Thomas, 189
excuse, *omit*, 76 (21)
express, *explicit*, 104 (27)
eyne, *eyes*, 28 (5)

F., T., xix
Fablel dou Dieu d'Amours, Li, 157
fact, *deed, action*, 10 (10, 14), etc.
fain (feign), 113 (34)
fall, *come to be*, 60 (29)
falsing, *proved false*, 13 (35)
falts, *false*, 60 (9)
fancy, *love*, 82 (27), 104 (2)
fantasy, *fancy, imagination*, 25 (22), 51 (20)
fardell (fardel), *bundle*, 105 (17)
farforth, *to a great extent*, 27 (37)
Farmer, Richard, xv
Farr, Edward, 194
fast, *quickly*, 107 (10)
fast, *fasten*, 8 (23)
Fates, the three, 60 (19) n., 64 (28) n., 105 (30) n.
fayne. *See* fain
fear, *frighten*, 94 (29)
feature, *shapeliness*, 56 (27)

GLOSSARIAL INDEX

feere. *See* fere
fell, *deadly, terrible*, 22 (27), 23 (18), 32 (23), etc.
Fellowes, E. H., 168
Fenton, Sir Geoffrey, 164 f.
fere, *companion, mate*, 36 (28), 74 (22)
feriman (ferryman), *Charon*, 60 (20)
fet, *fetch, draw*, 36 (23)
fie, 100 (12) n.
Fielding, Henry, 193
filde (filled), 87 (15), 112 (17)
file, *thread (of life)*, 60 (19)
filed, *polished, elegant*, 15 (5), 84 (2)
fine, *to end*, 15 (8); *the end*, 87 (6, 12), 89 (14), 94 (11), 99 (11), 113 (26)
fined, *refined*, 69 (7)
flagrant, *glowing, colorful (red)*, or more probably (cf. line 35) a misprint for *fragrant*, 119 (34)
flames of love, 26 (5)
flat, *level to the ground*, 110 (34)
flaunting, *showy, gaudy*, 91 (15)
flearing (fleering), *mocking*, 60 (34)
flee (flie), *fly*, 21 (29)
Fleece, the Golden, 75 (11)
fleet, *flit*, 13 (3), 17 (11), 20 (33), 49 (22)
Fletcher, Arthur, epitaph on, 52 f.
Fletcher, John, 191. *See* Beaumont
Fletcher, Phineas, 181
flit, flyt. *See* fleet
flurt (flirt), 81 (19), 84 (18)
flushing, *quickly flowing*, 74 (9)
fly, care not a, 65 (14)
foil ('foyle'), *repulse, defeat*, 4 (4), 8 (7), 95 (23)
folded, *encircling*, 110 (18)
follow, *obey*, 20 (11)
fond, *foolish, infatuated*, 60 (17), 90 (4); fondly, *foolishly*, 65 (11)
fool, *a term of endearment*, 103 (22) n.
for that, *because*, 60 (36), 61 (10)
for why, *because*, 33 (3), 116 (28) n.
force, *care for, regard*, 61 (15), 116 (13) n.
force, *power, strength*, 4 (11), 9 (11), 11 (23), 19 (33), etc.; *criminal assault*, 64 (18); of force, *necessarily*, 50 (21), 59 (8), 60 (37); of no force, *it doesn't matter*, 14 (17)
forcing, 116 (13) n.
ford ('foord'), *afford*, 47 (23)
forduld, *deadened, stupified*, 106 (36)
foreign, *strange, unfamiliar*, 60 (32)
forepassed, *already passed*, 92 (27)

[223]

GLOSSARIAL INDEX

forgo, *leave*, 112 (26)
forsid (forced), *cared, wished*, 65 (6)
forthink, *regret, repent*, 10 (14)
Fortune's wheel, 46 (26)
Foxwell, A. K., 167
fraight, *freighted* (= *fraught*), 55 (23) n.
frame, *construct, form*, 10 (16), 12 (4), 13 (8), 24 (31), 103 (11), etc.; *shape one's actions*, 6 (32)
frame, *construction*, 63 (12); *contrivances*, 48 (4); *out of frame, without order or form*, 74 (4), *out of one's due place*, 27 (41)
fraud, *defraud*, 28 (31)
fraught, *supplied*, 3 (8)
frayght, *freight, load*, 21 (17)
fresh, *youthful*, 14 (26)
friend, *lover*, 5 (10), 10 (11), 13 (10), etc.
frighted, *frightened*, 112 (20)
frisking, 26 (11) n.
Froissart, Jean, 197
Fry, John, xix n.
full, at (the), *completely, fully*, 15 (9), 101 (9)
Furnivall, F. J., xiv n., 153, 172, 177, 180 f., 190 f., 193
furth, *forth*, or perhaps a misprint for *further*, 77 (8)

G., W., 204
Gale, Dunstan, 198
game, *sport, pleasure*, 29 (37); *get the game, win*, 21 (3)
gan, *began*, 4 (25), 21 (21). *See* can, 112 (7)
Gascoigne, George, xxiv, 150, 159, 177, 184, 205
gastly (ghastly), 7 (14)
gathering wind, *sailing nearer to the wind*, 32 (18)
Gayton, Edmund, 186
Gemini, 65 (21) n.
genitive forms without ending, 5 (23) n.
genorositie (generosity), *excellence of race or lineage*, 53 (26) n.
Genzmer, Felix, 188
germayne (german), *relative (native)*, 74 (18)
gest. *See* guest
geue (give), 9 (9)
ghost, *spirit, soul*, 10 (3), 35 (22), 52 (19), 105 (22), 108 (3), etc.
Gibson, Leonard, 152, 189
Gifford, Humfrey, 146, 162, 195
Gifford, William, 151
Gilbert, W. S., 183
gin, *snare, trap*, 26 (31)
Ginevra and Dom Diego, 41 (8) n.

GLOSSARIAL INDEX

gins, *begins*, 22 (20), 111 (29)
giues (gyves), *shackles, fetters*, 13 (17)
glad, *gladden*, 11 (35), 89 (25), 103 (31)
glancing, *gleaming, flashing*, 87 (4, 19)
Glauce, 189. *See* Creusa
glose. *See* gloze
glove, take the, 8 (30) n.
gloze, 90 (5) n.; *pretence, false show*, 81 (24, 33), 87 (4, 17, 19), 88 (24), 94 (3), 101 (16); *gloss, commentary*, 86 (15)
glush, *?gush*, 114 (27) n.
glut, *glutted*, 80 (7)
go, *walk*, 21 (9); go pack, *go away*, 86 (23)
goast. *See* ghost
Godfrey of Viterbo, 188
Golding, Arthur, 198
Gollancz, Sir Israel, 162
Gorgeous Gallery of Gallant Inventions, A, bad grammar in, 182, 196, 199 f.; ballads in, xxii; borrowing from, by Thomas Howell, 184; borrowings in, from *A Handful of Pleasant Delights*, xxi f., 147, 158, 160–164, from Thomas Churchyard, 172, from Thomas Howell, 147 ff., 186, from *The Paradise of Dainty Devices*, xxii, 168, 182, 184, 197, from Tottel's *Miscellany*, xxii, 155, 158 ff., 165 f., from George Whetstone, 146; contributors to, xxi, 168, 172; editions and reprints of, xv ff.; editorial methods of the present edition of, explained, xviii; Elizabethan compilers of, the, xix f.; Elizabethan references to, xxii f.; licensed, xiv; Malone's copy of, xxv, described, xvi ff.; metrical forms in, xxiv f.; misprints in, listed, 121; Northumberland copy of, described, xvii f.; notes to, 143; quality of poetry in, xxiv; style of, xxiii; subjects discussed in, xxiii f.; tunes used in, 26 (9) n., 31 (9) n., 35 (21) n., 38 (3) n., 39 (21) n.; unpopularity of, xiv f., xxii; variant readings of, list of the, 121
Gorgons, the, 52 (20, 21) n.
goring gripes, *piercing pains*, 82 (28), 95 (11)
Gower, John, 155, 188, 197 f.
grafte, *grafted*, 56 (32)
granted, *declared, adjudged*, 69 (27)
grasshopper and the ant, the, 79 (11) n.
graue, *engrave*, 62 (30); *bury*, 113 (23), 116 (6)
Gray, G. J., xx n.
gree, *agree*, 18 (14)
Greene, Robert, xxi, 146, 151, 173, 184, 192, 194, 198
Greg, W. W., 173
Gregory of Tours, 188
Grierson, H. J. C., 176
gripes, *pains*, 10 (5), 82 (28), 95 (11)
gripte (gripped), *seized*, 118 (11)
grisled, grisly, *horrible*, 31 (12), 35 (22), 42 (3), 52 (19)

GLOSSARIAL INDEX

Grosart, A. B., xxiii n., 146 f., 151, 153, 161, 172 f., 178, 180 f., 184, 192, 194
groth, *groweth*, 47 (29)
Grove, Matthew, 194
Gruffith, William, epitaph on, 116 (9, 11 n.)
guerdon, 88 (25), 91 (29), 110 (7), 114 (19)
guest, *a new (stranger) lover*, 36 (35)
gyles, *guile*, 56 (32)

H., I., 198; author of a lost epitaph on Gruffith, 117 (34) n.
hale, *draw, pull*, 23 (26)
Hales, J. W., 191
Halliwell-Phillipps, J. O., 154, 157, 167, 186, 189, 192. *See Wit and Wisdom*
halt, *deceive, trick*, 91 (21)
Handful of Hidden Secrets, A, xiv
Handful of Pleasant Delights, A, xiii f., xxiii f., 155 ff., 162, 165, 169 f., 174, 179, 186, 188 ff., 206; borrowings from, in the *Gorgeous Gallery*, xxi f., 147, 158, 160 ff.
harbred (harbored), 9 (10)
hard (heard), 9 (22), 53 (20), 115 (5)
harp, *speak at length about*, 78 (8)
Hart, Georg, 198
Harvey, Gabriel, 151, 172, 180
Haslewood, Joseph, 164, 167, 191
hault (halt), 91 (21) n.
Hazlitt, W. C., xvi, xx n., 146, 150 f., 155, 159, 161, 173, 190 f., 196, 205
Health to the Gentlemanly Profession of Servingmen, A, 146, 151
heap, *increase*, 73 (11)
heare, *hair*, 52 (20); *here*, 109 (6)
heastes (hests), *commands*, 10 (35)
Hector, 63 (19), 116 (29); Hector's sister, *Polyxena*, 63 (19)
heeding, *heedful*, 9 (20)
heer, heere (her), 107 (19), 113 (21)
Helen of Troy, 5 (10) n., 14 (37), 56 (4), 59 (17), 63 (17), 81 (2) n.
Helicon, Mount, 63 (10)
helm, hold the, 10 (33)
Helmichis and Rosamund, 188
Hending's *Proverbs*, 180
Henry, Matthew, 167
Henryson, Robert, 153
Henslowe, Philip, 173
hent, *snatch, lay hold of*, 107 (19), 115 (37)
here (hear), 29 (10), 102 (5), 103 (26)
Hero and Leander, 77 (26) n.
hewing knife, 8 (10)
Heywood, Jasper, xxi, 72 (9) n., 117 (34) n.
Heywood, John, 189; *Works*, 151, 155, 166, 173, 179, 182, 190, 195, 197, 199

GLOSSARIAL INDEX

Heywood, Thomas, 162, 200
hie (high), 8 (16)
hight, *be called or named*, 103 (13)
Hill, Richard, 155, 180, 196 f.
Hippolytus, 39 (6) n.
hire, *reward, benefit*, 91 (21), 94 (9), 117 (17)
Histoires des Poètes, Les, 198
hit, *it*, 115 (5)
Hoby, Sir Thomas, 162
Hoccleve, Thomas, 181, 193
hold, *stronghold*, 62 (12); *support*, 17 (31), 37 (15), 46 (30), 62 (7); take hold of, *attain*, 93 (9); in hold, *in possession*, 60 (2)
hold, *follow*, 10 (26), 11 (2), 18 (16); *restrain*, 96 (9)
hole (whole), *wholly*, 31 (14), 36 (11)
homeliest, *most familiar (as in the home)*, 33 (19)
Homer, 177 f., 206
Horace, 80 (2) n., 152
hould (hold), *stronghold*, 62 (12)
hovering, *unfixed, inconstant*, 87 (17)
How a Man May Choose a Good Wife from a Bad, 185
Howell, Thomas, xxi f., 153, 161, 182, 189; a poem by, imitates the *Gorgeous Gallery*, 184; poems by, borrowed by the *Gorgeous Gallery*, 147 ff., 186
hugy, 22 (11) n.
Hunnis, William, xiii
Hunterian Club, 146, 164, 168, 172, 186. *See* Lodge
Huntington, Henry E., xix
hurtful, *malicious, harmful*, 117 (14)
hutch, *chest, coffer*, 89 (23), 99 (20)
Huth, Henry, 193
hyer (hire), 60 (9)
Hyginus, Caius Julius, 154

I, emphatic repetition of, 86 (27) n.
Jack Juggler, 191
Jason, 36 (24), 75 (10, 13) n., 83 (25) n.
Icarus, 12 (7) n.
Ide, the walls of, *Mount Ida*, 63 (23)
ielous (jealous), *watchful*, 12 (13), 15 (30)
jet, 65 (21) n.
ikorve, 105 (16) n.
Image of Hypocrisy, The, 172
imbost (embossed), 3 (5), 87 (21)
imbrew (embrew), *saturate (with blood)*, 20 (17), 112 (18)
imp, *youth*, 104 (4)
impart, *divide*, 106 (4)

GLOSSARIAL INDEX

impersid (empierced), 108 (7)
Inchbald, Mrs. Elizabeth, 151
indrowned, 104 (34) n.
infected, *infectious*, 55 (24)
intend, *design*, 17 (5)
Jones, Robert, 189
Jonson, Ben, 152, 174, 180, 182, 194
Jove, 15 (4), 64 (15) n., 76 (22). *See* Jupiter
joy, *enjoy, delight in*, 4 (13), 13 (17, 25), 20 (5), 40 (32), 60 (35), etc.
joyed, *joyful*, 61 (9)
Iphis, 83 (2) n.
irksome, 19 (33)
ist (is't), 92 (11)
Italy, 76 (15); a letter to a husband in, 74 ff.
Itrascus, 82 (32) n.
Jubinal, Achille, 157
Juliet and Romeo, 41 (12) n.
Juno, 178
Jupiter, 14 (34) n. *See* Jove
Juvenal, 180
I wis (iwis), 108 (34)

keep, *stay or remain in*, 114 (33) n.
Kendall, Timothy, 195
kept, *remained in*, 114 (33) n.
kerchief, 112 (20), 114 (29), 115 (5)
keyser (kaiser), *emperor*, 62 (11)
kick, *reject angrily, spurn*, 70 (3), 78 (9)
kind, *nature*, 19 (37), 24 (11), 25 (2), 43 (11), 44 (6), 59 (23), etc.; *Nature*, 105 (2); *class, sort*, 18 (7); after kind, *according to nature*, 28 (41)
Kingsley, Charles, 167
Kittredge, G. L., xxvi, 160, 169, 173, 178, 200
knap, *snap, break into pieces*, 105 (29)
knobs, 92 (16) n.
Kyd, Thomas, 152
kyte (kite), *a vulture*, 58 (3)

lad, *led*, 112 (21)
lake, *a small running stream*, 98 (31) n.
lamentable, *doleful, mourning*, 7 (2)
large, at, *in full*, 12 (35), 58 (25)
lasar. *See* lazar
lastest, *last*, 115 (24)
latest, *last*, 52 (24)
Latimer, Hugh, 193

GLOSSARIAL INDEX

latter, *last*, 94 (6)
lawre, *?laure = laurel*, 65 (22) n.
lay, *law*, 58 (31)
lazar, *leper*, 18 (9)
Lazarus and Dives, 90 (18) n.
leady ('ledy'), *lead-like*, 13 (21)
Leander, 77 (26) n.
learn, *teach*, 90 (20), 92 (26), 102 (17)
least (lest), 3 (13), 12 (13), etc.
leave, *permission (to live)*, 93 (8)
Lecky, W. E. H., 162
Lede (Leda), 10 (21), 14 (24)
ledy. *See* leady
lee, *leeward*, 32 (17)
leese, *lose*, 44 (7), 100 (5)
lenght (length), 99 (21)
length, *lengthen*, 19 (31)
less, *lessen*, 103 (22)
let, *hinder*, 12 (31), 107 (5)
let, *hindrance*, 103 (30), 111 (35), 112 (5)
leue (leave), 13 (31), 65 (9)
levid, 69 (28) n.
lewd, *ignorant, foolish*, 79 (22), 92 (26), 95 (25), 101 (11)
lewdness, *ignorance*, 92 (5)
lickering, 73 (9) n.
lickerous, *lecherous*, 66 (24)
licour salt, *sea water*, 31 (33)
lief (life), 22 (5)
lightiloue, *light of love, inconstancy*, 38 (5 n., 21), 84 (14)
lightly, *easily*, 62 (25); *immodestly*, 118 (20)
lights, *the eyes*, 108 (18)
like, *be pleased with*, 16 (32), 78 (5); *please*, 4 (17), 16 (3), 17 (15), 103 (12), etc.; *compare*, 59 (19)
liking, *pleasing, dainty*, 19 (24)
Lilly, Joseph, *Ballads*, 152, 162, 180, 189, 201
limbo, 81 (3)
Linche, Richard, 165
lively, *life-like*, 24 (31), 89 (7); *necessary to life*, 113 (5)
living, *necessary for life*, 11 (28), 12 (26), 14 (15), 15 (6), 18 (23)
Locrine, 153
Lodge, Thomas, xxi, 146, 168, 186, 192
loe (low), 52 (28)
long, *during a long period*, 95 (21)
Longfellow, H. W., 183
loose, *lose*, 9 (13), 97 (11)

GLOSSARIAL INDEX

looze, *lose*, 62 (32)
lose, *loose*, 24 (18)
losing from bandes, 65 (25) n.
lotted, *allotted*, 97 (33)
love, Elizabethan definitions of, 173
loveday, 104 (23) n.
lower, *frown on, threaten*, 21 (13), 48 (17), 57 (28), 82 (24)
lowres (lours), *frowns*, 85 (22)
Lucifer, 54 (20) n.
Lucrece, the rape of, 64 (18) n.
Lucretius, 152
lukers (lucre's), 86 (29), 97 (3)
lulled ('luld'), *lolled, reclined idly*, 101 (11); *soothed to rest*, 84 (14)
lurch, lie at, *lie concealed or in wait*, 4 (3)
lure, *apparatus used by falconers to recall their hawks*, 34 (19)
lust, *desire*, 45 (48), 49 (4), 103 (19); *list (impersonal)*, 106 (17)
lusty, *vigorous, flourishing*, 19 (34), 91 (11), 105 (6)
Lycophron, 178
Lydgate, John, 172, 188, 192
Lyly, John, 146, 153, 167, 172, 180, 186, 190, 193, 195 f.
lynck (link), the, of love, 8 (2)

M., Mrs., poems in honor of, 57 (14) n.
Mænads, 185
Maidment, James, 161
make, *manifest*, 7 (32), 17 (30); *prepare for*, 111 (19); *collect*, 5 (27); *do*, 110 (32); make and mar, *cause either the complete success or the ruin of a person*, 93 (19)
make, *mate*, 25 (31), 46 (12)
Malone, Edmond, xv ff.
Malone Society, 151, 180
mamtam, *?child's word for love-prattling*, 103 (26)
man, be thy, *i. e., thy servant (lover)*, 27 (39)
Mann, F. O., 175, 189, 196
Mannington, George, 188
Manuscript Additional *15,233*, 154, 157
Manuscript Additional *38,599*, 160
Manuscript Ashmole *48*, 150
Manuscript Bannatyne, 172
Manuscript Durham, Hoccleve's poems, 181, 193
Manuscript Egerton *2009*, 178
Manuscript Percy Folio, 191
Manuscript Sloane *1210*, 182
Map, Walter, 205
mar and make. *See* make
Marlowe, Christopher, 185, 200

GLOSSARIAL INDEX

Mars and Venus, 105 (34) n.
mask, *disguise (adorn)*, 81 (27); *hide*, 84 (30)
masking, *gay and festive*, 79 (4); *frivolous, fond of pleasure*, 81 (23), 87 (5)
mast, *the fruit of trees*, 52 (12)
maste (mayest), 102 (7)
match, *equal*, 15 (3)
matched, *?having a match or equal*, 64 (17), 72 (19) n.
mate, *checkmate, subdue*, 59 (16) n., 63 (28), 64 (17), 72 (19) n.
mate, *companion*, 52 (21), 118 (21)
maugre, *in spite of*, 36 (8), 114 (6)
may chaunce, *maybe*, 62 (7)
mayes, *mazes (labyrinths)*, 68 (17), cf. 72 (24)
mazed, *bewildered*, 12 (10), 82 (20), 86 (24)
McKerrow, R. B., xxiii n., 146, 178, 188, 205. *See* Nashe
mean, *moderation*, 10 (26); *means (of living)*, 106 (31)
meat, *food*, 3 (28), 4 (13); *to meet*, 15 (31) n.
Medea, 75 (11, 12, 13 n.), 83 (25) n.
Medusa, 52 (21)
mend, *improve*, 24 (15)
Menelaus, 5 (23) n.
Meres, Francis, xxi
mestive, *mournful*, 92 (15) n.
Midas, 96 (8)
middest of, in, 45 (13)
Milton, John, 197
mind, in, *with the intention of*, 108 (19)
minds, *thoughts, intentions*, 105 (16) n.
Minerva, 9 (17), 64 (15) n., 116 (25) n., 119 (19). *See* Pallas
Minotaur, 12 (5), 68 (15) n.
Minus, 111 (4) n.
Mirror for Magistrates, xiii, 167, 191
misdeem, *misjudge*, 17 (8), 48 (20)
mislike, *be displeased*, 4 (24); *dislike*, 10 (23), 15 (23), 16 (19), 17 (2), etc.
misliking, *displeasure*, 83 (13)
miss, *fail to happen*, 3 (23)
moan, *bemoan*, 79 (23)
mo(e), *more*, 25 (23), 52 (7), 83 (2), 90 (20)
mold, *the earth*, 55 (22)
molde (mould), 56 (23)
Momus, *son of Night, famed for his censoriousness, especially for his lampoons on the gods*, 4 (3, 32), 118 (22)
mone. *See* moan
Monsieur dom Diego, 41 (8) n.
Montgomerie, Alexander, 180
moone, *moan*, 29 (8)

[231]

GLOSSARIAL INDEX

moossell (muzzle), 112 (18)
more hardier, *more boldly*, 111 (34) n.
more longer, 8 (8)
Morris, Richard, 180
Morton, James, 152 f.
most, *chiefly*, 14 (19)
motion, *impulse, emotion*, 84 (30), 89 (3)
mought, *might*, 75 (33)
move, *make proposals to*, 27 (28); *provoke to anger*, 48 (12)
mundaine, 43 (8)
Munday, Anthony, xix, 145, 151, 180
muse, *wonder*, 54 (30) n., 58 (2), 61 (4), 78 (5)
Muses, the Nine, 9 (18), 116 (18)
musing, *wondering*, 13 (8), 115 (3)
must, *misprint for* muse, 54 (30) n.
Mynotaure. *See* Minotaur

naked we came, naked we return, to the earth, 89 (27) n.
Narcissus, 55 (26) n., 119 (31)
Nashe, Thomas, xxi, xxiii, 146, 178, 188, 194, 205
naythless, *nevertheless*, 110 (35)
ne (a negative), 18 (17), 26 (5, 7), 35 (29), 36 (22, 26), etc.
need, *necessarily, needs*, 95 (20)
Nemrod (Nimrod), 90 (19) n.
Nestor, 63 (15) n., 80 (26)
Neville, Alexander, 196
New English Dictionary, cited, xxiii, 167 ff., 177, 184, 190, 192, 199, 202 f., 206
newfangleness, 39 (10)
Nichols, J. G., 172
nie (nigh), 35 (31)
nill, *will not*, 114 (20)
Nimrod, 90 (19) n.
Ninus ('Minus'), 111 (4) n.
noise, *sound (of music)*, 14 (6)
nonce, for the, *for the time being*, 37 (41)
none, *no*, 55 (3), 106 (29); *not at all*, 110 (37)
nonne (nun), 75 (32) n.
North, Sir Thomas, 162
Northumberland, Duke of, his copy of the *Gorgeous Gallery*, xvii f.
nothing, *not at all, in no way*, 4 (31), 5 (7), 43 (27), 47 (4)
noughts, at, 26 (29)
noyce. *See* noise
nymphish aid, *the aid of the nymphs (or rather of the Muses)*, 116 (20)

observe, *keep (faith)*, 75 (16)
Occleve. *See* Hoccleve

[232]

GLOSSARIAL INDEX

of, *at*, 87 (3, 19); *by*, 37 (21) n.; *from*, 28 (45), 91 (20); *off*, 19 (25), 28 (39), 58 (11), 87 (9), 94 (17), 99 (19), 114 (35), etc.; *that*, 57 (12) n.
oftenly, 109 (6)
Olrik, Axel, 188
on liue, *alive*, 53 (23)
or, *ere*, 35 (18), 65 (13), 103 (8)
orderly, *regularly*, 104 (8)
Otto, August, 146
ouerlyuing. *See* overliving
ought, *owed*, 16 (33)
out alas! 31 (30)
outchast, 114 (4) n.
overliving, *living too long (or possibly a misprint for* overloving), 112 (32)
overpass, 103 (16)
overrun, *read through*, 118 (22)
overslip, *omit*, 103 (15)
overthrow, *fall down*, 47 (21)
Ovid, 64 (35) n., 152 f., 180, 188, 193, 197 ff.
Oxford, Earl of (Edward de Vere), xiii
Oxford Spelling Book, 199

paint, *color, beautify*, 24 (12), 38 (26), 100 (8); *portray, describe*, 53 (16), 117 (3)
Painter, William, 164 f.
Palfreyman, Thomas, xx
Pallas, 15 (4) n., 64 (14), 119 (14). *See* Minerva
palm, yield the, 15 (5)
pampered plumes, ?*luxurious dress*, 79 (21)
Paradise of Dainty Devices, The, xiii f., xx ff., 152, 182, 186, 203, 205; borrowings from, by the *Gorgeous Gallery*, xxii, 168, 182, 184, 197; imitation of, by the *Gorgeous Gallery*, 145
pardy (par dieu), 28 (28)
Paris, 56 (10), 63 (26) n., 64 (31), 81 (15)
Paris, Gaston, 188
Park, Thomas, xv ff., 158 f., 167, 169, 171, 174 ff., 179, 182, 185, 187, 190, 196, 200 f., 206
Parker, Martin, 157
Parker Society, 194
Parnassus, 63 (8), 116 (26)
part, to her, *for her share*, 56 (11)
pass, *regard, care for*, 5 (7), 23 (13), 117 (20); *surpass*, 63 (7, 14, 21)
passing, *surpassing, great*, 10 (12), 31 (29), 81 (13), 108 (28)
passing bell, *a bell that rings at the hour of death to call for prayers for a passing soul*, 14 (9)
Passionate Morrice, The, 180, 190, 193
Patch, H. R., 156

GLOSSARIAL INDEX

pate, *head*, 117 (17)
path, *?go on, pursue one's course*, 70 (17) n.
Patterson, R. F., 174
pause, *delay*, 43 (13)
Pawles, 117 (36) n.
pay, *reward, payment*, 58 (28); *the pleasure of the gods*, 55 (7)
pay one's pate, 117 (17) n.
paysd (peised), *weighed*, 41 (28)
pealfe (pelf), 96 (12) n.
pearce (pierce), *strike*, 12 (31), 53 (5)
pearching, *parching*, 44 (5)
Peele, George, 156, 167, 177, 190 f., 205
Peele, Stephen, 171
peevish, *silly*, 86 (23)
peised ('paysd'), 41 (28)
pelf, 96 (12) n., 98 (16)
pellets, *bullets*, 32 (5)
pendant, *the end of a lady's girdle that hung down after passing through the buckle*, 107 (19, 21, 33), 108 (6)
Penelope, 59 (16) n., 64 (16 f.) n., 88 (7)
Percy, Bishop Thomas, 189, 191
Percy Society, 151, 154, 159, 192
perfixt, *determined*, 35 (5)
Pernassus. *See* Parnassus
perpend, *consider, ponder*, 81 (4)
Persius, 200
Pettie, George, 162
peuish. *See* peevish
Phaedra, 39 (2) n.
Phaedrus, 183
Phebe. *See* Phoebe
philed. *See* filed
Philistines, 90 (17)
Phillip, John, 174, 192
Phoebe, 111 (31). *See* Diana
Phoebus, 63 (30). *See* Apollo
Phoenix Nest, The, xxi, 161
phrase, *phraseology*, 117 (28)
Piers Ploughman, 167
pinch, *torment*, 117 (29), 118 (12)
pine, *suffer*, 20 (2); *fade away*, 116 (5); *torment*, 61 (19), 72 (26), 105 (22), etc.
pining, *painful*, 14 (4), 104 (32)
pipes, pack up one's, *cease from action or speaking*, '*shut up*,' 75 (11)
Pirhus. *See* Pyrrhus
pistle (epistle), *letter*, 12 (34), 13 (8, 13), 15 (25), 16 (19, 20)

[234]

GLOSSARIAL INDEX

place, in, *on the spot*, 16 (11), 19 (10)
plain, *complain*, 115 (4)
plat, *plot (of ground)*, 73 (17)
Plautus, 193
playfeares, *playmates*, 103 (25)
playne, *complain*, 57 (11)
pleasure, to, 35 (10) n.
pliant, *yielding, compliant*, 78 (6)
Pliny the Elder, 146
plumes, *plumage (of pride)*, 79 (3, 21), 81 (27)
Plutarch, 157, 162
Pluto, 81 (4), 114 (7, 21)
ply, *yield*, 61 (29)
Polívka, Georg, 192
Polyxena, 14 (36) n., 56 (8) n., 63 (19)
pome, *apple*, 81 (14)
Poor Knight His Palace, A, xv, 162, 165
port, *deportment*, 26 (21), 56 (31), 105 (10)
Porter, Henry, 155, 193
post, a peevish, *used contemptuously of a man*, 86 (23)
posy, *a motto for inscription on a jewel or for embroidery on a handkerchief*, examples of, 67 (34) n., 77 (30)
Powell, Thomas, 154
prates, paint one's, 100 (8) n.
pray, *prey*, 34 (21); *pray for*, 60 (15)
pray, *a prey*, 101 (20), 112 (34)
preace. *See* press
prefer, *advance, promote*, 37 (23, 46)
press, *rush, hurry*, 17 (25), 58 (9), 116 (24)
press, *crowd, company*, 47 (8)
prest, *ready*, 32 (5), 60 (20), 88 (5), 102 (7), 117 (30)
preter, *past*, 90 (20) n.
pretty, *fine, pleasing*, 3 (9), 65 (2), 79 (1)
prevail, *avail*, 13 (16), 81 (33), 91 (27)
Priam, 41 (9) n., 81 (11)
price, have one's life in, *esteem highly*, 20 (10); make of no price, *have little esteem for*, 6 (28)
prick, *incite forward*, 38 (6), 78 (9); *spur forward*, 65 (15)
Pridioxe, Thomas, 154
prime, *height*, 88 (28); *springtime (of life)*, 79 (10, 26), 81 (19), 91 (11), *(of love)*, 103 (23)
prince, *princess*, 52 (28)
printers: Allde, John, xix; Disle, Henry, xiii; Griffith, William, 203 f.; Hacket, T., 203; Jones, Richard, xiii f., xxi f., 152, 204; Proctor, Thomas, xviii ff., 79 ff., 145, 168, 187, 191, 204; Tottel, Richard, xiii, xix

[235]

GLOSSARIAL INDEX

Proctor, John, xix
Proctor, Thomas. *See* printers
procure, *bring about, produce*, 18 (4), 73 (12), 77 (20), 82 (25, 30); *secure*, 78 (30)
Prometheus, 64 (2, 3 n.)
proof, 55 (21) n.; *experience*, 89 (4)
prooft, 69 (31) n.
proper, *pretty*, 26 (2), 67 (34), 93 (2)
prove, *experience*, 17 (15); *find out by experience*, 91 (10)
proverbs and proverbial phrases: *aeger dives habet nummos*, 96 (2) n.; after a storm comes a calm, 51 (3) n.; after showers the sun shines, 51 (4) n.; beat the bush, miss the birds, 65 (17) n.; beggars have no choice, 9 (30) n.; bird in hand is worth two in a bush, 27 (22) n.; blind, the, eat many a fly, 57 (29) n.; bull, the savage, in time bears the yoke, 9 (31) n.; burnt child dreads the fire, 65 (23) n.; crow is white, to say that the, 97 (5) n.; death is common to all men, 99 (34) n.; *donec eris fœlix, multos numerabis amicos*, 100 (19) n.; dripping water wears away a stone, 11 (26) n.; fairest, the, without are the foulest within, 66 (26) n.; *fœlix quem faciunt, aliena pericula cautum*, 92 (25) n.; for better or for worse, 62 (4) n.; grass, a serpent lies in the greenest, 79 (32) n.; grass, all flesh is, 93 (7) n.; happy is he who can beware by another's harms, 92 (25) n.; he who fights and runs away, etc., 77 (11) n.; highest seats have the most wind, 10 (24) n., 70 (28) n.; *invidus alterius rebus macrescit opimis*, 80 (2) n.; *latet anguis in herba*, 79 (32) n.; lingering love, misliking grows in, 88 (22) n.; loath to depart, 77 (29) n.; *memento mori*, 96 (27) n.; *mors omnibus communis*, 99 (34) n.; *ne sutor ultra crepidam*, 4 (28) n.; necessity (need) knows no law, 9 (30) n.; of sufferance cometh ease, 69 (18) n.; out of sight, out of mind, 82 (19) n.; plow the sea, 65 (25) n.; *respice finem*, 99 (9) n.; rule the roast, 34 (4) n.; sheep young as well as old come to market, 94 (20); shoemaker shouldn't look above shoes, 4 (28) n.; snake, a, lies in the grass, 79 (32) n.; soon hot, soon cold, 86 (8) n.; sow in the sand, 65 (25) n.; spare to speak, spare to speed, 16 (30) n.; speak and speed, 6 (6), 16 (30) n.; strive against the stream, 17 (17) n.; sunshine follows the rain, 51 (4) n.; sweet is sour (sweet meat, sour sauce), 89 (33) n.; *tempus edax rerum*, 9 (31) n., 93 (2) n.; things are not what they seem, 69 (33) n.; time consumeth all things, 93 (2) n.; time past can't be recalled, 102 (8) n.; time trieth all things, 6 (24), 15 (34) n.; try before you trust, 65 (19) n.; wind, the most, is round the highest places, 10 (24) n., 70 (28) n.; wooing, the, that's long a-doing, etc., 88 (22) n.; words are wind, 36 (34) n.
provoke, *advance, effect*, 44 (28)
Psyche, 170
Publilius Syrus, 151
puppet-show, 198
put one's hand to, *set to work, offer help*, 10 (8)
Puttenham, Richard, *The Art of English Poesy*, 195
Pyramus, 13 (34), 78 (30); the "History" of, 103 ff.
Pyramus and Thisbe (1562), 203

[236]

GLOSSARIAL INDEX

Pyrrhus, 14 (36) n.; Pyrrhus's father, *Achilles*, 63 (19)
Pythias, 117 (31) n.

quail, *put an end to*, 31 (29), 32 (37)
quaint, *fastidious, prim*, 53 (18)
quere (quire), *letter*, 16 (6)
quight, *aquite (acquit)*, 64 (30)
quires (choirs), 26 (9)
quite, *requite*, 52 (11)
quiuring (quivering), 74 (8)

race, *course (of virtue)*, 17 (21)
rafte, 63 (8) n.
Raleigh, Professor Sir Walter, 184, 189
ramp, *climb, scramble*, 117 (37)
rare, *rarely*, 6 (29)
rashly, *quickly, hastily*, 4 (4)
raste, 63 (8) n.
reave, *split, cleave*, 43 (29); *take away*, 113 (35)
red (read), 61 (12, 14 n.)
Redford, John, 167
redust, 108 (3) n.
Reed, Joseph, 151
regard, *look at, pay attention to*, 34 (24, 30)
reign, *kingdom, realm*, 114 (7, 22)
rejoice, *pleasure, enjoyment*, 93 (14)
reketh (recketh), *careth*, 67 (5)
releasement, 33 (11)
relent, 25 (39) n.
Reliquiae Antiquae, 182
remorse, *compassion*, 74 (11), 119 (28)
remove, *move (the lips in speaking)*, 24 (25)
rend, *rent, torn asunder*, 53 (9)
renew, *change*, 6 (25), 48 (13)
rent, *rend*, 7 (24)
repair, *place of meeting*, 109 (4)
repute, *believe*, 27 (16)
require, *ask for, beg*, 13 (7), 48 (27), 59 (22, 27), 104 (3)
respect, *in comparison with*, 108 (35) n.
rested, *arrested*, 44 (18)
retier (retire), *return*, 75 (22)
Return from Parnassus, The, 153
reue. *See* reave
revoke, *recall*, 75 (3)
rhetoric, 106 (25) n.

GLOSSARIAL INDEX

rid, *remove, take away*, 5 (24), 10 (3), 14 (3), 17 (36), 18 (23), 20 (21), etc.
ride, *float*, 11 (13), 59 (26)
rime ruff, 117 (35) n.
Ritson, Joseph, xix n.
roast, rule the, 34 (4) n.
Robinson, Clement, xxi.   See *A Handful of Pleasant Delights*
roche (roach), *a fish*, 51 (16)
Rollins, H. E., xiii n., 153 f., 160, 185, 188, 191, 195
Romance of the Rose, 180
rome (room), 32 (21)
Romeo and Juliet, 41 (12) n.
Rosamund and Helmichis, 82 (30) n.
rossy (rosy), 108 (21)
rout, *company, people in general*, 4 (37), 35 (24)
Rowe, Addie F., xxv
Rowlands, Samuel, 159, 193
Rowley, William, 151
Roxburghe Ballads, 154, 157, 167, 173, 179, 189, 193, 198
Roxburghe Club, 150; its edition of the *Gorgeous Gallery*, xv ff., 169, 175 ff.   See Collmann's *Ballads*, *A Poor Knight His Palace*, and *A Special Remedy*
Roydon, Matthew, xxi
Roydon, Owen, xx f., 3 (21)
Rucellai, Giovanni, 188
ruddocks, 99 (20) n.
rudely, *clumsily*, 4 (4)
rue on, *have pity on*, 20 (8)
Ruphilus, his epistle to Elriza, 9 ff.
rush, *dash out (? fly) rapidly*, 65 (18)
Russell, Thomas, 151
ruth, 25 (7), 108 (8)

S., E., xxi, 183
S., F., 198
S., S., 151
sad, *serious, steadfast*, 48 (25) n.
St. Paul's Cathedral, elegies pasted upon, 205
salfely (safely), 111 (15)
salve the sore, 7 (16) n.
Samson, 90 (17)
sance (sans), 100 (14) n.
Sandys, Archbishop Edwin, 183
Sannazaro, Jacopo, 180
sans, 100 (14) n.
savor, *relish*, 65 (11)

[238]

GLOSSARIAL INDEX

scace, *scarce*, 49 (19), 91 (18)
scalde (scaled), 63 (9)
scale, *flint*, 62 (27) n.
scant, *live meagrely*, 91 (14)
scantly, *scarcely*, 12 (10), 17 (7)
scapte, *escaped*, 12 (11), 16 (12)
Scherer, Hans, xxiii
science, *knowledge*, 106 (24)
scorn, have a, *be scorned*, 58 (12)
Scott, Sir Walter, 175
Scottish Text Society, 180
scry, *descry*, 7 (7)
Scyrens. *See* Sirens
scyte (site), 110 (23)
seed, *offspring*, 29 (13)
seel(l)y. *See* silly
seemings, *appearances*, 17 (27)
seems, *beseems*, 34 (32), 53 (2)
seethe (seeth), *third person singular of see*, 33 (23)
seilde, *seldom*, 27 (21)
seldom, *infrequent (adjective)*, 13 (24)
Sempill, Robert, 180
Seneca, 196
senge, *singe*, 64 (33)
septier (sceptre), 62 (18) n.
serbillitie, 53 (28) n.
serve, *work (prepare) for*, 92 (2)
set, *proclaim, reveal*, 108 (2)
shade, *conceal, veil*, 17 (21)
Shadwell, Charles, 151
Shakespeare, xiii, xxiv, 160, 162, 165, 182, 189; cited, 153, 155, 164, 182; quoted, 151 f., 160 f., 167 ff., 183, 186 f., 190, 194, 196 f., 199, 202, 206
Shakespeare Society, 162, 167. *See* Halliwell-Phillipps
Shakspere Society, New, 180, 190, 193
shaling, 52 (12) n.
shame, *modesty*, 56 (28)
shape, *cause*, 119 (24)
shent, *disgraced, ruined*, 39 (16)
shift, have no, *have no means of effecting an end*, 75 (28)
shine, *cause to shine*, 10 (17)
Shirley, James, 151
short, for, *in brief*, 109 (8); in short of, *lacking, in the absence of*, 106 (31)
should, 15 (13) n.
show, *deceptive appearances in general*, 93 (19)
shrine, *conceal*, 9 (6), 19 (17), 59 (10), 94 (4, 14); *hide myself (be buried)*, 95 (20) n.

GLOSSARIAL INDEX

shroud, *hide*, 79 (20); *bury*, 94 (3), 99 (15)
shun, *?hide, screen*, 87 (22) n.; *keep away, refrain from*, 93 (19)
Sidney, Sir Philip, xxi f.
sight, *ability to see, the eyes*, 19 (20), 28 (54), 87 (10), 107 (13); *appearance*, 24 (3), 61 (7), 108 (15), 112 (7); *seeing*, 72 (25), 82 (26), 104 (2, 30); *sigh*, 115 (4); *something shown or exhibited*, 103 (14)
sightly, *finely*, 108 (18)
silk, soft as, 111 (11)
silly, *innocent, harmless*, 4 (12), 11 (27), 14 (25), 60 (5), etc.; *foolish*, 95 (15)
Simpson, Richard, 151
Sinnatus and Camma, 38 (32) n.
Sir Giles Goosecap, 189
Sirens, 75 (27), 86 (16)
sith(e), *since*, 8 (28), 17 (4), etc.; *?sigh or sight*, 104 (33) n.
skale. *See* scale
skantly. *See* scantly
Skeat, W. W., 155, 167, 172, 205
Skelton, John, 166, 173, 204
skill, *comprehend*, 22 (26)
skill, *judgment, reason*, 91 (22) n.; *can some skill, have skill at*, 4 (28)
slea (slay), 8 (18)
slide, *change, vary (in love)*, 15 (23), 38 (15)
slidingly, *in danger of sliding (falling down from a high estate)*, 70 (32)
slights (sleights), *trickery*, 23 (4), 64 (8) n., 97 (4)
sloe, *the fruit of the blackthorn*, 52 (9)
smart, *pain*, 15 (21), 18 (31), etc.
smeared, *smudged (with tears)*, 76 (3)
smilings, 63 (33)
smoking, *steaming (with blood)*, 112 (22) n.
Smollett, Tobias, 157
smoothest, *most plausible*, 67 (22), 69 (7)
sole, *solitary*, 111 (32)
Solomon, 99 (2)
sonnet, *a song or short poem*, 31 (7); examples of the Shakespearean, 171, 182, 201; irregular form of, 202
sorrowing sobs, 82 (29), 86 (18), 87 (12), 92 (14)
sort, *kind, class (of people)*, 4 (6), 9 (26, 29), 18 (8), 20 (9), etc.; *manner*, 61 (2), 88 (19)
sound, *?words with a seductive sound*, 64 (19)
sound, *resound*, 81 (9, 25)
Southwell, Robert, 181
sowter (souter), *shoemaker*, 4 (22, 28 n., 29, 30)
spaste (spaced), 63 (29) n.
Special Remedy against Lawless Love, A, xv, 150, 168
Speculum Stultorum, 193

[240]

GLOSSARIAL INDEX

speed, *be successful*, 16 (30), 65 (4); *give success to*, 48 (19); *smite, destroy*, 19 (25)
speed, *fortune*, 11 (8)
speeding, *prosperity*, 65 (3)
spending days, *days that are spent (passed)*, 17 (36)
Spenser, Edmund, xx, 153, 157, 161, 179 f., 182
Spenser Society, 146, 206. *See* Heywood, John, *Works;* Taylor
spent, *occupied, took up*, 13 (30) n.; *ended*, 31 (15)
spight, *despite, harm*, 78 (12 f.)
spill, *destroy*, 8 (16, 24), 77 (4), 78 (32); *perish*, 46 (3)
spleen, words spoken of the, *i. e., spoken in jest or play*, 17 (33)
splint, *splinter*, 62 (27)
spoil, *despoil, injure*, 64 (19)
spoiling, *harmful*, 44 (9)
spot, *a moral blemish*, 54 (26)
spot, *sully (one's reputation)*, 29 (19), 61 (10)
sprent, *sprinkled (with tears)*, 31 (17)
spright. *See* sprite
spring, *be produced or brought forth*, 7 (17), 64 (12); *grow*, 11 (16); *jump*, 26 (11)
sprite, *spirit, soul*, 16 (16), 21 (8), 61 (6), 120 (6)
stain, *blemish, i. e., surpass*, 15 (5)
staming (stamming), 63 (12) n.
stand, *be or 'go,'* 15 (18), 110 (32) n.
stark, *completely*, 53 (9)
start, *turn aside, go away*, 8 (19); *be unfaithful to*, 25 (42), 77 (18)
starve. *See* sterue
state, *condition of prosperity*, 100 (16)
stay, *exist*, 114 (22); *remain quietly*, 107 (22, 28); *restrain*, 90 (21), 108 (22), 112 (5); *support*, 109 (21)
stay, *delay*, 77 (10); *obstacle, hindrance*, 33 (29), 74 (8), 107 (5); *state*, 46 (26)
stealing, *stealthily moving, noiseless*, 13 (22), 59 (29), 111 (27)
steres (steers), *goes*, 107 (4)
sternles, *rudderless*, 11 (12) n.
Sterrie, D., 193
sterue (starve), *die*, 49 (28), 60 (22), 62 (2)
sticking place, 119 (37) n.
still, *continually*, 9 (8)
stint, *bring to an end, stop*, 12 (19), 13 (15), 37 (12); *come to an end*, 33 (28–30)
stir, *stir up*, 12 (14)
stock, *stem*, 63 (12) n.
store, *abundance*, 90 (14), 96 (6), 106 (22), etc.; *have in store, possess*, 117 (32)
strain, *constrain*, 72 (11); *torture*, 109 (18)
strake, *struck*, 116 (2) n.
stratch (stretch), 8 (10)
Stubbes, Philip, 193
sturdest (sturdiest), 67 (25)

GLOSSARIAL INDEX

suffisde (sufficed), 91 (14)
surnamed, *previously named*, 75 (8)
surpassed, *bygone*, 74 (24) n.
Surrey, Earl of (Henry Howard), xiii, xxv, 63 (9) n., 169, 171. *See* Tottel's Miscellany
suspect, *suspicion*, 69 (26), 104 (6), 110 (34), 111 (14)
sute (suit), *entreaty*, 55 (14), 60 (12); *wooing*, 35 (5), 58 (10, 12), 72 (19), 73 (12), etc.
suters (suitors), 27 (3, 28), 64 (12)
swage, *assuage*, 22 (18)
swagement, *assuagement*, 15 (21), 60 (33)
swap down, *fall (flop) into a swoon*, 115 (37)
swarue (swerve), 15 (26), 17 (11), 61 (33)
swell, '*puff up' with anger or boasting*, 4 (7, 22); *rise, increase*, 5 (23), 7 (29), 55 (28), 104 (21), etc.
swifted, *quickened*, 107 (4)
Swinburne, A. C., 188
sycophants, *critics*, 3 (22) n.
Synorix and Camma, 38 (32) n.
syue (sieve), 49 (12)

tail, climb to another's, 71 (30)
take, *endure, suffer*, 4 (2), 12 (6)
tane, *taken*, 32 (22), 113 (10)
Tantalus('s), 119 (7)
Tarquin, 64 (18)
tattling, *prattling*, 75 (7), 100 (7)
Taurus, 65 (21) n.
Taverner, Richard, 193
Taylor, John, the Water Poet, 146, 175, 179, 182, 187, 198
Tell-Troth's New-year's Gift, 153
tend, *attend*, 15 (30)
Tennyson, Alfred, Lord, 162
Teucer, King, 188
than, *then*, 6 (12)
that, *what*, 14 (15), 15 (12, 14 f.), 17 (11), 21 (26), 29 (33, 35), 30 (25), 44 (34), etc.
the, *thee*, 59 (16), 61 (5), 79 (23), etc.
then, *than*, 4 (33), 5 (20), etc.
Theocritus, 157
Theseus, 12 (7) n., 39 (6) n.
Thesiphon, 64 (28) n.
thicke, *thicket*, 52 (8)
Thisbe, 13 (34), 38 (30), 78 (29); the "History" of, 103 ff.
Thompson, E. M., 194
thoughtful, *anxious*, 112 (4)
thrall, *thraldom, bondage*, 5 (10)

[242]

GLOSSARIAL INDEX

throngs (throes), *woe, affliction*, 43 (7)
throwes, 115 (24) n.
Thynne, Francis, xix
tickle stay, *unsteady, inconstant state*, 46 (26) n.
tiger's milk, fostered with, 55 (22), 60 (2) n.
Time, Truth's daughter, 159
Tisiphone, 64 (28) n.
to, *as, for*, 28 (9), 56 (11), 72 (27); *too*, 15 (8, 32), 19 (6), 37 (9), 51 (17), 79 (23), etc.
tomb, *entomb*, 20 (19), 99 (3)
too, *to*, 26 (23), 27 (31), 101 (19), etc.
too too, *exceedingly*, 97 (30)
Tottel's *Miscellany*, xiii, xxi, xxiv, 150, 152 f., 156 f., 172, 174, 177, 186, 188, 190, 192; borrowings from, by the *Gorgeous Gallery*, xxii, 155, 158 ff., 165 f.
towards, *in regard to*, 7 (3)
toy, *whim*, 84 (32)
trace, *track*, 112 (31)
trade, *customary mode of action*, 56 (30)
traste (trac'd), 112 (29)
travail, 48 (22)
trayde, *betrayed*, 14 (25)
trayne (train), *snare*, 73 (14)
trede (tread), 56 (22)
tristive, *tristful, sad*, 119 (25)
Troilus, 14 (36), 41 (9) n., 46 (12), 56 (12), 59 (14). *See* Cressida
trope (troop), 35 (34)
troth, of, *truly*, 75 (35)
Troy, 63 (18), 81 (8)
Tudor Facsimile Texts, 155, 193
tunes named in the text, 26 (2), 31 (9), 35 (21), 38 (4), 39 (23)
Turbervil, Hodg, 186
Turbervile, George, xxiv, 146, 151, 156, 185, 188, 195
turn, serve one's, 75 (15)
twain, 103 (24) n.
tween, *between*, 53 (27), 76 (11), 104 (20)
two, *to*, 59 (19)
Tyndale, William, 151

vade, *fade, vanish*, 79 (7, 21), 87 (11), 89 (10), etc.
vading, *fading, i. e., drooping and lustreless*, 79 (3)
vailing foretop, *lowering the foretopsail*, 32 (16)
vain, *vanity*, 89 (35), 90 (21), 92 (10), 95 (15)
Valerius Maximus, 146
valiaunst, valiaunts, *most valiant*, 92 (19), 94 (30), 99 (27 n., 31)
Vaux, Thomas, Lord, xiii, xxi, 155, 158 ff., 183
vayne. *See* vain

[243]

GLOSSARIAL INDEX

Udall, Nicholas, 177
ventre, *venture*, 5 (9), 64 (17)
Venus, 55 (23) n., 56 (10) n., 81 (14), 103 (18) n.; hymn of Pyramus to, 105 (15, 18, 34 n.), 107 (25)
vilde, *vile*, 81 (7, 20)
"Vilikins and his Dinah," 170
Virgil, 169, 174, 185 f.
Vlisses (Ulysses), 59 (16), 64 (16), 88 (9)
vncouth, *unknown*, 79 (29)
vncoynd, *deprived of one's coin (wealth)*, 99 (21)
vngaynd, *not yet gained or possessed*, 87 (10)
vnholpen, *unhelped*, 8 (20)
vnkind, *unnatural*, 12 (25), 15 (29), 45 (43)
vnlose, *unloose*, 107 (19), 109 (17)
vnlusty, *listless, without strength*, 19 (26)
vnment, *unthought of, i. e., never thought at all*, 89 (10)
vnright, *misdeed, sin*, 11 (3)
vnsaciate (insatiate), 80 (20), 95 (33)
vnsheathd, *disembodied*, 61 (7)
vnstorde, *unsupplied with wealth*, 91 (11)
vnsure, *not fixed or certain (as to time)*, 94 (26)
vntill, *unto, upon*, 58 (32)
vntwinde, *untwine*, 49 (26)
void, *ineffectual*, 4 (8)
vouch, *call to witness*, 17 (10)
vrge, *incite, provoke*, 7 (13)
vse, *be accustomed to*, 20 (24), 118 (2)
vsing, *usage*, 24 (27)
Usk, Thomas, 167
vsuall, *usually*, 90 (6)
Vulcan, 12 (7) n., 105 (34) n., 112 (24)

W., Is., 204
wade, *go on (to describe further)*, 64 (2)
wage, *fight*, 53 (7)
waight (weight), 55 (21) n.
wake-a-bed, *wakefulness*, 50 (8)
Waller, A. R., 176
wamenting, *lamenting*, 52 (22)
wan (won), 15 (2), 56 (10)
want, 64 (32) n.; *lack*, 106 (22), etc.
Wapull, George, 198
ware (were), 108 (34)
Warton, Thomas, 203
waste, *pine away*, 117 (25)

GLOSSARIAL INDEX

Watson, Thomas, 152, 170, 179
wave, *vacillate*, 100 (11)
way (weigh), *consider*, 46 (25), 55 (6) n., 75 (2), 78 (23), 81 (22), 94 (19)
wayght (wait), 32 (32)
weary, 104 (7) n.
weed, *garments*, 40 (18), 79 (4), 105 (10); *harm*, 65 (25) n.
ween, *think*, 62 (7)
weighed, *regarded*, 35 (14)
weighing, *considering*, 46 (30)
well, *safely*, 5 (21)
Wells, J. E., 194
were (wear), 91 (5)
werst, *wert*, 54 (7)
what stone (whetstone), 62 (29)
Wheatley, H. B., 189
whelm, *throw over and cover*, 10 (32)
where, *whether*, 70 (13)
whereas, *where*, 35 (9), 52 (5), 54 (3)
Whetstone, George, xxiv, 146, 151, 165, 168, 180, 184, 189, 196
which, *that which*, 26 (16)
whight (white), 63 (31)
while, *a space of time*, 15 (17), 17 (27)
white, 57 (32) n.; hit the white, *hit the center or mark at which an arrow is aimed, i. e., succeed*, 36 (41)
whorepools (whirlpools), 79 (31)
whot, *what*, 17 (19); *hot, angry*, 46 (13)
Whyte, Nicholas, 189
wield, *have power against*, 3 (24)
wight, *creature (human)*, 8 (3), 9 (7), etc.
Wilbye, John, 206
will, *wish*, 14 (19), 61 (12, 15, 32)
Williams, R., xiv, xx
Williams, Richard, xiv n.
Willobie his Avisa, 178
Willoby, Thomas, 178
willow, the token of a deserted lover, ballad on, 83 (11) n.
Wilson, Robert, 151
wink at, *overlook*, 30 (25)
wise of, by, *by means of*, 56 (10)
wished, *longed for*, 75 (22)
wishly, 59 (16) n.
wist, *known*, 9 (7)
wit, *with*, 71 (35)
Wit and Science, 154, 157, 167, 189
Wit and Wisdom, 162

GLOSSARIAL INDEX

witty tale, *wise speech*, 96 (20)
woe worth, *woe be to*, 44 (8)
woe's me, 110 (15), 113 (14), 115 (14)
womb, *belly*, *stomach*, 113 (23)
women, poems supposed to be by, 16 (27) n., 57 (8) n., 116 ff.
wone, 79 (14) n.
woodlike, *as if crazy*, 112 (35)
Wordsworth, William, 195
wot, *know*, 11 (18), 20 (14), 54 (31), 62 (20), etc.
would, *wish*, 15 (12), 52 (4), 57 (30), 103 (13)
Wright, Thomas, 150, 193, 205
wring, *blast*, *destroy*, 11 (17)
writh(e), *vary*, 65 (5) n.
wrye, *twist aside*, 45 (20)
wun, 79 (14) n.
Wyatt, Sir Thomas, 167, 169

ye, *the*, 60 (19), 104 (3)
ye(e), *yea*, 62 (2), 64 (17), 103 (30), 108 (33), 110 (35), 111 (2)
yet, *that yet*, 105 (30) n.
yield, *grant*, 60 (33), 61 (25), 88 (6), etc.
youthly, *youthful*, 31 (17)
ypast, *passed*, 7 (21)

Zoilus, 118 (20) n.